The
Politics of British Defense Policy,
1945—1962

The
Politics of British Defense Policy, 1945–1962

By WILLIAM P. SNYDER

ERNEST BENN LIMITED

To Lou

Foreword

THIS BOOK is the first of a series of publications to be sponsored by the Mershon Social Science Program in National Security. Directed to the large public concerned with international developments, as well as to specialists in military affairs, the substance, conclusions, and implications of this study merit careful attention.

Major Snyder presents in detail the series of adjustments Great Britain has made since World War II to bring into balance domestic capacities and international commitments. That the war adversely affected relative national power and loosened the bonds of empire is well known; not so familiar to Americans is the process by which British policy-makers have shaped and reshaped military capacities amidst recurrent crises at home and abroad. Certain to provoke discussion is the author's conclusion that, given the complex of interrelated problems forcing themselves on British attention, elements of military statecraft have been logically chosen and, on balance, unusually successful. Implications abound for American, as well as British, organizational behavior. Without the ever-burgeoning, technical, structural, even intellectual, paraphernalia that is our own Defense Department, the British system has still managed to function in a fashion judged acceptable by most of the standards of measurement established by this scholarly investigation as well as by an overwhelming proportion of the electorate, and, while Britain's role on the world stage is now far smaller than that of the United States, the relatively meager accoutrements available to play that role have made satisfactory performance in many respects much more difficult.

One should not slide by this aspect of Major Snyder's work. Although focused on military policy-making, it also is a case study in the complicated consequences that ensue when a country's ability to manipulate the international environment to its own advantage declines swiftly, considerably, dangerously. Imperial systems of the West have all been placed in analogous situations. Moreover, in the sense of decreased influence, the same problem has beset even the most powerful countries, including the United States and the Soviet Union—which is but another way of saying that the simple confrontation of the bi-polar, "cold-war" world has given way to less rigid, multi-faceted layering of international relationships. How particular governments have responded, in terms of change in popular attitude as well as modification of statecraft, has been insufficiently studied. Only out of such an empirical analysis as *The Politics of British Defense Policy* can scholars begin to construct testing concepts for comparing operations of national and international systems.

None of the problems of foreign policy-making has greater contemporary significance than patterns of civil-military action in the formulation and execution of national-security policy. The need for many Western countries, especially the United States, to maintain large military forces in peacetime, to alter ceaselessly their organization and equipment in an effort to keep pace with technological innovations, has called into question traditional social-science notions concerning relative civilian and military responsibilities, to say nothing of how the two terms can meaningfully be defined. Behind the governmental issues raised lies a new form of the old question of accountability of elected and appointed officials within a democratic society. Major Snyder goes beyond an analysis of how military officers and civil servants worked together in defining British defense policy to reveal some of the ideas each group had of its own role and that of its counterpart. Both, he demonstrates, enjoyed a large degree of autonomy in policy-making, as regards other groups within the executive branch, Parliament, parties, pressure groups, public opinion leaders, the "attentive" public, and so on down the scale to the mass electorate. Readers of *The Politics of British Defense Policy* may well hope that other scholars will follow the lead of Major Snyder and re-examine such currencies as "civilian control" in "stable democracies."

EDGAR S. FURNISS, JR.

Columbus, Ohio

Acknowledgments

I AM ESPECIALLY INDEBTED TO Colonel George A. Lincoln, head of the Department of Social Sciences at the United States Military Academy, for his help and encouragement throughout the period in which I worked on this project. I am also grateful to my colleagues in the Department of Social Sciences at West Point who assumed my duties during several absences in connection with this work.

Professor Harold Sprout of Princeton University first suggested the study, and his numerous suggestions were extremely useful. Professors Harry Eckstein, H. H. Wilson, and Sidney Verba, also of the Princeton faculty, and Colonel DeWitt C. Armstrong III, of the Policy Planning Council of the Department of State, were kind enough to comment on an initial draft.

Financial support for the project was provided by the Mershon Center for Education in National Security of the Ohio State University. I owe a special obligation to the director of the Social Sciences Program of the Center, Professor Edgar

S. Furniss, Jr., for the many useful suggestions he made concerning the final manuscript.

Finally, particular thanks are due to my wife and sons. They suffered a preoccupied member of the family for many months; yet they always managed to provide encouragement when it was most needed.

None of the above, of course, is responsible for any of the judgments or errors of fact that appear herein. The views expressed are my own. They do not necessarily represent the views or policies of the United States Army or any other governmental agency.

WILLIAM P. SNYDER

West Point, New York

Contents

I   *Introduction*   **3**

II   *The Evolution of Defense Policies since 1945*   **9**

III   *Parliament as a Critic of Defense Policy*   **43**

IV   *The Influence of Parliament and the Articulate Public on Postwar Defense Policies*   **65**

V   *Pressure Groups and Defense Policies*   **81**

VI   *The Policy Elites*   **105**

VII   *The Service Departments*   **123**

VIII   *The Politics of Decision-Making*   **151**

IX   *The Politics of Defense Spending*   **181**

X   *Defense and the Balance of Payments*   **205**

XI   *Defense and Politics*   **227**

XII   *Conclusions*   **245**

Bibliographic Note   **261**

Index   **273**

Figures

1/   *The Development of British Air-Transport
      Capacity, 1950–60*   /13

2/   *Table of Organization of the British
      Ministry of Defense*   /facing 153

Tables

1/   *British Military Manpower for the Years 1950–63,*
by Branch of Service   /36

2/   *Civilian Work Force in the British*
Service and Supply Departments   /38

3/   *Attitudes of the British Public toward Nuclear*
Weapons, 1960–61   /60

4/   *British Defense Expenditures on Production, by*
Percentages in Industrial Sectors   /89

5/   *Allocation of the British Defense Budget for the*
Years 1949–50 through 1962–63, by Percentages **/170**

6/   *British Spending for Social Services and Economic*
Services, Expressed as a Percentage of Total
Governmental Expenditures   /192

7/   *British Debt-Servicing Charges, 1946–60*   /193

8/   *Prewar and Postwar Current Accounts of British*
Imports, Invisibles, and Exports   /207

9/   *Percentage of Total British Exports by Value*   /210

10/   *Types of British Defense Purchases, for the Years*
1949–50 through 1960–61   **/211**

11/   *Current Accounts of Balance 'of Payments and*
British Military Expenditures Abroad, 1948–60   /217

The
Politics of British Defense Policy,
1945–1962

1 / Introduction

ON DECEMBER 5, 1962, Mr. Dean Acheson, Secretary of State during the Truman administration, addressed delegates to a student conference at the U.S. Military Academy at West Point. He gave special attention to the three problems he considered most significant to a conference discussing the Atlantic Community—NATO military strategy, German reunification, and European colonial policies. His speech, however, did not provoke among Western political leaders and commentators the further discussion of these issues that, apparently, Mr. Acheson both hoped for and believed to be necessary. The possibility of subsequent discussion was, in fact, effectively foreclosed by a sharp protest from London. The passage that evoked the British protest ran as follows:

> Great Britain has lost an empire and has not yet found a role. The attempt to play a separate power role—that is, a role apart from Europe, a role based on a "special relationship" with the United States, a role based on being the head of a "commonwealth" which has no political structure, or unity, or strength, and enjoys a fragile and precarious economic relation-

ship by means of the Sterling area and preferences in the British market—this role is about played out. Great Britain, attempting to work alone and to be a broker between the United States and Russia, has seemed to conduct policy as weak as its military power. H. M. G. is now attempting—wisely, in my opinion—to reenter Europe, from which it was banished at the time of the Plantagenets, and the battle seems about as hard-fought as were those of an earlier day.[1]

London's protest was reasonable. Negotiations on the British application for entry into the European Economic Community were at a critical stage at the time of Mr. Acheson's speech, and British officials complained that his remarks damaged the United Kingdom's bargaining position. The speech also weakened the position of the leadership in both major political parties in the domestic debate on the merits of joining the Common Market. The Macmillan government had repeatedly assured its back-bench critics that neither Britain's "special relationship" with the United States nor the country's "Great Power" status would be adversely affected if Britain were admitted. The Labor party, which had recently been told by its leader, Hugh Gaitskell, that in a choice between Europe and the Commonwealth, Britain must choose the Commonwealth, approved the decision to join the Common Market, subject to certain "conditions." These conditions were so stringent, however, that the party leadership—to the discomfiture of many of its backbenchers—obviously did not want Britain to follow Mr. Acheson's suggestion.

But these valid political reasons obscured the more basic psychological cause of the British protest. The "loss of empire" is the fundamental fact of Britain's postwar international position. The application for membership in the Common Market dramatized Britain's international decline—in less than a quarter of a century, Britain had been reduced from a position of world leadership to that of a supplicant for partnership in a Europe dominated by France and Germany. For British politicians and officials it was a subject that could be talked around but not about.

"Losing an empire" is a complex process, one that demands many adjustments in policies. New foreign policies are needed to recognize the complexity created in international affairs by the formation of weak and politically unstable states and to acknowledge the differences involved in dealing with newly sovereign nations rather than politically dependent areas. Economic policies also need revision; new trade arrangements and economic development programs are often required. In addition to the changes generated by the formation of new states, adjustments of similar magnitude are required in the relations with established powers. These policies are critically dependent upon the attitudes and pattern of politics within the society itself which undergo subtle changes as ties with dependent areas are severed. The political elite, for example, must become accustomed to the nation's diminished ability to control or influence events abroad after dependent territories obtain sovereignty. The intellectual and economic communities face a similar decline in importance and international prestige. The consequence of a decline in international influence leads to a concern for the lack of national purpose within elite groups. Constant adjustment of policies to a changed situation generates a sense of frustration over the inability to devise stable policies. Chauvinistic and nationalistic policies have a strong appeal to large sections of the population.

The implications of the severance of political ties with dependent areas are particularly great for military policies. Establishment of new states is normally accompanied by the employment of military power. Force has been used to prevent or forestall the declaration of sovereign status by an insurgent movement, as in Kenya. In other cases, Malaya for example, force has been employed, not primarily to prevent the cutting of political ties, but to insure that political control was turned over to a particular group in the new state. Finally, military forces have maintained law and order during the transition from dependent to sovereign status, as in Nigeria.

Military policies are also a central issue in the definition of a "new role." Military power is one of the key relationships in post–World War II international politics: types of forces, their equipment, and the strategies guiding their use are major foci in communist-Western relations. These same considerations, plus the weapons and deployment of forces, are of fundamental importance even within the communist and Western blocs.

Because military forces perform two important but different roles during the process of international decline, defense policies constantly need revision. The adjustment is complicated because the types of military forces necessary to terminate successfully colonial relationships may not be appropriate to support policies with older states. The constantly decreasing scope of policies—to an ultimate role not yet defined—is compounded by psychological changes and tensions that develop in the military establishment. For these reasons, post–World War II British defense policies are intimately concerned with, and can only be understood against, the background of Britain's international decline. Indeed, judgments of the effectiveness of these policies and the processes by which they were formulated are themselves not immune to the assessment of Britain's international decline.

There are two additional sources of uncertainty that contribute to the complexity and difficulty of formulating effective defense policies. The first is the indeterminacy of scientific and technological development. Military research and engineering utilize the latest products of a rapidly expanding technology. Modern military equipment is designed a decade in advance for purposes that are themselves uncertain, and its development almost always depends on processes and techniques that are unknown when contract decisions are made. Second, defense policies are intimately involved with domestic political and economic affairs. Military forces, at least in a stable and well-integrated society like Great Britain's, are created to influence the external environment, the world outside the nation. They contribute to "security" or "defense" against external "threats" and also gain for the country power and prestige in international affairs. Military forces, however, are a consumer of resources. Domestic goals and programs—social welfare, consumption, investment—require the same limited resources. Military policies are thus involved with two sets of equally legitimate, but often conflicting, goals. Neither set is absolute; resources can be traded between the two broad alternatives, but the conversion rate is highly uncertain.

This study is concerned with British defense policies since the end of World War II. It has two purposes: to analyze the formulation of policies and to indicate the main pressures which have helped shape the substance of policy since World War II. In this sense it is a case study designed to illuminate one area of governmental activity in Great Britain. Several broader questions are involved, however. First, international decline is a relatively common phenomenon. For the reasons previously enumerated, military policies provide a particularly useful focus for studies that compare the adjustment of different national political systems when sharp changes in international position have taken place. A second area of some interest is how different political systems relate and respond to the simultaneous demands of international and domestic politics. Again, military policies provide a useful focus. Hopefully, this study will be valuable to those interested in examining these broader questions, either as they apply to a single society or to several societies.

1. Dean Acheson, "Our Atlantic Alliance: The Political and Economic Strands," *Vital Speeches*, XXIX, No. 6 (1963), 163–64.

2/ The Evolution of Defense Policies since 1945

AT THE END of World War II, the United Kingdom faced a new and uncertain configuration of international forces. Britain's foreign-policy objectives needed revision and re-definition. Modifications were required in the instruments of foreign policy to permit manipulation of these new forces. Policy objectives and the instruments of policy needed to be meshed and related with one another. There was an additional complication attendant to military policies: the costs of military forces had to be kept compatible with the economy's limited resources.

Historically Britain used military forces only infrequently in the conduct of its foreign affairs, although they were normally available to support other instruments of policy. A maritime strategy was the central concept in the creation and employment of these forces. Defense of the home islands—assisted by the United Kingdom's geographic separation from Europe—required a strong navy, one that could control the adjacent sea approaches. The maintenance of Britain's vital trade links with the territories overseas rested on secure sea communications, again a job for the Royal Navy. The navy's task was facilitated by an extensive system of overseas operating bases which commanded the strategic points, Gibraltar and Suez, for example, on the sea routes linking the Empire. There was, in contrast, little need for a large army. Internal security in the colonial possessions could be maintained by native troops led by small British cadres. In the absence of long-term military commitments in Europe, an army sufficient to train leaders for the colonial forces and to act as a mobilization base in the event of an emergency on the Continent was adequate.

By World War II, there had been many modifications in the traditional maritime strategy. Adjustments of much greater magnitude have been made since 1945. The postwar changes have been characterized, first of all, by extensive delays between the conception of new policies and the creation of forces that give them operational substance. Second, the technological developments necessary to maintain modern operational forces have lagged in recent years. Finally, competition for resources among the major components of the defense program—overseas security, European defense, and strategic nuclear force—has intensified in recent years. All three patterns have a common source: resources made available for defense have been inadequate to maintain a diversified spectrum of military capabilities and deployments. Indeed, the shortage of resources has not only prompted policy adjustments, it is at the heart of the substantive weaknesses in policy.

OVERSEAS SECURITY

Overseas security refers to the requirements for military forces in territories external to, but owned or controlled by, Britain. With few exceptions, these are located in the Mediterranean, Africa, and Southeast Asia. Since 1945, beginning even before wartime demobilization was completed, there have been extensive and continuous military operations in these overseas areas. The brunt of the burden has fallen on the army. In 1946 and 1947 there were extensive internal-security commitments in Palestine and Greece. Guerrilla warfare began in Malaya in 1948 and lasted for nearly a decade. In 1952 there was civil unrest in Kenya, followed in 1955 by the costly four-year civil war in Cyprus. At the same time, moreover, the overseas-base system deteriorated slowly. Particularly crucial was the loss in 1956 of Suez, an event that shattered British confidence in the future availability of other bases.[1] Suez constituted a major link in the communications route to the Far East; its loss resulted in the division of the area of British overseas operations into two unconnected parts. A large share of the deployed forces were in the Far East or East Africa—the areas most distant from Britain. Finally, except for a few African and Gurkha troops, colonial manpower was no longer available, and large numbers of *British* troops were deployed overseas.

The problem facing defense planners has been to reduce the manpower and financial costs of overseas security—without producing a corresponding decline in military capabilities. Ideally, any solution would minimize army deployments abroad, require few overseas bases, and afford flexibility in employment. Two methods have been devised: the air-lifted central strategic reserve, able to move rapidly from the United Kingdom to overseas trouble spots; and the naval task force with organic ground combat units, supporting transport and tactical aviation, and a limited logistic and resupply capability.

The air-lifted central strategic reserve was first mentioned in 1954. The white paper of that year noted that "it will be our aim gradually to reduce the total size of the Army and to reconstitute the strategic reserve at home, the lack of which is at present a serious, though unavoidable, defect in our defence readiness."[2] Although a press article in February, 1954, indicated that the Chiefs of Staff planned an air-mobile force, the first official announcement to that effect came in 1955. Two years later, in 1957, special emphasis was placed on the air-lifted strategic reserve:

> . . . It could be interpreted in many ways: there was something in it for nearly everyone. For those who favored British withdrawal in favor of local nationalisms it seemed to promise at least a start in that direction. . . . For those who favored active British intervention . . . hope was held out. . . .
>
> .   .   .   .
>
> The idea, dependent as it was upon air transportation, was inherently modern and thus implicitly neutralized criticism or fears that strategic plans might simply be extrapolations from past experience.[3]

Creation of an air-lifted strategic reserve involved two tasks. It was necessary first to free army manpower for the reserve force. By 1957 an army brigade had been designated for this purpose.[4] The second problem, air-lift capability, was more difficult. Before 1956 air-lift was very limited—*fifteen* C-123 transports, an aircraft in service in the U.S. Air Force since the early 1950's, approximated the capacity. After 1956 an increase in transport capacity competed for resources with the Bomber Command—then organizing the British strategic force. As a consequence, the expansion of airlift capability was relatively slow—and makeshift (see Fig. 1). Of the air-craft that entered into service with the Royal Air Force after 1956—Beverley freighters, Bristol Britannias, and Comet II's —the latter two types were military versions of commercial transports. Both had serious limitations on the kinds of military equipment they could carry. Neither was designed to operate from unimproved tactical airstrips or for air-drops of troops or equipment.

The threefold expansion in lift capacity between 1955 and 1960 proved rather less productive than was at first anticipated. Within this short period, conditions changed very radically. The first and most important development was the "air barrier."[5] It was not altogether a new problem—after World War II the British were denied overflying rights in parts of the

MILLIONS

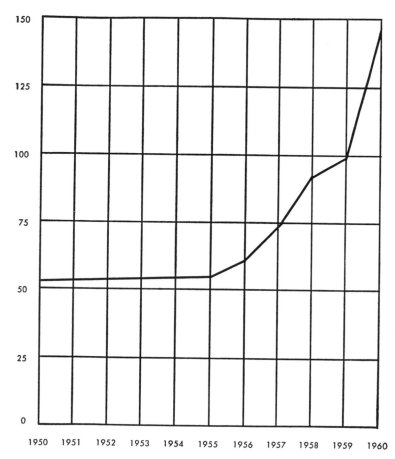

FIG. 1.—The development of British air-transport capacity, 1950–60. The calculation is based on the capacity of each type of aircraft over the range appropriate to its role. The figures assume normal utilization rates; in an emergency, these might be almost doubled. (Adapted from Cmd. 673, "Memorandum by the Secretary of State for Air to Accompany Air Estimates, 1959–60.")

Middle East and South Asia. But alternative routes were devised without difficulty, and overflying rights did not become
significant until after the Suez intervention. By way of an
example, air movements to Aden, a major base about fifteen
hundred miles south of Suez at the entrance to the Red Sea,
now involve: a flight to Malta, on to El Adem (Libya), due
south, parallel to the Egyptian border, then east to Aden; or
to Kano (Nigeria), east to Entebbe (Uganda) and then north
to Aden. Both routes may well be unavailable in future emergencies; a third alternative is via the Canary Islands, Ascen-
sion Island, Salisbury, Entebbe, and then on to Aden. This
third route, incidentally, is about ten thousand miles long, as
compared to the direct (with a stop at Malta) distance of
three thousand miles.[6]

Along with the air barrier other problems became apparent
as more careful analysis was given to air movement of forces.
Troops can be moved easily but are ineffective without heavy
equipment and supplies. If equipment and supplies are to be
moved, the number of troops that can be transported in an
initial movement is greatly reduced. In 1958 the government
announced that "in order to facilitate air transport, heavy
equipment, vehicles and other supplies will be stored at focal
points, such as Singapore." [7] Three years later a number of local
stockpiles had been established. Although a valuable innovation, prepositioned supplies are but a partial solution. Aside
from the costs of providing extra equipment, maintenance is a
difficult and endless problem. Stored items must also be replaced as equipment changes. However, the major problem,
especially in an area as extensive as that east of Suez, is the
movement of prepositioned items from storage to battle areas.

While the limitations on the strategic reserve are very
great, recent procurements have greatly increased transport
capability. The availability of long-range, turbo-jet Britannias,
has made it possible to shift the older Hastings to tactical
transport operations. Fifty-six Argosys, an aircraft designed
to carry bulky equipment or paratroopers, were delivered in

1962 and 1963. In early 1963 an estimated fifty jet STOL transports (the AW 681) were ordered; these aircraft will replace both the Hastings and Beverleys in the late 1960's. Also on order are five Comet 4C's and five tri-jet VC-10's. The Short Belfast (ten are expected by 1965) will increase capability to transport heavy equipment over long distances. In addition to greater lift capacity, a more comprehensive program of joint army–air force training is being carried out. Finally, the strategic air-lift mission has been given greater emphasis by the RAF.[8] While the air-lifted strategic reserve was too late to allow significant manpower reductions overseas during the 1950's, the larger capability planned for the late 1960's will make possible a more rapid response than in the past and thereby partially compensate for smaller forces and fewer bases.

The second attack on the costs of overseas security came from the Royal Navy. The navy's solution is the "Commando" ship. Commando ships are aircraft carriers modified to carry the personnel and equipment of a Royal Marine Commando, a battalion-sized force of about eight hundred men. Each Commando ship is equipped with helicopters for air-landing and supply; an aircraft carrier to provide air cover and tactical support aviation would normally accompany each Commando ship. Logistic support is furnished by fleet tankers and freighters, grouped in what is called an "Underway Replenishment Group."[9] The Commando, the carrier, and the supporting logistic vessels together form an amphibious task group and constitute a highly mobile and relatively self-contained combined arms force. The task group avoids the political problems implicit in fixed land bases. The size of the Commando and its lack of heavy equipment limit its employment to small brushfire incidents or internal security missions, however.

The Commando ship was developed by the Royal Navy after the Suez intervention. During that operation two aircraft carriers, "HMS Ocean" and "HMS Theseus," were used to transport Royal Marines to Suez. Possibly because of the shortage of landing craft, these units were landed by helicopter, the British use of which the navy pioneered in Malaya. The helicopter-borne landing was one of the few bright spots in the Suez intervention, and within a year the navy decided to convert a carrier, "HMS Bulwark," to Commando duties.

Previous decisions were important in the development of the Commando. By 1955 the navy had settled on the carrier as the capital ship, the "core of the modern fleet," and the following year it adopted a related program, "afloat support." Afloat support refers simply to arrangements that enable vessels to provision and refuel at sea. Afloat support reduced the navy's reliance on fixed land bases, which had declined in numbers and were considered highly vulnerable to nuclear attacks. In addition, it permitted a smaller operational fleet to maintain the same strength on patrol stations, because the number of trips to and from home base for fuel and supplies was reduced.

The Commando ship meshed easily with the carrier task group and afloat support. But before the Commando became an operational reality it was necessary to overcome a new hurdle: The 1957 white paper imposed stiff financial restrictions on all the services. The Navy Estimate for the financial year 1957–58 was £25 million less than for the previous year. Increased costs of materials and higher salaries further reduced the buying power of these funds. Manpower cuts were also ordered. The navy, like the other services, made sharp cuts in shore establishments:

. . . Resources are being rapidly diverted . . . from the shore support of the Navy to the fighting ships themselves. This policy will not only give the Fleet greater mobility and immediate readiness but . . . the reduction in the number of our seagoing ships will be much less than the proportionate loss in manpower over the next few years.[10]

Reductions in the carrier or afloat-support component were fortunately unnecessary, and sufficient slack was created to proceed with the first Commando.

By 1961 the amphibious task group was an established part of the operational fleet. A Commando had been employed successfully in modified form in the summer of 1958 in Jordan and in Kuwait in mid-1961. A second carrier has been converted to a Commando ship, and the size of the Royal Marines has been nearly doubled (to 9,200 men) in recent years. An assault ship especially designed for beach landings is under construction, as are several supply vessels. These new vessels will be formed into an "Amphibious Warfare Squadron," which, with embarked tanks and artillery, will increase the size and effectiveness of the ground combat forces that can be landed by an amphibious task group.

The air-lifted strategic reserve and Commando ships do not replace the army as the principal component of military capability in the overseas areas because there are severe limitations on the size of the forces that can be deployed by these methods. Neither Commandos nor air-lifted units are capable of sustained operations. But if the two are coupled with army units and the present base structure, Britain has the ability to employ rapidly small combined forces in the area from Aden to Hong Kong.

Two related aspects of the overseas security mission deserve brief mention. The first is that the development of the Commando and the strategic reserve have made it likely that all three of the services will be involved in any given military operation overseas. This has increased the desire for unified overseas commands to provide central planning and operational control. The first unified command was established in Aden in late 1958, and subsequently a Mediterranean Command was organized. These integrated headquarters proved useful, especially during the Kuwait operation in late 1961, and on the basis of this experience, the government announced in early 1962 that it would establish a unified command in the Far East.[11]

The second aspect concerns tactical air support. Although the overseas security mission centers on the army, tactical air support must come from another service—in the past, from the RAF. The RAF's job has become a difficult one; with the loss of base rights and overflying privileges, many areas in which the army expects to operate are beyond the operational radius of land-based fighters. The navy has argued that carrier-based strike aircraft are the only reliable method of furnishing this support. The decision to build a new aircraft carrier, announced in July, 1963, hinged mainly on this argument. The navy's solution was chosen over the alternative advanced by the air force—tanker aircraft and long-range fighters with an in-flight refueling capability—primarily because the loss of even one of the existing bases east of Suez would make it impossible to give the army the necessary support in many areas.

EUROPEAN DEFENSE

"On the Continent of Europe we have stationed large forces for the last 16 years in complete contrast with our previous military dispositions." [12] This statement from the 1962 Defense White Paper suggests the continuing surprise of officials at the permanent nature of the commitment of British military forces in Europe. The NATO obligation is indeed a radical departure from established principle of the past; a permanent military commitment within the framework of a multinational alliance is clearly not part of the traditional maritime strategy.

The commitment of a sizeable portion of the nation's military forces to the Continent culminated a series of earlier decisions. The first step was the wartime invasion. At the end of the war British troops were in Europe and thus available for peacetime occupation duty. Before this requirement ended the cold war intensified, and the initial arrangements for collective security under the North Atlantic Treaty Organization had been formulated. With the outbreak of war in

Korea, the British rearmament effort was channeled mainly
into NATO, for although a contingent was also dispatched to
Korea, a Soviet attack in Europe was then considered very
likely; moreover, the Far East was regarded as a sphere of
primarily American responsibility. More important, many
British officials believed that a contribution to European
defense would help persuade the United States that the
American military effort was worthwhile and would be
matched by Europe's own efforts.[13]

The final and critical step in Britain's military entry into
Europe came in 1954. In an effort to salvage a German military contribution to NATO after the French rejection of the
proposed European Defense Community, the Churchill government agreed to maintain in Europe for fifty years a force of
four divisions and a supporting tactical air force element.
This "unprecedented commitment," as Sir Anthony Eden
called it, was necessary to build "an effective defence system
in Western Europe, which in turn is essential for the security
of the United Kingdom. . . . " By "giving the new commitment, we may succeed in bringing in the Germans and the
French together, and keeping the Americans in Europe."[14]

Although it is reasonable to think that the British expected
that the size of the NATO contribution could be reduced after
a few years, British strategists initially assumed that the
commitment of 80,000 men to NATO could be sustained in the
face of immediate plans for military manpower reduction.
This expectation was based on two other policies then being
developed—the air-lifted central strategic reserve, discussed
above, and the strategic nuclear force. Both new programs
were expected to reduce manpower needs in the overseas areas.
The air-lifted reserve would hopefully allow rapid deployments from the U.K. and thus balance smaller forces at
overseas bases. The strategic nuclear force, announced only
a few months earlier in the 1954 Defense White Paper, would
be a deterrent and

. . . should have an increasing effect upon the cold war by making less likely such adventures on the part of the Communist world as their aggression in Korea. This should be of benefit to us by enabling us to reduce the great dispersal of effort which the existing international tension has hitherto imposed upon us.[15]

In short, over-all manpower reductions would also be possible because requirements in NATO could be met by forces released from the overseas areas.

This, of course, was a miscalculation. A strategic nuclear capability was largely irrelevant to the internal security problems normal in the overseas areas.[16] Therefore, European defense and overseas security needed the same general types of forces: they were competitors.

Before 1957, when the army enjoyed a relative abundance of manpower, the competition between European defense and overseas security was not important. The 1957 plan to end conscription in 1960 disrupted this easy coexistence. Both programs were reduced. Cuts of one battalion were ordered in Korea. Forces in Libya were to be "progressively reduced"; other British overseas garrisons would, "wherever practicable," undergo "considerable reductions."[17] In contrast, the British Army of the Rhine (BAOR) was to be cut by 13,000 in the next twelve months. Additional reductions were forecast "thereafter" [18] with BAOR's eventual strength planned at about forty-five thousand. During this same period the other British element in Europe, the Second Tactical Air Force, was reduced in size by one-half. Strong pressures from the United States and West Germany prevented the reduction of BAOR that had originally been envisaged, and it has been maintained at a strength of about fifty-five thousand men since 1958.

The British advanced a number of reasons to justify their force reductions in Europe. The most prominent was the economic argument: a reduction was necessary because of the high foreign-exchange costs. Even after the German contribution, the British Army of the Rhine had cost an average of £50 million annually since 1951.[19] The return of sovereignty to West Germany made the extent of future German support problematic. This economic argument was only thinly veiled in discussions of NATO strategy: British officials argued that NATO needed a relatively small ground-force component; indeed, overlarge conventional forces were thought to detract from the credibility of the then predominantly American strategic capability.[20]

The concept of "interdependence," endorsed by NATO in late 1957, provided yet another rationale for a smaller conventional contribution: it was argued that the maintenance of "independent overseas responsibilities" provided "unquestionable benefits to the common cause." [21] The British also viewed their slowly increasing nuclear capability as a contribution of common benefit. Finally, the political climate on the Continent had greatly improved since 1954. With the French tied closely to the Germans, the political need for a large British contribution had disappeared.

To soften the impact of the manpower cuts it was announced that there would be an increased reliance on tactical nuclear weapons in BAOR: ". . . Atomic rocket artillery will be introduced which will greatly augment . . . fire-power"; tactical air force units "will be provided with atomic bombs." [22] The decision to provide British units with tactical nuclear weapons again meshed with NATO strategy, which since 1954 had assumed that these weapons would be used in any attack. Force reduction, however, proceeded independently of the provisioning of BAOR with tactical nuclear weapons. Two surface-to-surface missile units equipped with the seventy-five-mile range American Corporal were planned for 1957 and 1958. The first of these did not arrive in Europe until 1959. There were other complications, as Colonel George Wigg noted to the House of Commons in February, 1961:

There is a shortage of manpower in BAOR and to fill the gap there are discussions about the use of atomic tactical missiles. We have not got any. What atomic tactical missiles are there under British control in Germany at the present time? There is the 47th Guided Weapons Regiment. There are three Royal Artillery regiments armed with Honest Johns, and with 8 in. howitzers, all of which are American and under American control. Our independent atomic potential inside the Army of the Rhine does not in fact exist at all. I will go further. I say that there is not a kiloton weapon in Germany, not even in the Air Force, that does not belong to the Americans and that is not under American control. The high falutin' arguments that are put forward when we are discussing whether we should use atomic weapons in Germany are entirely academic in character.[23]

While the commitment to NATO signified important changes in army and air force deployment, the consequences for the Royal Navy were less pronounced. NATO naval missions were much the same as two of the traditional tasks of the Royal Navy—maintenance of shipping and ocean communication routes, and the blockade of enemy territorial waters. Missions formerly the unilateral responsibility of the Royal Navy were now to be undertaken in co-operation with other navies, and since 1950 almost all maneuvers in the Atlantic and Mediterranean have been joint exercises. In 1957, for example, there were over twenty such exercises.

Because of the flexibility of naval forces and the difficulty of making a meaningful distinction between NATO and national missions, the extent of the British naval contribution to NATO is difficult to determine. The bulk of NATO naval forces, however, have been furnished by Britain and the United States. And in 1961, a year by no means unique in terms of naval deployments of the last decade, the Minister of Defense noted that 85 per cent of Britain's naval strength was assigned to NATO.[24]

The Royal Navy has made a significant contribution to NATO naval doctrine in two fields—antisubmarine warfare and minesweeping. In response to the German successes in these aspects of naval warfare during World War II and to the very large number of Soviet submarines after 1945, great emphasis was placed on these missions. Also, during Korean rearmament only small vessels which could be completed in a relatively few months were ordered by the Admiralty, vessels useful mainly for these purposes.[25] Despite the recent emphasis on carriers, the concern for antisubmarine warfare has continued because carriers and Commando ships are particularly attractive submarine targets.

The basic British maritime strategy relied on geography and a strong navy to buy sufficient time to mobilize against an attacking force. The weaknesses of this strategy were evident in World War II—Britain was subjected to heavy air attacks and faced a serious invasion threat in the early months of the war. Subsequent developments in nuclear weapons and delivery systems destroyed much of the remaining significance of the Channel as a barrier against strategic nuclear attack. Hopefully, such an attack can be prevented by the retaliatory capability of the United States and Britain. If deterrence fails, such defense as is possible rests on a collective effort located, as Stanley Baldwin implied in 1936, east of the Rhine, not the Channel. In the nuclear age the defense of "these islands" means interdependence and NATO, not a maritime strategy.

The implications of the Soviet threat and advances in military technology were met by steady revisions in the home-defense forces. During Korean rearmament, measures similar to those employed during World War II were instituted. By 1954, however, it was evident that these were of little value. Realization of this, and heavy commitments in Europe and overseas, caused the government to disband a number of the elements of the home-defense force. The first unit deactivated was the Army Antiaircraft Command. A year later, in 1955, the Home Guard, reactivated in 1951, was demobilized and put on a reserve basis. In 1956, ending a tradition of 150 years of service, the Coast Artillery was ordered to transfer responsibility for port defense to the navy and RAF.[26] Culminating these changes, the Defense White Paper of 1957, in a famous passage, noted the limitations of defense against strategic attack:

It must be frankly recognised that here is at present no means of providing adequate protection for the people of this country against the consequences of an attack with nuclear weapons. Though, in the event of war, the fighter aircraft of the Royal Air Force would unquestionably be able to take a heavy toll on enemy bombers, a proportion would inevitably get through. Even if it were only a dozen, they could with megaton bombs inflict widespread devastation.[27]

At the same time, Fighter Command was reorganized to provide improved air defense on the bases used by Bomber Command.

The growing vulnerability to strategic air attack also required changes in the civil defense program. Expenditures on civil defense between 1950 and 1956 amounted to about £400 million, with some two-thirds of the outlays directed to stockpiling.[28] An extensive organization was established in 1950 and 1951; and as late as 1954 it was manned by about 380,000 volunteers.[29] In 1955 it was decided to augment the volunteer organization by a Mobile Defense Corps of forty-eight reserve army and RAF battalions "trained and equipped to perform fire-fighting . . . rescue and ambulance duties." [30] These duties were later transferred to Territorial Army units. The present pattern of civil defense, costing some £15 million annually, was announced in 1957 : [31]

. . . The country's economic capacity limits the effort which can be devoted to [civil defense]. . . . The main task will be to keep the existing local organisation in being. . . . The necessary training equipment will be provided. Essential research will proceed; and work on emergency communications . . . the fall-out and warning and monitoring system will go on. These preparations will provide a framework for expansion, should that later be necessary.[32]

THE STRATEGIC NUCLEAR FORCE

In the 1953 defense debates the government hinted that it intended to develop a strategic nuclear force. The decision was confirmed in the 1954 Defense White Paper:

The primary deterrent, however, remains the atomic bomb and the ability of the highly organised and trained United States strategic air power to use it. From our past experience and current knowledge we have a significant contribution to make both to the technical and to the tactical development of strategic air power. We intend as soon as possible to build up in the Royal Air Force a force of modern bombers capable of using the atomic weapon to the fullest effect.[33]

The policy was initially greeted with wide approbation. The concept of deterrence was a familiar one in British military thinking, and the strategic nuclear force promised to utilize the latest developments of an advanced technology. A decade later, however, the strategic nuclear force is the central issue in British defense policy. One aspect of the issue is whether or not the strategic nuclear force is an effective deterrent. There is also a second question, closely related but more complex: Are the political advantages of a national strategic nuclear force worth the cost, it being assumed that any such British strategic force is at best of only limited usefulness as a deterrent?

The decision to build a strategic nuclear force evolved from several earlier policies. The first was the wartime effort at strategic air bombardment. After World War I the Royal Air Force emphasized air bombardment, partly in the hope that this mission would prevent the loss of its identity as a separate service. During his long tour as Chief of the Air Staff (1919–29), Lord Trenchard articulated the doctrine to the generation of young air force officers who rose to high command during and after World War II. Although the contribution of strategic bombing to the Allied victory in World War II has since been questioned, in the early postwar years the RAF believed that air bombardment had been of great importance in the German defeat. Also, the development in 1945 of atomic weapons removed any qualifications suggested by the wartime experience. Next, the American federal executive, under the provisions of the U.S. Atomic Energy Act of 1946, was unable to share with Great Britain the results of the joint, wartime Manhattan Project. Partly because they wanted atomic weapons, and partly in the expectation that a demonstration of their independent capability would qualify them for sharing atomic secrets in future years, the British subsequently initiated an atomic-development program. By 1952 the first device had been exploded; by 1954 atomic weapons were "in production in this country and delivery to the forces has begun." [34] Third, the air force decided in 1947 to build a series of long-range bomber aircraft. These included the Vulcan and Victor medium bombers, due for service after 1956, and, as "further insurance," the Valiant, to be available in 1955. [35] An interim aircraft, the Canberra light bomber, was expected in 1950. It would fill the requirement for a strategic bomber until the "V" series aircraft were available. A doctrine of strategic air bombardment, the availability of atomic weapons, and a series of advanced bomber aircraft were the essential components of the decision to build a strategic nuclear force, while the United States Strategic Air Command, formed in 1946 and after 1949 the dominant organization in the American defense structure, provided a relevant and attractive model on which to pattern Bomber Command.

The buildup of the strategic nuclear force proceeded rather slowly. The 1955 Air Estimates stated that bombers would begin to enter service in "the next twelve months." Added, however, was the caution that

more is involved than re-equipment. . . . We must select personnel of the highest quality and train them specially. We must provide the bases required in peace and war, bearing in mind that the "V" bomber force must be capable of completing its mission even though a surprise attack might first have been launched upon this country. We must perfect methods of operation. . . . [36]

Force expansion continued in 1956; by this time some Valiant squadrons had been formed. [37] In 1957, Bomber Command was "building up steadily"; Vulcan aircraft were now entering service and "stocks of nuclear weapons are increasing." [38]

Equipment deliveries to Bomber Command continued in 1958—megaton bombs were "in production and deliveries to the Royal Air Force have begun." [39] Equipment, communications, and base facilities apparently became available as needed. Under the able leadership of Air Chief Marshal Sir Harry Broadhurst, a wartime fighter commander, Bomber Command made rapid improvements in operational readiness; in 1958 RAF entries made highly respectable showings (ninth and twelfth of 164 crews) in U.S. Strategic Air Command bombing competition.[40]

Concurrently with the buildup of Bomber Command, supporting capabilities were developed. Work started in 1955 on an early warning and reporting system. After 1957 air defense was considered an "essential complement" to the bomber force; by 1958 most of the RAF's fighter interceptors had been shifted to the defense of airfields used by Bomber Command. Between 1959 and early 1963 the RAF operated sixty Thor missiles in conjunction with the U.S. Air Force; in this same period efforts were made to co-ordinate the employment plans and target lists of SAC and Bomber Command. In 1960 Britain joined with the United States in building the Ballistic Missile Early Warning System (BMEWS).

Even before the decision to build a strategic nuclear force was made public, British policy-makers recognized that the V series aircraft would be obsolescent by the early 1960's. Thus, the development of delivery systems to follow the V-bombers was commenced in the early 1950's. The major project was Blue Streak, a liquid-fueled ballistic missile "designed for launching from underground." [41] It was to have a range of 2,000 to 2,500 miles—between that of the intermediate (Thor and Jupiter) and intercontinental (Atlas and Titan) systems then under development in the United States. The second project was Blue Steel. It was a "standoff" weapon, similar in principle to the more recent Skybolt, and would allow the attacking aircraft to launch its attack 100 miles from the target, out of range of local air defenses. Blue Steel was expected to prolong the period of service of the V-bombers already in use by reducing their vulnerability to air defenses in the period immediately prior to the availability of the Blue Streak.

The Blue Streak project was cancelled in 1960. There seem to have been two main reasons for the decision. First, costs were too great for the defense budget. The delivery of aircraft to Bomber Command had proceeded somewhat slower than had initially been expected. And since development costs had been underestimated, aircraft expenditures began to snowball in the late 1950's. At the same time, the cost of the Blue Streak project exceeded initial estimates; when the system was cancelled it had already cost an estimated £100 million, with expenditures for procurement and installation still to come. Second, a cheap alternative appeared to be available; Skybolt, an airborne and air-launched ballistic missile system of 1,000-mile range, was then under development in the United States. Following the cancellation of Blue Streak, the Eisenhower administration agreed to sell Skybolt missiles to the Royal Air Force, provided only that Britain furnish its own nuclear warheads. For the British, the agreement was ideal: Skybolt extended the period of useful service of the V-bomber fleet at very little cost. There was apparently little concern that the United States might someday cancel Skybolt—a reasonable attitude in light of U.S. defense policies during the 1950's.

The British cancellation of Blue Streak had important implications: it signaled an end to Britain's technical capability to build a long-range ballistic missile system. It also raised an important new question: Was it now desirable for Britain to attempt to maintain a strategic nuclear force, even assuming a measure of American assistance? The question had not received much attention. The major concern before 1960 was how the strategic nuclear force would be employed, not whether Britain should have one.[42]

A central issue in discussions of the strategic nuclear force is its military effectiveness. In the comments below it is assumed that the force would be employed unilaterally in a second-strike role. This is the most pessimistic situation; first-strike employment is militarily more advantageous, as is joint employment with Strategic Air Command.

Three interrelated problems are at issue: the size of the force, its vulnerability to surprise attack, and its ability to penetrate enemy air defenses. In its present status the firstline or operational force comprises, roughly, one hundred eighty bombers, a large portion of which are Mark II versions of the Victor and Vulcan aircraft.[43] Existing facilities enable this bomber force to be dispersed to some thirty or forty secondary airfields; there are, therefore, the same number of unprotected targets presented to an attacker. Vulnerability is somewhat reduced by dispersal; it is, however, difficult to believe that a significant proportion of the force would escape destruction in a surprise attack, when the aircraft would probably be concentrated on even fewer airfields.

While vulnerability to surprise attack has increased with the shift in Soviet strategic capability from aircraft to ballistic missiles, the government has held that Bomber Command is less subject to destruction than this summary suggests. One reason for the government's calculation is the low order of probability placed on a surprise attack. Unlike the United States, where military planning is predicated mainly on an assessment of enemy *capabilities,* British planning gives somewhat greater weight to enemy *intentions.* It is therefore assumed that Soviet preparations would be evident before an attack could be launched. It is argued, therefore, that sufficient time would be available to alert and disperse the force. Although the protection afforded by dispersion is not very great, a number of special measures enable the force to be airborne very quickly. Through the use of multiple engine starters and certain special equipment stocked at dispersal airfields, bombers can be airborne in about three minutes. Multiple crews permit maintenance of ground alerts for protracted lengths of time. Assuming that the force is alerted and that countermeasures (such as high altitude nuclear explosions) do not disrupt the warning system, British planners anticipate that many of the bombers could be dispatched.

In any conceivable second-strike employment, the attacking force would be reduced in size by takeoff failures and losses from the enemy's strike. As the force enters target areas and is brought under fire by alerted air-defense forces, its size is reduced again. Because the force is small, it probably will not be able to "saturate" air defenses and thereby reduce its own vulnerability. The probability that an attacking aircraft will reach the target area decreases rapidly with improvements in air-defense systems. The government has argued that "enough"—an undefined figure—would penetrate Soviet air defenses to inflict "unacceptable" damage on the enemy. The Labor opposition and many outside commentators question this assertion.

Judgments about the effectiveness of the force as a deterrent depend on numerous assumptions relating to vulnerability, penetration ability, and the effectiveness of defensive countermeasures. These assumptions are seldom made explicit by critics; a reliable analysis is perhaps limited to those who possess detailed technical data, i.e., the government itself.

The question of whether to maintain a strategic nuclear force is difficult to answer, partly because its military effectiveness is not easily ascertained. But the complexity of the problem is greatly compounded by the highly uncertain and incommensurable side effects that are involved. Some critics have maintained that the force is unnecessary.[44] The U.S. strategic capability is assumed to be adequate. The resources devoted to the British deterrent ought, therefore, to be transferred to conventional forces, which, critics feel, are badly needed by the West. The assertion that a strategic nuclear force increases Britain's influence in Washington is questioned. Even if some influence does exist by reason of the force, the critics suggest that larger conventional forces would buy an even greater amount of influence with the U.S. Finally, it is argued that if Britain did not have a strategic nuclear force, there would be less pressure on other countries to build their own nuclear weapons. Preventing the spread of nuclear weapons would be a major contribution to arms control and would enhance Britain's prestige in many parts of the world.

Another group of critics argues that the V-bomber force should become the nucleus of a NATO or joint-European strike force. In their view Britain cannot afford to maintain indefinitely an effective and independent deterrent; however, they see no point in scrapping the present bomber force. There is also, because of the uncertainty of American response to a Soviet attack in Europe, a military need for a NATO strike force. The European members of NATO could reasonably undertake the task of building one. Three benefits are usually attributed to the proposal: Britain would have a greater voice in European affairs; Europe would gain added authority vis-à-vis the United States in NATO affairs; and a joint nuclear force is the only feasible way to prevent the West Germans from building their own independent force. A major drawback in the proposal is the difficulty of devising a means to maintain effective political control over the force; French participation, doubtful under President de Gaulle, would be necessary.

Defenders of the government's policy have argued that the force is effective as a deterrent. The political benefits—increased influence in Washington and, perhaps, Moscow—are considered highly valuable. Moreover, they doubt that Britain's prestige would be greater or that there would in fact be a reduced desire by other countries to build their own national nuclear forces if Britain reversed its current policy. Finally, there is the question of the shift of resources. The relevant constraint on conventional forces is manpower, not money. The striking characteristic of the three analyses is less their originality or brilliance than the enormous uncertainties and incommensurables implicit in them.

If a force deters because the enemy *fears* it will be effective, it may be that the British force is now fulfilling a "passive" or second-strike role. There is no doubt, however, that the credibility of the bomber force is declining rapidly. Skybolt was expected to provide the necessary technological upgrading. It was designed to be launched some one thousand miles from the target. At that range, the vulnerability of the transporting bomber to air defenses would be negligible. Skybolt would therefore extend the useful period of service of the British V-bombers until 1970.[45] The United States cancelled the Skybolt program in December, 1962. Except for Blue Steel—also launched from a bomber and now being improved so as to provide a capability until 1966–68—there are no other replacement systems under development in Britain.[46]

Following the cancellation of Skybolt, President Kennedy agreed to make available to the United Kingdom Polaris missiles and technical data relating to nuclear-powered, missile-firing submarines. The Macmillan government thereupon decided to build a fleet of Polaris-firing submarines consisting, it was recently announced, of five boats. The Polaris is an especially attractive system since it is relatively invulnerable to surprise attack. But with only five boats, the force on station will be very small: two or three submarines carrying thirty-two or forty-eight missiles. The submarines will not be available until 1968 or 1970—by which time the V-bomber force will be highly vulnerable to air defenses—and there will perhaps be a period of a year or two in which Britain will be unable to attack the Soviet Union with nuclear weapons. A much more important issue, however, is the cost of the program. Under the Nassau Agreements, Britain must build its own submarines. Estimates of the cost of a nuclear submarine run from £60 to £100 million; a five-boat fleet would cost between £300 and £500 million. The costs of maintaining a strategic nuclear force have thus increased greatly over the relatively inexpensive Skybolt arrangement. Are the military and political benefits of a Polaris force worth the price?

Another issue must be considered simultaneously: What are

the costs and benefits—and the prospects—of the Mixed-Manned Nuclear Force proposed by America? [47]

DEFENSE RESOURCES

A review of postwar defense policies would be incomplete without brief mention of the resources that have been consumed by defense. The shortage of resources has prompted defense planners to decrease continually the scope of defense policies. Further, many alleged deficiencies in policy would disappear if more resources were made available. But it may be the critics' expectations that need revision, not the policies.

The Costs of Defense [48]

Historically security programs were never very expensive. Except for periods of active war or acute emergency, defense expenditures seldom exceeded 3 per cent of the Gross National Product. In contrast to this pattern, defense cost 11.8 per cent of the national income in 1952 and has not fallen below 7 per cent of the GNP since World War II. The higher costs are largely explained by the fear of Soviet aggression in Europe and the turbulent conditions in the overseas areas. But rapid technological change and the loss of inexpensive manpower and overseas bases that were available before World War II have also pressed the cost of security programs upward.

Postwar force and budget reductions were generally completed by mid-1947. Since that time British defense allocations have progressed through six reasonably well-defined financial stages. The salient features of each are noted below.

Pre-Korean stability. By mid-1947 the defense budget had been reduced to about £740 million. There was a small increase —about £40 million—in 1948. This followed the new tensions in Europe after the communist coup in Czechoslovakia. Spending levels, however, remained below £800 million through 1949 and the first half of 1950.

Korean rearmament. There was a sharp increase in defense spending after the outbreak of war in Korea. In the early fall of 1950, the government announced a rearmament program to cost £3,400 million over the next three years. Subsequently, UN reverses in Korea and, possibly, pressures by the United States prompted the Attlee government to increase the original rearmament program; thus, in January, 1951, it was announced that £4,700 million would be spent on defense over the following three years. This latter figure was somewhat misleading—the operative constraints on rearmament were over-all industrial capacity, the need for a smooth transition from civil to military production in the manufacturing sectors, and the competing demands of exports.

The Churchillian "Stretch." In the general election in November, 1951, the Conservative party defeated the Labor party. One month later Sir Winston Churchill, the new Prime Minister, announced that the £4,700 million, three-year program would be carried out over four rather than three years. This extension came at the end of a severe balance of payments crisis that lasted through most of 1951 and was an acknowledgment that the £4,700 million program was well behind schedule.

The "New Look." Despite the cessation of hostilities in Korea, defense spending in 1953 exceeded £1,700 million; in 1954 expenditures began to decline. This "New Look" followed closely the "New Look" of the Eisenhower administration, which cut nearly $4 billion from the U.S. defense budget in 1954. Budget reductions were accompanied by other policy shifts, e.g., the decision to develop a strategic nuclear force and a sharp downgrading of the army's claims on resources.

"MacSandys." During the period of the "New Look" the defense budget declined from about £1,700 million to about £1,600 million. The aberration in this pattern occurred in 1956 when the Suez operation raised costs again to about £1,700

million. The real reduction during this period was greater, however, since price levels increased by about 10 per cent. In early 1957, following the resignation of Sir Anthony Eden, Mr. Duncan Sandys was appointed Minister of Defense by the new Prime Minister, Mr. Harold Macmillan. The new government emphasized defense economies. An expenditure ceiling was imposed, and budgets between 1957 and 1959 increased only £25 million. In 1959 defense cost 7.6 per cent of the GNP.

"A stabilized share of the GNP." Defense spending has increased each year since 1960. In effect, defense has been alloted between 7 and 7½ per cent of the GNP, and security expenditures have grown at about the same rate as the national income. In 1963 the estimates were £1,830 million. The decision of December, 1962, to build a Polaris nuclear submarine force has intensified and strengthened defense claims for more resources.

Manpower [49]

Postwar service manpower levels, like defense spending, have been unusually high. In 1950 force levels were 690,000. Service strengths of 875,000 in 1952 declined slowly to about 700,000 by early 1957. A sharper reduction has taken place since 1957: there were about 425,000 persons in the forces in mid-1962. In contrast, the average strength during the interwar period was about 330,000. The larger postwar levels, as compared to the prewar peacetime strengths, are due to the extensive commitments in Europe and overseas, exacerbated by the loss of colonial manpower and the inefficiencies of a conscript army.

Postwar manpower policies have centered around one problem—National Service or conscription. The British services were traditionally volunteer forces; not since 1815 had there been peacetime conscription. But the Attlee government felt it necessary to continue conscription after World War II. This policy was initially justified by the desire to maintain large reserve forces, but by late 1948 conscripts represented an increasing share of the strength of operational units overseas. Because of growing international tensions and since training and transportation time consumed a large share of the conscript's short career, the period of service, set at twelve months in 1947, had been increased to eighteen months by 1949 and to two years by 1950.

Table I below indicates service manpower levels since 1950. The figures in parentheses are the number of conscripts in each service. Of the three services, the army was most dependent on National Service: between 1951 and 1957 about half its manpower was conscript. The share in the air force was somewhat lower, about one-third, while the navy used very little National Service manpower. The large percentage of conscripts in the army and air force created difficult problems in these services. The army, for example, had heavy operational commitments abroad and was faced with the administrative task of constantly rotating personnel back and forth to overseas stations. The two-year period of service also provided a constant inflow of recruits into the services and made it necessary to maintain a large training establishment. National Service was also detrimental to service morale and, consequently, inhibited regular recruiting. In short, conscription was considered an inefficient system for meeting manpower requirements. Over-all force levels were inflated, and by impairing regular recruiting National Service insured its continued existence.

A constant and major objective of personnel policies before 1957 was to increase the flow of regulars into the forces. It was reasoned that any increase in the regular component would allow a corresponding reduction in total manpower levels. To stimulate recruiting and raise retention rates, pay increases were granted in 1950, 1954, 1956, 1958, 1960, and 1962. The extent of the increases is suggested by the fact that military pay has occupied a relatively constant share of the total defense budget. In the financial year 1950–51 and

TABLE 1 *

BRITISH MILITARY MANPOWER FOR THE YEARS 1950–63,
BY BRANCH OF SERVICE †
(000 Omitted)

Year	Royal Navy		Army		Royal Air Force		Total	
1950	135		360		193		690	
1951	141	(7)	433	(224)	251	(89)	827	(320)
1952	146	(5)	451	(224)	272	(89)	872	(318)
1953	143	(7)	442	(228)	178	(78)	864	(313)
1954	132	(8)	443	(221)	261	(69)	839	(298)
1955	126	(10)	422	(205)	253	(70)	803	(285)
1956 ‡	120	(12)	398	(202)	242	(76)	761	(290)
1957	114	(10)	366	(174)	221	(69)	702	(253)
1958	105	(5)	322	(145)	184	(46)	614	(196)
1959	102	(2)	304	(125)	173	(26)	580	(153)
1960	98	(1)	264	(98)	164	(18)	526	(117)
1961	95		231	(65)	158	(13)	485	(78)
1962	95		201	(26)	148	(5)	445	(31)
1963	96		183		147		426	

* Sources: Central Statistical Office, Statistical Annexes to the annual "Statements on Defense" and *Annual Abstract of Statistics*, Nos. 93 and 96 (London: H. M. Stationery Office, 1956 and 1959).

† Strengths (men and women) as of June 30 each year except conscripts' which are as of March 31 each year. The aggregate total contains nurses of the various nursing corps not included in the individual service strengths.

‡ Estimates. In 1956 some 30,000 reserves were mobilized during the summer for the Suez operation.

1951–52, for example, military pay represented 25 per cent and 24 per cent respectively of the total defense budget. In 1959–60 and 1960–61, with manpower levels reduced by 20 per cent and 35 per cent over the earlier years, military pay took 23 per cent of all funds allocated to defense. The attempts to buy volunteers have raised service pay and benefits to levels directly competitive with standards of remuneration in civil life; to maintain comparability of civil and military pay, biennial pay reviews based on the cost-of-living index are now statutory.

In addition to pay increases, a number of other measures have been employed to make service life more attractive. The most important is an extensive program to build new barracks and family quarters. The army, as an example, was constructing some 1,500 new family housing units annually in the early 1960's—and was renting 10,000 family units in Britain and West Germany.

The effort to "regularize" the forces was unsuccessful. Conscripts made up between 35 and 40 per cent of the forces with little change between 1950 and 1957. Despite these disappointments, the government in 1957 decided that conscription would be abolished and that there would be "no further call-up . . . after the end of 1960." [50] This decision, which must rank as one of the major policy choices since 1945, was conditional: the Macmillan government promised to reinstitute National Service if the army failed to recruit at least 165,000 regulars. It was common knowledge, however, that the figure of 165,000 represented an actuarial estimate of the number that could be recruited and was well below the level of 200,000 the War Office felt it needed.

The progress of army recruiting attracted considerable attention in Parliament and the press. Some critics nonetheless suspected, perhaps hoped, that the government would not achieve its goal of 165,000 regulars.[51] As a consequence of the decision, service public relations and recruiting activities, particularly in the army, were considerably more active than before 1957. By mid-1962 the transition to all-regular forces was completed. Between 1957 and 1962 aggregate force levels had fallen from 690,000 to 425,000.

The 1957 force reduction had its greatest impact on the army, and it was the only service in which a reorganization of the operational elements was necessary. In all three services, however, support and service facilities were closely reviewed. In the navy, for example, over sixty small installations were closed. The activities of two home commands and two major dockyards were transferred to other establishments. The dockyards at Hong Kong and Trincomalee were closed, while the yard in Malta was sold to a civilian firm. As a result of these measures, some 23,000 civilian and 7,000 naval positions were abolished. As part of these reviews, each of the services instituted so-called civilianization programs, under which duties assigned to uniformed personnel were transferred to civilian employees. The reduction in military strengths thus overstates somewhat the decline in combat effectiveness of the forces. The levels of civilian employment and the total civil work force as a percentage of the uniformed establishment are shown in Table 2 below.

TABLE 2 *

Civilian Work Force in the British Service and
Supply Departments †
(000 Omitted)

Year	Industrial	Non-Industrial	Total	Military Strengths	Per Cent §
1951	275	126	401	827	48
1952	297	139	436	872	50
1953	307	138	445	864	51
1954	302	140	442	839	53
1955	301	134	435	803	54
1956	296	135	431	761 ‡	57
1957	284	133	417	702	59
1958	259	128	387	614	63
1959	242	125	367	580	63
1960	237 ‡	131 ‡	368	526	70
1961	232 ‡	133 ‡	365	485	75

* Sources: Central Statistical Office, *Annual Abstract of Statistics*, Nos. 93, 96, and 98 (London: H. M. Stationery Office, 1956, 1959, and 1961).

† As of April 1 each year. Included are a small number of employees in the Ministry of Aviation (formerly the Ministry of Supply) who perform duties not connected with defense.

‡ Estimated.

§ Civilian work forces as a per cent of military strengths.

Despite the compensating features of civilianization, force reductions accentuated the competition among the different programs. When the government wanted to increase BAOR manpower during the Berlin crisis of late 1961, there was very little slack. The choices were limited. A buildup in BAOR required either a reduction overseas or in the strategic reserve. As alternatives, the government could mobilize by proclamation Territorial Army units, or could extend the period of service of a limited number of the conscripts still on duty. The

second alternative was chosen, and it resulted in the contro-
versial Army Reserve Bill of 1961. This bill was symptomatic
of many of the difficulties facing defense planners. The government had achieved a compromise between limited resources
and extensive commitments, but the balance was so finely
drawn that policy was, in fact, relatively inflexible.

1. DeWitt C. Armstrong III, "The Changing Strategy of British
Bases" (Ph.D. dissertation, Princeton University, 1960), pp. 295–309.

2. Cmd. 9075, "Statement on Defence 1954," p. 6.

3. Armstrong, "The Changing Strategy of British Bases," p. 222.

4. Cmd. 150, "Memorandum of the Secretary of State for War Relating to the Army Estimates, 1957–58," p. 10.

5. Very briefly, an "air barrier" is created whenever one government
refuses another permission to overfly its territory.

6. Sir William Hayter, "Forces Too Few and Far Away," *Observer*,
December 10, 1961.

7. Cmd. 363, "Report on Defence: Britain's Contribution to Peace
and Security," p. 7.

8. Cmd. 1630, "Memorandum by the Secretary of State for Air to
Accompany Air Estimates, 1962–63," p. 6.

9. These formations are depicted in some detail in Cmd. 1629, "Explanatory Statement on the Navy Estimates, 1962–63," pp. 14–15.

10. Cmd. 371, "Explanatory Statement on the Navy Estimates, 1958–
59," p. 4.

11. Cmd. 1639, "Statement on Defence, 1962: The Next Five Years,"
p. 15.

12. *Ibid.*, p. 3.

13. Denis Healey, "Britain and NATO," in Klaus Knorr (ed.), *NATO
and American Security* (Princeton: Princeton University Press, 1959),
p. 214.

14. Anthony Eden, *Full Circle: The Memoirs of Anthony Eden* (Cambridge, Mass.: Houghton Mifflin, 1960), p. 186.

15. Cmd. 9075, p. 5.

16. Except that opposing strategic forces of approximately equal capability may be a basic condition for engaging in "brushfire" operations.

17. Cmd. 124, "Defence: Outline of Future Policy," p. 5.

18. *Ibid.*, p. 4.

19. See Table 11 below, p. 217.

20. Healey, "Britain and NATO," p. 222.

21. Cmd. 363, p. 4.

22. Cmd. 124, p. 4.

23. 635 H. C. Deb. 1285.

24. 635 H. C. Deb. 1202.

25. Cmd. 9396, "Explanatory Statement on the Navy Estimates, 1955-56," p. 5.

26. Cmd. 9688, "Memorandum of the Secretary of State for War Relating to the Army Estimates, 1956–57," p. 9.

27. Cmd. 124, pp. 2–3.

28. Central Statistical Office, *National Income and Expenditure, 1961* (London: H. M. Stationery Office, 1961), p. 42.

29. Cmd. 9075, p. 21.

30. Cmd. 9391, "Statement on Defence, 1955," p. 23.

31. Because of disinvestment of stockpiles, the total expenditure is much smaller.

32. Cmd. 124, p. 3.

33. Cmd. 9075, pp. 4–5.

34. *Ibid.*, p. 5.

35. Cmd. 9388, "The Supply of Military Aircraft," p. 4.

36. Cmd. 9397, "Memorandum by the Secretary of State for Air to Accompany Air Estimates, 1955–56," p. 4.

37. Cmd. 9696, "Memorandum by the Secretary of State for Air to Accompany Air Estimates, 1956–57," p. 4.

38. Cmd. 149, "Memorandum by the Secretary of State for Air to Accompany Air Estimates, 1957–58," p. 4.

39. Cmd. 363, p. 5.

40. Cmd. 673, "Memorandum by the Secretary of State for Air to Accompany Air Estimates, 1959–60," p. 2.

41. Cmd. 363, p. 6.

42. See Chapter III.

43. The data in this and the following paragraphs are drawn from The *Guardian*, May 12 and 13, 1961.

44. These are the general arguments used by critics and defenders of the policy, not the specific analysis of any one individual.

45. Skybolt, however, would have increased the vulnerability of the force to surprise attack.

46. Two aircraft, the Buccaneer (which recently entered service with the Fleet Air Arm) and the TSR2 (due about 1966), have a strategic capability and reduced vulnerability because of their low-altitude penetration capability. Whether these aircraft have sufficient range for service in the strategic nuclear force is unknown; the adoption of the Polaris suggests that they do not.

47. See Chapter VII.

48. See below, Chapter IX.

49. See below, Chapter XI.

50. Cmd. 124, p. 7.

51. The 1957 white paper announced plans for forces of "about 375,000." The 1958 white paper stated that "the Services have been given authority to recruit up to the following ceilings: Navy 88,000; Army 165,000; R.A.F. 135,000. The fact that these three ceiling figures for recruiting together total 388,000 does not mean that it is intended to increase the planned strength of the combined forces beyond the figure of 375,000 mentioned above. But the Government have felt it right for the present to maintain some flexibility" (Cmd. 363, p. 10). Following a most satisfactory recruiting effort in 1958, the 1959 white paper explained: "Since in any voluntary force fluctuations in the level of recruitment are inevitable, it has been decided to accept recruits [in the army] in excess of . . . [165,000], up to an overall ceiling of about 180,000" (Cmd. 662, "Progress of the Five-Year Defence Plan," p. 5). There were frequent attempts at the end of 1962 to interpret these statements as authorization for an army strength of 180,000. In the event that this higher level was not reached, the government could be criticized for (1) a poor job of recruiting, and (2) reneging on its promise to reintroduce conscription if service strength was not up to the prescribed level. An additional element of uncertainty was interjected because it was not always clear whether the army's limit included women and boys, who together number about 15,000. Finally clearing the confusion, the 1961 white paper spoke of an army "of the order of . . . 165,000 to 180,000" and added that these figures "exclude boys and women" (Cmd. 1288, "Report on Defence, 1961," p. 8).

3/ Parliament as a Critic of Defense Policy

MAJOR DEFENSE POLICIES—the size and composition of the forces, the defense budget, and the broad strategic concepts governing force employments—are announced by the government in the annual statement on defense, more commonly known as the defense white paper. This document and the service estimates, which detail the expenditure programs for each service in the approaching fiscal year (April 1–March 31), are normally submitted to Parliament early in each calendar year. Policy proposals that appear on an irregular basis— defense organization changes are an example—are announced in special white papers.

Parliamentary action is mainly limited to debate of the policies formulated by the government. The clash in debate of government and opposition provides a constant stream of information and criticism that serves to publicize the activities of the parties and the problems and policies of the day. This division of political labor is well recognized by British constitutional theory, and procedural rules for the two Houses of

Parliament limit their ability to modify government proposals. These limitations are particularly evident in respect to control of expenditures. Unlike the United States, where Congress can and does change both the total size and the item allocations in an Executive budget, Parliament lacks these fundamental powers. Although Parliament—specifically, the House of Commons—must approve policies that involve financial expenditures or changes in organization, this action is normally little more than a formality. The tight discipline of the party system insures the votes needed for Parliamentary approval of government proposals. Disapproval is extremely unlikely since it would entail the fall of a government.

THE LIMITATIONS ON PARLIAMENT
AS CRITIC OF DEFENSE POLICIES

The custom of Parliament is to raise issues of general national importance; debates seldom become enmeshed in masses of financial or technical detail. Parliament would thus seem to provide a particularly effective national forum for discussion and debate of defense policies. In fact, it suffers several handicaps which limit its ability to inform the larger public of the important security issues facing the nation. One is the concentration of defense debates in a period of a relatively few weeks (what Colonel George Wigg calls the "defence season" [1]), normally in February and March of each year. For the remainder of the session—unless there is an opposition motion or a special white paper—Parliament says little or nothing about defense.

A more serious problem is the lack of information. MP's of all political leanings consider that the lack of information weakens seriously their ability to engage in intelligent debate and hence properly to inform the larger public of defense-policy issues. Except for those members who hold political office, MP's are not privy to classified information. Nor are Parliamentary

committees able to receive regularly the secret testimony of
political and military leaders on policy matters.[2] Illogical and
paradoxical as it may seem, parliamentarians obtain most of
their information—even unclassified data—from the press and
other news media. There are, according to Mr. Shinwell, other
sources, but these do not necessarily provide a balanced or reliable flow of information:

> I am one of the few people now in this House . . . who is not in the
> confidence of military experts. Not a single general, not a single air
> marshal, not a single admiral, not a single military correspondent of *The
> Times* . . . or of any of the reputable organs of the Press ever comes to
> me and says, "I know that you are interested in defence. Would you like
> to have some information?" Not a bit of it.[3]

The end result is that the quality of Parliamentary discussions
suffers: lack of access to classified data limits Parliament's
effectiveness in debate of defense policies. Even though classified materials might not necessarily be relevant or even useful
in discussions of general national goals and policies, few members feel themselves adequately informed when they lack such
restricted information.

The granting of access to classified information to members
of Parliament poses a difficult problem, and an effective procedure to provide interested MP's with the information they
desire has yet to be devised. During periods of crisis, opposition *leaders* are usually given access to classified materials—
Mr. Churchill, for example, was briefed by the Attlee government following the outbreak of the Korean War [4]—but there
is still a need for information during less critical periods. In
response to a proposal by Mr. Shinwell, Minister of Defense
in the latter years of the Attlee government, Prime Minister
Macmillan offered in 1958 to hold regular consultations with
opposition leaders on defense matters. The Labor leadership
declined the offer, arguing that consultations would imply
Labor endorsement of government policy and hence weaken the
party's effectiveness as critic.[5] Neither of these proposals, in-

cidentally, improve the situation of the interested back-bench MP.

The executive or closed session has also been suggested as a way of providing Parliament with classified information and was strongly advocated by Mr. Churchill during the early period of the Korean War.[6] While this process would inform Parliament, its proceedings could not be reported in the press or *Hansard* and would contribute nothing of benefit to the general public.

Parliament's lack of information is matched by its lack of interest in defense matters. It is pointless to maintain that a given percentage of time ought to be spent in debate of defense policies; it does seem, however, that the time allocated to defense might profitably be increased. Over the last decade the House of Commons has devoted about seven or eight days in each session to defense. Two days are spent on the defense white paper; one day is allowed for each of the three service estimates; and two or three days are usually spent on special white papers, opposition motions, and adjournment debates. Since the normal session runs to about one hundred seventy meetings, debates of defense policies receive about 4 to 5 per cent of the available time in the House of Commons. Yet defense is the most expensive of all public policies; since 1945 it has consumed between one-fourth and one-third of all expenditures by the national government.

Defense debates in the House of Lords suffer from many of the same shortcomings. Speakers in the House of Lords very often possess qualifications that are absent in the House of Commons—military or scientific achievements of high order, for example—and the caliber of debate is excellent. The Lords, however, gives even less time to defense than the House of Commons. Except for Lord Montgomery's always provocative (and well-publicized) comments on current policies, the debates are lacking in excitement. Finally, much of the impact of these debates is lost because few people believe the Lords to be of any real importance.

As might be expected, defense debates seldom attract much Parliamentary interest. Sustained interest is even more limited: In the nine debates of defense white papers in the House of Commons between 1952 and 1960, there were 113 speakers (including government spokesmen). Forty per cent of the speeches, including most of the long ones, were made by *sixteen* members—eight from each party; over two-thirds of the speeches were made by forty-four members. The limited time for debate makes it impossible to have many speakers; the limited interest in defense makes it unnecessary to have additional time for the subject. And those few members with a continuing interest in defense (they could perhaps be described as a *de facto* defense committee) operate without adequate information, without sufficient time, and without the privilege of examining expert witnesses.

The Labor Party's Weaknesses in Opposition

Parliament's informing or lyrical role depends to a considerable degree on the party in opposition. The Opposition shares responsibility for scheduling Parliament's time, and the value of debate rests largely on the skill and vigor of its critique of government policies. The political opposition since late 1951 has been the Labor party. Two special problems have restricted its effectiveness as critic of defense policy. The first limitation arose because Labor leaders and defense spokesmen were in basic agreement with the policies of their Conservative opponents. Moreover, those aspects of policy with which the opposition leadership disagreed provided Tory spokesmen with an opportunity to discredit the Labor party. Second, a number of back-bench MP's disagreed sharply with the views of the party leadership on defense policies, thereby splitting the party internally.

On many of the major policy issues after 1952 the front-bench or official Labor party position has been close to that of the government.[7] Labor initially endorsed Tory policies, which had, after all, been initiated by the Attlee government.

The principal modifications subsequently brought forward by
Conservative governments were also generally acceptable to
Labor. These modifications included such critical matters as
the size of the defense budget, the decision to build a strategic
nuclear force, and the ending of National Service. The agreement among front-bench spokesmen of both parties was
sufficient to provoke from Mr. Konnie Zilliacus, a Labor backbencher and a "unilateralist," [8] the following protest in the
1959 defense debate:

. . . All the way through, the debate has seemed to me to be very much
of an "Annie, Get Your Gun" debate, with my right hon. Friend the
Member for Belper . . . [Mr. George Brown, then Labor's principal defense spokesman] and supporting cast singing in chorus with the right
hon. Gentleman the Minister of Defence [then Mr. Duncan Sandys] and
his troupe, to the theme of
      "Anything you can do I can do better,
      I can do anything better than you." [9]

The general support of the Labor party and especially its
leadership has presumably strengthened the conviction of successive Conservative governments that their policies were both
objectively correct and politically feasible.
   The consensus on policy has not been complete, however.
After 1956 Labor differed sharply on one important issue, the
balance between conventional and nuclear capabilities. This
complex situation, in bare outline, took shape as the government formulated and announced its plans for employing the
strategic nuclear force. The government's doctrine, "massive
retaliation," emerged piecemeal in defense debates and white
papers beginning in 1955, appearing in its most explicit form
in paragraph 12 of the 1958 Defense White Paper.[10] The government indicated that a major conventional attack by the
Soviet Union would cause the employment of the British
strategic nuclear force. Whether the force was to be employed
alone or in conjunction with SAC was never made clear;
neither was it clear whether this response was applicable only

to the NATO area or to other geographic regions as well. The Labor leadership, drawing indirectly on earlier American criticisms of Secretary of State Dulles' ideas, affirmed the need for a strategic nuclear force but rejected this Conservative doctrine of its use.[11] Labor spokesmen Healey, Strachey, and Brown argued that massive retaliation was suicide. What was needed was a policy of "graduated deterrence," [12] a doctrine that admitted the existence of a lesser range of threats and responses.

Graduated deterrence, however, raised other complex issues involving tactical nuclear weapons and conventional forces. In accord with the 1954 NATO policy and as a corollary of their strategic nuclear doctrine, the government held that tactical nuclear weapons would be required in the event of a Soviet ground attack in Europe. Indeed, the British Army of the Rhine was then being reduced in size. Concurrently, organization and doctrine were being revised in anticipation of receiving tactical nuclear weapons from the U.S. The Labor leadership thought that tactical nuclear weapons were necessary but feared that an overreliance on them would make it more difficult for NATO forces to respond to an ambiguous threat, such as a border incident, or something less than a full-scale attack. In Labor's view, larger, better-equipped forces for conventional or non-nuclear operations provided the solution.[13] But it was accepted, almost as an article of faith, that it would be impossible to obtain larger conventional forces without a return to conscription.[14]

Labor's critique of the doctrines on the use of the strategic nuclear force and tactical nuclear weapons in Europe was an interesting and useful contribution to the public discussion of defense policies. But much of its impact was lost, since the critique provided Conservative spokesmen an opportunity to discredit the Labor party. The Labor critique also led to an internal dispute in the Parliamentary Labor party. Both situations served to weaken the party as a critic of government policy.

One of the attractions of a strategic nuclear force was that it was believed to increase Britain's influence on American decisions concerning the use of the Strategic Air Command. Britain could thereby presumably insure the United States strategic commitment to the NATO area; equally important, British leaders would be able to prevent a rash or overrapid employment of SAC. A second attraction was that the strategic nuclear force would help counterbalance the much larger Soviet conventional strength in Europe, and fewer British conventional forces would then be necessary. Labor recognized and agreed with the need to influence American decisions on the use of SAC. Labor also wanted to end National Service.[15] Acceptance of the need for a strategic nuclear force and commitment to an early end to National Service were two basic premises that could not easily be reconciled with Labor's critique of government policy. Thus, the Labor front-bench position, especially after 1957, was either incomplete or inconsistent. Government speakers did not fail to notice and publicize the dilemma.

The question of the balance between conventional and nuclear forces was also the subject of a dispute. Labor backbenchers, particularly Messrs. Wigg and Crossman, argued that if larger conventional forces were indeed necessary, National Service had to be reinstated to provide the requisite manpower.[16] Mr. Crossman, the intellectual architect of the back-bench analysis, also asked why a British strategic nuclear force was necessary: given the country's resource limitations and the size of the American strategic force the resources allocated on the V-bomber force could, he felt, be better utilized on conventional forces.[17]

The Labor back-bench critique received a more sympathetic hearing from Tory backbenchers than from Labor defense spokesmen. Brigadier Antony Head, the Minister of Defense for a few months in late 1956, Nigel Birch, Sir Fitzroy Maclean and a few younger Conservatives held similar views.[18] The discussions on the balance of conventional and nuclear forces thus produced strange divisions and alliances within the House of Commons. The government and the Labor leadership agreed on the need for a strategic nuclear force and the desirability of an end to National Service. However, they disagreed on strategy and the Labor leadership was highly critical of the massive-retaliation doctrine. A few Labor backbenchers accepted the party's graduated-deterrence concept [19] but argued that conscription was therefore necessary to obtain larger conventional forces, and, finally, that the strategic nuclear force was not necessary. Several Tory MP's held similar views. The complex divisions and alliances that developed during the debates aroused as much interest as the underlying issues of defense policy.

After 1957 the question of the balance between conventional and nuclear forces progressively divided the Labor party. The issue reached a climax in 1960, when forty-four Labor backbenchers failed to support the party's Motion of Censure of government defense policy. This split was the fourth in ten years to be caused by differences within the Parliamentary party on defense or foreign policies. In 1950 Aneurin Bevan and two junior ministers—one of whom, Mr. Harold Wilson, is now the party leader—resigned from the Attlee government over the issue of defense costs during Korean rearmament. A related problem, German rearmament, was the cause of a split in 1954. One year later fifty-seven Labor MP's, including Aneurin Bevan, failed to support the party's censure motion which read that

[the Labor party] regrets that the Statement on Defence, 1955, while recognising that thermonuclear weapons have effected a revolution in the character of warfare, and that until effective world disarmament has been achieved it is necessary as a deterrent . . . to rely on the threat of using thermonuclear weapons, fails to make proposals for the reorganisation of Her Majesty's Forces and of Civil Defence, to indicate what future defence expenditure may be . . . or to explain the grave and admitted deficiencies in the weapons with which Her Majesty's Forces are at present furnished, in spite of the expenditure of some £4,000 million for defence purposes over the past three years.[20]

The seemingly irreconcilable divisions within the Parliamentary Labor party stem partially from the diverse social, educational, and occupational backgrounds of Labor members.[21] When classified by occupational backgrounds members form three approximately equal groups. The "Workers," usually trade-union officials of working-class backgrounds, normally have no more than a secondary-school education. They are interested primarily in higher welfare grants, improved health and educational standards, and increased wages and pensions. The second group, the "Professions," is university educated, with backgrounds in law, journalism, or teaching. Ideological moderates, these members adopt middle-ground positions on most foreign-policy issues and are less concerned with economic matters than the Workers. The remaining members, midway in educational levels between the Workers and the Professions, form a group called "Miscellaneous Occupations." Although lacking a common occupational background, this group nevertheless embodies and articulates a common ideological theme— the anticolonialist, anticapitalist, and pacifist strands of British socialism. Its membership includes most of the Labor party's unilateralists (numbering about fifty) and the bulk of those who opposed German rearmament. Thus, on issues of foreign, colonial, or defense policies, the Miscellaneous Occupations adopt a different position from that of the Workers and the Professions. On economic issues, the Workers become the party's left wing, the two remaining groups again adopting a more moderate position. The extremes do not cancel each other; one group always rests to the left of the majority of the party. Internal party cohesion, so necessary in British politics, is lacking.[22]

Defense debates have tended to highlight the internal divisions of the Labor party rather than to publicize the deficiencies in government policies or to arouse public interest in defense issues. In commenting on the 1958 defense debates, for example, the *Observer* noted that the opposition, "torn by internal divisions, was able neither to comment intelligibly nor to offer any alternative policy." [23] The revolt in 1960, alleged the *Daily Herald*, permitted the government to evade opposition charges of excessive missile and aircraft costs and ". . . made a Tory holiday of the second day of the debate. . . ." [24] In contrast, the differences within the Conservative party, admittedly not as sharp as in Labor, went unnoticed. Conservatives who believed that larger conventional forces were needed and that a strategic nuclear force was unnecessary were able to direct their criticism at the opposition front bench, thus maintaining a facade of Tory unanimity.

Recent general elections reveal the failure of defense debates to arouse public interest in defense issues. In the 1955 general election, for example,

such interest as there was unquestionably tended to shift from foreign to domestic affairs.
. . . Those Labour candidates who made the attempt found surprising little response to their expositions of the horrors of atomic warfare. . . .[25]

Nor, despite previous discussions in Parliament of British nuclear strategy, was the story any different in the 1959 general election: "The main questions of defence—the H-bomb, conscription, and military inter-dependence–were ignored." [26]

THE CONSEQUENCES OF PARLIAMENTARY DEBATE

British governments enjoy great latitude and autonomy. Governments are expected to govern, and autonomous but responsible institutions and habits of decision-making are grounded on ideas of political deference by which each constituency expects its Member in Parliament to act in accordance with his individual interpretation, or his party's interpretation, of the national interest. Yet there is also an assumption that one of the requisites for a democratic political system is an enlightened electorate. An informed public provides an additional check on political power by establishing broad limits on the choices that can be made by political leaders. Although it is not the only source of information and criticism, Parliament is supposed to play a central role in informing the public. However, defense-policy debates do not appear to create an informed or critical public. In fact, public opinion places few limitations on policy choices. Public attitudes are weakly held, and mass opinion tends to shift rapidly following changes of policy to support government decisions. Finally, public attitudes are relatively unresponsive to criticisms of defense policies—but highly responsive to government pronouncements on defense issues.

Whatever deficiencies public opinion polls may have, they remain the best available index of attitudes in the mass public.[27] Poll data are reasonably clear and unambiguous in their major outlines, and it may be assumed that they provide a reasonably accurate description of mass public opinion. To explore the consequences of Parliamentary debate, the following section examines public opinion poll data on: conscription, 1949–56; the magnitude of the defense effort, 1949–52; the magnitude of the defense effort, 1955–61; and nuclear weapons and unilateralism, 1955–61.

Conscription, 1949–56. Polls in 1949 indicate that conscription was approved by a majority. In January, in response to the question "Do you think that conscription should be continued or discontinued in peacetime?", 57 per cent thought it should be continued, while 33 per cent wished it discontinued.[28] The same question was asked in November, and the response was 53 per cent and 38 per cent, respectively. Before the government announced an extension of the period of service to two years, a sample was asked in September, 1950: "Would you approve or disapprove if the period for conscription were increased from eighteen months to two years?" A majority, 55 per cent, approved and 33 per cent disapproved. A poll in early 1953 posed the following question: "Some people argue that conscription should be decreased from two years to eighteen months. Do you think that it should be decreased or left as it is?" Forty-five per cent wanted a decrease, while the same percentage wanted the period to remain at two years. In May, 1954, the question was: "Some European countries now have less than two years' conscription. Churchill says it would not be wise for us to cut our own two-year period. Do you agree or disagree with him?" Forty-nine per cent agreed and 35 per cent disagreed.[29] Following an announcement of service manpower cuts in October, 1955, only 34 per cent agreed that it was wise not "to cut our two year call-up period and . . . [to raise] the age of starting." Forty-seven per cent disagreed. By September, 1956, supporters of National Service were a minority: "Do you think that the party which gets your vote should support or oppose these proposals? Abolish conscription?" Forty-four per cent supported the proposal (i.e., end conscription), and 38 per cent opposed.

The foregoing data suggest that public attitudes on conscription were transient and sensitive to pronouncements by national political leaders. In the period 1949–54 a majority or near majority approved peacetime conscription; public support, in short, was anchored in the firm commitment of both government and opposition to National Service. By 1956, one year before the government announced its plan to end conscription, public support had fallen somewhat, much as the support for National Service had declined among political leaders. The Labor party persistently questioned the need for conscription and the length of the period of service, and their criticism was especially sharp in 1955 and 1956. Despite Labor's criticism and the somewhat equivocal support of the government—the Tories also wanted to end National Service but there seemed no easy way to meet military manpower needs without maintaining the period of service at two years—the mass public only mildly disapproved of what was generally thought to be an intensely unpopular policy.[30]

The magnitude of the defense effort, 1949–52. In a poll in July, 1949, respondents were asked, "If the Government has to make cuts in the money it is spending, what . . . should be cut first?" Fifteen per cent indicated the armed forces; 73 per cent selected other areas of government expenditure. Of a sample questioned in September, 1950, 78 percent agreed "with the Government's increased spending on defence" while only 14 per cent disagreed. In July, 1951, the British Institute of Public Opinion (BIPO) asked: "If the Korean war ends soon, do you think that Britain should continue her defence programme as planned, or should it be reduced?" Sixty-four per cent thought the program should be continued as planned; only 22 per cent favored a reduction. In February, 1952, after Mr. Churchill had extended the £4,700 million rearmament effort over an additional year, 58 per cent favored "continuing the present [i.e, the extended] rearmament programme." Twenty-eight per cent wanted the program reduced. "Some people say that we should not spend so much money on armaments at the present. Do you agree or disagree . . . ?" In September, 1952, 47 per cent responded by noting that arms expenditures were "not too high," while 36 per cent indicated they were "too high." Even when asked, in March, 1951, to choose between defense and housing, a very scarce commodity in postwar Britain, public support for defense was remarkably high: "Mr. Dalton has said that rearmament must not interfere with housing. Do you agree with him or should defence come before housing?" [31] "Housing first" was the choice of 44 per cent; "Defence first" was the choice of 41 per cent.

The pattern in the period 1949–52 is thus reasonably clear: The public supported rather decisively the government's decisions on the magnitude of the defense effort. Public support continued throughout the period despite one of the major intraparty struggles in recent political history—the Bevanite revolt. Defense expenditures were the focus of Bevanite criticism, if not necessarily the only reason for the revolt. The consequences of this split for the Labor government aside, the Bevanite revolt did not have a significant impact on public attitudes toward the rearmament program. Indeed, the single exception (the "Dalton" question) to the pattern of majority support appeared in March, 1951—*before* Mr. Bevan and his followers made public their dispute with the Attlee government.

The magnitude of the defense effort, 1955–61. A poll in September, 1955, showed a noticeable change from three years earlier. Thirty-two per cent of the public believed that defense should be reduced "if the Government wants to cut down its spending." All other major public policies mentioned for reduction totaled 49 per cent. "Do you think that the party which gets your vote should support or oppose these proposals: Cut down on defence expenditures?" In September, 1956, 49 per cent indicated they supported the proposal and 34 per cent opposed; a year later 50 per cent supported and 32 per cent opposed. In February, 1958, BIPO asked: "Do you think the Government should increase, decrease . . . , or keep expenditures at the present level on: Arms and Armaments?" Only 12 per cent favored an increase and 51 per cent favored a decrease, while 37 per cent believed present expenditure levels were satisfactory. In January, 1959, a status quo pattern grew stronger: "Do you think the Government is or is not spending enough money on: Armaments and Defence?" Seventy-one per cent thought the present level was enough; 9 per cent indicated approval of larger expenditures. To summarize, after 1955 an overwhelming majority of the mass public was opposed to any increase in the size of the defense effort.

In recent years there has been another change. In February, 1960, 27 per cent approved the decision to increase spending on defense while 54 per cent disapproved. By November, 1961, public opinion was still more favorable to increased defense spending: 18 per cent, the largest number in several years, thought the government was spending "too little" on armaments and defense. Twenty-nine per cent indicated that expenditures were "about right." Only 26 per cent thought the government was spending "too much."

The course of public opinion after 1955 traces much the same pattern as the government's attitudes toward defense economies. With the financial crisis of 1955 the government exerted strong efforts to "hold the line" on defense spending. The Prime Minister, Sir Anthony Eden, and Mr. Harold Macmillan, his Chancellor of the Exchequer, believed over-all government spending excessive and defense especially costly.[32] A "general examination" of government expenditures was ordered, one of the results of which was the 1955 service manpower reductions. Subsequent white papers gave special emphasis to defense economics, especially in 1957, and government spokesmen frequently noted that the economy could not support a larger defense effort.[33] In addition, these efforts were supplemented by an occasional dramatization of the burden of the defense effort. One of the most important was Mr. Macmillan's "two rifles" speech on May 16, 1956. In this address to the Foreign Press Association, the Chancellor of the Exchequer claimed that Britain, as compared to her European allies, was carrying a "second rifle"; and although he admitted it was a "pipe dream," he spoke of a £700 million cut in defense expenditures.[34] This speech was especially important in shaping public attitudes on the size of the defense program both before and after the Suez intervention:

One of the curious results . . . is the extraordinary kind of neutralist emotion which is growing, not least in the party opposite [i.e., the Conservative party]. There is in every speech that is made, in every newspaper that one reads, even the more responsible ones, an emotion that Suez has shown that all this money has been wasted, that it has not produced [*sic*] effective results, a feeling of, "Let us cut it; let us do away with it. Nothing is of any use, anyway."

This assessment of the climate of post-Suez opinion came from George Brown, the Labor spokesman on defense. He continued:

The Prime Minister began all this recently. This was not done by irresponsible newspapers. It was not done by uninformed back benchers. It was not done by ill-intentioned Front Benchers on this side of the House.

. . . .

From the first £700 million pipe dream the thing has been changed to £350 million and £500 million in the *Observer* and in *The Times* on the day when . . . the Minister of Defence came back from America.[35]

The government, to support its decision to maintain a stable level of defense spending, suggested that sharp reductions were possible and desirable. Its argument that defense economies were a "good thing" was rapidly confirmed by mass public attitudes. The responsiveness of public opinion is also demonstrated after 1960: The defense budget was increased in 1960 and each year thereafter, and the mass public subsequently began to support the increased defense effort.

Nuclear weapons, 1955–61. The structure of public attitudes toward nuclear weapons was first suggested by public opinion polls in February and March of 1955. In these samples 31 per cent and 32 per cent, respectively, disagreed with the decision to make the hydrogen bomb. In 1958 attitudes were roughly the same. An April poll indicated that 25 per cent would approve if Britain were "to give up her H-bomb without waiting for America or for Russia to move." Subsequent polls in 1958 and 1959 indicated that one-quarter to one-third of the public supported unilateral nuclear disarmament.

Since 1960 the British Institute of Public Opinion has asked a standard series of questions on nuclear weapons. The responses to one such question in 1960 and 1961 are shown in Table 3 below.

Since 1955 support for unilateralism has varied between a low of 19 per cent and a high of 33 per cent. By 1958 the Campaign for Nuclear Disarmament had become a well-publicized element in British life, but subsequent polls reveal no important surge of support to unilateralism. Indeed, percent-

TABLE 3

Attitudes of the British Public toward Nuclear Weapons, 1960–61 *
(Percentage Favoring Each Response)

Date	Response			
	1	2	3	4
1960				
April................	26	19	31	24
May................	33	27	24	16
July................	27	34	28	11
September...........	21	31	36	12
October.............	21	32	37	10
1961				
January-April........	19	26	36	19
June................	20	30	35	15

* Question: What policy should Britain follow about nuclear weapons?
Responses: 1. Give up nuclear weapons entirely.
2. Pool all nuclear weapons with other NATO countries and rely mainly on American production.
3. Continue to make our own nuclear weapons.
4. Don't know.

ages fell in late 1960 and early 1961. The decline began in September, 1960, at the time of the Trades Union Congress (T.U.C.) meeting, where Mr. Frank Cousins of the Transport and General Workers Union dramatically opposed the defense policies of the Labor party leadership with his form of unilateralism. Public support continued at a low level through early 1961, although this was a period of intensive activity by the unilateralist groups.

One reason for the decline in mass support was the sharp counterattack by Mr. Hugh Gaitskill, the Labor party leader, who, supported by most of the Parliamentary party, promised to "fight, fight, and fight again." In the course of Gaitskill's battle the case for a strategic nuclear force, membership in NATO, and defense in general was stated more forcibly by Labor party leaders than ever before. Moreover, organizations promoting unilateralism were less effective in molding public opinion than the groups they challenged. Only 37 per cent of the public was even aware of the debate on nuclear policies within the Trades Union Congress. A large majority of knowledgeable respondents saw the T.U.C.'s concern over defense policies as "improper": defense policies are legitimately the responsibility of the government and the political parties; the T.U.C.'s "proper" concern is trade unionism.[36] Similarly, the semiviolent activities of the Committee of 100, a militant splinter group of the CND, contributed in 1961 to the decline of mass public support for unilateralism: "The Committee of 100 demonstration . . . recruited some powerful support for their opponents," noted Dr. Henry Durant of the British Institute of Public Opinion in December, 1961. "Support for unilateralism slumped from 30 per cent to 21 per cent." [37] The reason was that the public disapproved the tactics employed by the Committee—in October, 1961 over 60 percent viewed "direct action" with disfavor.

Those four brief surveys suggest the difficulties faced by critics of defense policies. The Bevanite revolt in 1950 produced little change in public support for Korean rearmament. Labor's persistent attack on National Service after 1954 resulted in somewhat weakened public support, but hardly massive opposition to conscription. Popular sympathy for unilateralism has increased little since 1955. Mass public attitudes, in short, have been relatively unresponsive to criticisms of defense policies.

Criticism provokes a subsequent explanation and justification of policies. Whether the debate takes place between the government and the opposition or is centered within a party, the critic speaks with less prestige and authority than the defender of policy. Any government is likely to have important advantages, as, for example, its command of recognized expertise and information. Defense is also viewed as a national problem properly the prerogative of the government of the day, not that of its critics. Since to criticize policy is to call into action an opponent more effective as an agent of opinion formation, procritic public attitudes are subsequently converted into support for official policy.

The inherent weaknesses of the opposition's position have

been exacerbated by the ambiguous critique and the persistent divisions within the Labor party. It is not surprising, therefore, that a majority of the public has consistently believed that the Conservative party is better able than the Labor party to handle the problems of defense and foreign policy.[38] Yet Labor, ironically, has probably made the best of a difficult situation. The party admittedly gave insufficient time and effort to the problem of defense.[39] But additional Parliamentary consideration would only tend to operate to Labor's disadvantage. Debates both initiated a Tory response and revealed that the Labor party's divisions and splits were far broader than simple issues of defense policy. Additional public interest and concern with defense issues would very likely have cost the party votes in election campaigns.

1. 682 H. C. Deb. 532.

2. The powers of Parliamentary committees are limited in scope, mainly to an ex post facto review of administration. Policy questions are specifically excluded from their purview.

3. 583 H. C. Deb. 579.

4. Reported in *The Times*, July 28, 1950.

5. For comments on the issue see Max Beloff, "Defence Talks between Party Leaders," *The Times*, April 29, 1958.

6. Reported in *The Times*, March 17, 1950.

7. This analysis of the Labor party's position is based on House of Commons debates. The Lords debate was much the same, except that the split within the Labor party was less evident.

8. One who urges that Britain unilaterally renounce nuclear weapons.

9. 600 H. C. Deb. 1393.

10. Cmd. 363, "Report on Defence: Britain's Contribution to Peace and Security," p. 2.

11. The best Labor critiques came from John Strachey and Denis Healey. Both had become interested in military problems and were familiar with the American literature. Labor speakers also owe a heavy debt to the Hon. Alastair Buchan, currently the director of the Institute of Strategic Studies. As Washington correspondent for the *Observer* until 1956, Buchan observed and reported the American debate on the Dulles doctrine, an experience which influenced his comments on British defense policies after his return to London in 1956.

12. This was sometimes called "minimum deterrence."

13. A short summary of these contrasting views may be found in Denis Healey, "Britain and NATO," in Klaus Knorr (ed.), *NATO and American Security* (Princeton: Princeton University Press, 1959), pp. 209–35.

14. Indeed, the question was whether the government would be able to recruit an all-regular army of 165,000. The leading skeptics were Colonel George Wigg (Labor) and Brigadier Antony Head (Conservative).

15. Labor speakers questioned the need for conscription in every defense debate after 1954, and in the 1955 general election the party unofficially promised to end National Service. See D. E. Butler, *The British General Election of 1955* (London: Macmillan, 1955), p. 88.

16. See, for example, 583 H. C. Deb. 638.

17. See, for example, his brilliant speeches in the 1958 and 1960 defense debates in 583 H. C. Deb. 632–41 and 618 H. C. Deb. 1058–67.

18. See 618 H. C. Deb. 921–97 and 600 H. C. Deb. 1166–76, 1338–41.

19. They accepted "graduated deterrence" as an appropriate NATO strategy, not as a national strategy for Britain.

20. 537 H. C. Deb. 1917.

21. A hypothesis advanced by Professors S. E. Finer *et al.*, in the important book *Backbench Opinion in the House of Commons, 1955–1959* (New York: Pergamon, 1961), pp. 14–75.

22. *Ibid.*, p. 75.

23. March 2, 1958.

24. March 2, 1960.

25. Butler, *The British General Election of 1955*, p. 74.

26. D. E. Butler and Richard Rose, *The British General Election of 1956* (London: Macmillan, 1960), p. 72. Defense issues were seldom mentioned in the critical by-elections of 1962.

27. Poll data were obtained from the Gallup Organization, Princeton, New Jersey, which maintains files of British Institute of Public Opinion Social Survey results. I am greatly indebted to George H. Gallup, Jr., for allowing me to use the data.

28. "Don't know" responses have been omitted from the text.

29. Invoking the name of Churchill, then the prime minister, may have been sufficient to reverse the slight decline in the previous (1953) poll.

30. David Butler has commented on the 1955 general election as follows: "The unpopularity of national service among large sections of the electorate was widely appreciated. Both sides acknowledged the demand for a cut. The Labour Party went decidedly further in promising one, but even it made no official commitment. Whether it harvested many votes on the issue is open to question" (Butler, *The British General Election of 1955*, p. 88).

31. Mr. Dalton, a former Labor chancellor of the Exchequer, was popular and widely known. At this time he was minister of local government and planning and a member of the cabinet.

32. Anthony Eden, *Full Circle: The Memoirs of Anthony Eden* (Boston: Houghton Mifflin, 1960), p. 350.

33. On January 17, 1957, less than a week after he became prime minister, Mr. Macmillan told a national TV audience that "we certainly cannot do without our defences. We have obligations to ourselves and to our partners. We must carry our fair share, but not more than our fair share. We are going to make sure that we are not spending money on things we do not need or commitments we cannot sustain. There must be no waste of money. No vested interests, however strong, and no traditions, however good, must stand in our way." (Reported in *The Times*, January 18, 1957.)

34. Reported in the London press on May 17, 1956.

35. 564 H. C. Deb. 1288–91. For a brief period after Suez, most of the quality press explicitly called for cuts in defense spending. The pattern soon shifted, however. The *News Chronicle* of February 5, 1957, said that talk of great reductions in defense was "silly." The *Daily Telegraph* of the following day was concerned over the impact of defense cuts on the aircraft industry. By midsummer most of the press was concerned about the reductions in conventional forces.

36. Data from BIPO, "Political Index," September, 1960.

37. BIPO, "Political Index," December, 1961.

38. Butler and Rose, *The British General Election of 1959*, p. 71.

39. Mr. George Brown once confessed to a reporter for the *Guardian* that "there are not enough votes in defence, I suspect, for us to give it the attention officially which we ought to give it (February 25, 1960).

4/ The Influence of Parliament and the Articulate Public on Postwar Defense Policies

PARLIAMENT is largely excluded from direct participation in the policy process. It has had no voice at all in many, probably most, of the major postwar policy decisions, such as the development of a strategic nuclear force and the commitment of British forces to NATO. Indeed, Parliament was not informed, much less consulted, by the Attlee government of its decision to build atomic weapons. It is thus easy to overlook Parliament's influence on the substance of defense policy. But the power and autonomy of a government does not mean that Parliamentary influence is insignificant. Its contribution to defense policies is something more than just debate and criticism. Parliament is both a source of influence, which is frequently accommodated by a government, and a part of the network of intellectual activities by which an articulate public external to the government attempts to influence policy decisions through commentary and criticism.

THE INFLUENCE OF PARLIAMENT

The most important test which a new government policy must meet is its reception by Parliament. The test is not the vote which the proposal must obtain to effect its passage; party discipline and energetic whips virtually insure the government the necessary votes. What matters is the mood and frame of mind, the sense of the House, that emerges as Parliament debates policy proposals. The comments of back-bench supporters and the nature of opposition criticism—because they help set the tone of public opinion in the nation as a whole—furnish an indication of what the government may expect as public reaction to its policies. The reception of a bill by Parliament is also evidence to a government of its own fitness to govern: its competence to recognize and to define national problems, and its capacity to formulate appropriate solutions. If a policy is well received, the responsible ministers are pleased, and the government's confidence in itself is stimulated. If Parliament's reaction is something less than enthusiastic, the government's elan is impaired, and its morale is lowered. Policies need not be popular or easy to pass this difficult and crucial Parliamentary test: to ignore the existence of difficult problems or to advance weak and compromising measures when hard and unpopular policies seem indicated is to lay open before Parliament weaknesses that are inexcusable in a government.

In the context of postwar defense policies, Parliament has had a significant influence, not directly in shaping policies, but rather in strengthening and confirming the commitment of each successive government to the policies it has formulated. Although it has become somewhat testy in recent sessions, Parliament's usual reaction to defense proposals—whether by Labor or Conservative governments—has been generally favorable. Except for the *post*-1956 critique of strategic doctrine, which was weakened by Labor's internal splits, defense policies have commanded the general support of the leadership

of the political opposition. Cases in which government proposals have been met by significant back-bench opposition are
hardly more numerous: the Attlee government's decision to
retain conscription in 1946; the size and financing of the
Korean rearmament effort that led to the Bevanite revolt; and
finally, strategic nuclear policy and conscription after 1957.
In two instances—the white paper presented by Sir Winston
Churchill in 1954 and the 1957 Defense White Paper—Parliament even approached enthusiasm. In short, the milieu has
been reinforcing: the basic assumptions of defense policies
have until recently gone virtually unchallenged and coherent
alternatives have only infrequently been put forward. In the
face of Parliamentary approbation, political leaders would
hardly be inclined to search for modifications or alternatives;
the addition of Parliamentary support dampens the incentive
of dissident officials and military officers to continue to press
for their preferred alternatives.

The mood of Parliament is neither precise nor tangible,
and its importance can be suggested only in general terms.
However, Parliamentary influence of a more direct nature may
be transmitted into the government through the party structure—specifically, though the back-bench committees.

In the Conservative party, backbenchers are organized into
a series of committees, known collectively as the "1922 Committee." [1] This organization includes a defense committee, sub-
committees on each of the various services, and—a recent
addition—a space subcommittee. Except for the MP's who
serve as chairmen, committee membership is reportedly somewhat fluid. Partly because of the relatively large number of
retired military officers who man the Conservative back bench,
interest tends to be relatively high. In the Labor party, which
has drawn few professional officers into its ranks, back-bench
committees concerned with defense policies were relatively
weak and inactive during its period in office.

The relation between party leaders and back-bench members
is one of mutual dependence. The leadership depends on its

back bench for the necessary votes to pass its policies. While it can, and on occasion does, command the support of back-benchers by the use of various sanctions, it much prefers that back-bench support rest on intraparty agreement and harmony. The backbencher's political career depends largely on the success of the party as a whole, and on most issues considered by Parliament his support may be taken for granted. Although he almost always submerges his personal dictates and votes with his party, he also prefers that party discipline be used sparingly. But in the case of policies in which he has an unusual interest or strong sentiments, or if the decision has implications for his constituency, the backbencher often feels that his views would be of interest and value to the government; in any event he will want to be consulted and forewarned of forthcoming policy announcements. Mutual dependence and a common desire for harmony within the party thus bring together interested backbenchers and responsible government ministers.

The frequency of contacts between ministers and interested backbenchers varies with time, personality, and issue. On occasion ministers are invited to present the government's views to a back-bench committee. At other times the committee meets privately, its chairman forwarding though the party whips a report to the responsible ministers on the "sense of the meeting." Finally, a minister may seek out the views of a back-bench committee. In short, interested backbenchers and responsible ministers are linked by the party structure, and the back-bench committee has ready communications into the government departments.

The backbencher interested in defense policies works under an important handicap—his lack of information. Unlike the "interested member," i.e., an MP who speaks for one of the many organized interests groups such as the Federation of British Industries, he is unlikely to have an outside agency to furnish him with materials.[2] Nor does he have the expert staff available to members who are in the government. As a consequence of his need for data and ideas, the backbencher is somewhat vulnerable to proffers of assistance or skillful arguments from other sources.

Although generally reliable information is available in the daily and weekly press, which is discussed below, two other sources are of special relevance to the backbencher. Probably the most important of these is the opposition. A shared interest in a particular area of public policy serves to bring MP's of the parties together. Indeed, the opportunities for discussion and contact among MP's is unlimited, and "Members Opposite" are often convenient and reliable sources of information.[3] There is even formal collaboration between members; a recent example is the series of study groups sponsored by the Army League in 1958 and 1959. The group that prepared the Army League's pamphlet *The British Army in the Nuclear Age* included two Labor MP's who were then front-bench spokesmen for the opposition, Messrs. Strachey and Paget, and two MP's from the Conservative back bench, Colonel Tufton Beamish and Mr. Richard Sharples.[4]

The second source of information especially relevant to the backbencher is the permanent research staff in the central organizations of the two political parties. Both party organizations have been interested in defense problems, and each has published a number of papers on aspects of current policy. The activities of the somewhat better-financed Conservative Research Center, however, are more extensive and influential than those of its counterpart in Transport House. A department of the Conservative Central Office, the Conservative Research Center, investigates a range of subjects of interest to the party. Included among its staff are several research associates who specialize in defense-policy matters. For the young backbencher without extensive military service or ministerial experience, the Center's research associates are useful sources of information and ideas. In fact, Center assistance may be pressed on a backbencher, since a back-bench client can bring the policy prescriptions of the researcher to an audience he could not otherwise command.[5] In somewhat this fashion the Center made an important although anonymous contribution to *Stability and Survival,* a collection of articles on defense policy by young Tory backbenchers and writers.[6] This widely circulated pamphlet, critical of government policies, was sponsored by the Bow Group, the organization of young Conservatives, following a series of study group meetings in mid-1960.

How important are the back bench and the attitudes that it channels into the government? Civil servants acknowledge that it is more important than any other non-economic group external to the government.[7] To say more than this is, of course, difficult—"humanly impossible," as the political correspondent of *The Times* once put it.[8] The proceedings of back-bench committees and meetings of the Parliamentary party are among the most discreet of political activities. They take place behind closed doors, and the details seldom leak to the press.[9] Some reasoned, if general, conclusions are possible, however.

The significance of back-bench opinion is related to three factors: the size of the governing party's majority, the degree to which back-bench opinions focus or coalesce, and the composition and leadership of the back-bench committees. Contrary to what might be supposed, back-bench influence is quantitatively greater when a government has a large majority. With as small a majority as both governments enjoyed between 1950 and 1955, the defection of a very few members creates a serious situation. Under these circumstances one would expect ministers to explain carefully the bases of government policies to party backbenchers.[10] At the same time backbenchers are inclined to be much more reserved. The spectre of a general election is a powerful deterrent—the casualties in an election are concentrated mainly among backbenchers— and even to think critically invokes the possibility of disciplinary action. With a large majority the backbencher is under far less pressure. He is willing to articulate his opinions and may even abstain from voting in a division without fear of bringing down the government.

The other factors are equally critical: If back-bench opinion is very scattered and only a few members contest any particular aspect of policy, a minister could perhaps ignore them. If all are concerned with one element of policy, a stronger challenge faces the government. Finally, the leadership of the back-bench defense organization may be non-representative of back-bench opinion or at least the most frequently voiced attitudes.

If these speculations are correct, it is reasonable to believe that back-bench opinions have become more important in recent years. The Conservatives have enjoyed a large majority since 1955, and Parliamentary concern has focused mainly on two problems, the strategic nuclear force and the balance between NATO and overseas commitments. It is to be suspected, however, that back-bench opinion has also tended to reinforce and support the government. Back-bench attitudes do not necessarily coincide with the patterns of opinions that are articulated in Parliamentary debates; the Speaker is obliged to give a fair hearing to all views. Back-bench attitudes, on the other hand, represent the consensus of a smaller, more homogeneous group whose leadership is concentrated in the hands of a relatively older group of MP's, few of whom appear to have a history of active or strong criticism of government policies. In the crucial defense debates on the Nassau Agreement of January 30–31, 1963, for example, Tory backbenchers split in their reaction to the government's decision to build a Polaris force. But support outweighed criticism among Conservative MP's with leadership roles in the back-bench committee structure: supporters of government policies included the Chairman of the Defense Committee, Air Commodore Sir A. V. Harvey, and the Chairman of the Navy Subcommittee, Sir John Maitland.[11] This action followed by a month a meeting of the Conservative Defense Committee with the Minister of Defense (Mr. Thorneycroft) in which the Committee sought assurance: first, that Britain would develop a stand-off weapon of greater range than Blue Steel in order to maintain the credibility of the British V-bomber force during the period in which manned bombers with gravity bombs would be highly vulnerable to air defenses and before the entry into service of the Polaris force; and second, that Britain would retain an "absolute right" to use Polaris independently.[12] Much the same pattern of support appeared about one month later in the debate of the 1963 Defense White Paper, when a majority of the most prominent members of the back-bench defense organization again supported the government's policies.[13] If these cases are representative, the back bench, a source of pressure to which ministers are particularly sensitive, may buttress government policy choices but not necessarily press on the government the new or different proposals most frequently voiced by the critics of policy.

THE INFLUENCE OF THE INTELLECTUAL COMMUNITY

There are in Britain few organizations that are concerned with security problems. Private organizations which undertake research under contract from the service departments or the Ministry of Defense (such as the RAND Corporation in the United States) are nonexistent in the United Kingdom. Private institutions like the Royal Institute of International Affairs and the Royal United Service Institution have until recently been concerned more with historical or descriptive studies than with current military-policy issues. Similarly, there are no university centers that specialize in military policies; there are only a few university courses dealing with national security affairs.[14] Individual scholars with an interest in security problems are only slightly more numerous; the fifteen or so books dealing with current security policy or organization published in Britain between 1946 and 1960 were the product of half that many authors. These authors, a few commentators, and some ten or twelve MP's also contribute most of the commentary on defense-policy issues that appears in the daily and weekly press. In addition to being very small, this articulate public does not include (with the possible exception of P.M.S. Blackett, one of Britain's most distinguished physicists), individuals competent in the technical aspects of military policy—for example, weapons-system costing theory and techniques, systems analysis, and the economics of national security.

If security problems have attracted rather minimal interest in the intellectual community, it is not because of inadequate press reporting. The large London daily papers, *The Times,* the *Guardian,* and the *Daily Telegraph,* employ competent and experienced full-time (or nearly so) Defense or Military Correspondents. Their thorough and outstanding reporting of defense affairs is supplemented by the news that appears in the Sunday papers (the *Sunday Times,* the *Sunday Telegraph,* and the *Observer*) and the nationally circulated weeklies (the *Economist,* the *New Statesman,* the *Spectator,* and a recent addition, the *New Scientist*).[15]

Englishmen are voracious newspaper readers, and most policy-makers are probably exposed daily to one or more of the better papers. It is reasonable to believe that press reports are important in defining for policy-makers the larger political worlds, international and domestic, in which defense policies are shaped. Press reports, rather than official documents or briefings, are also likely to be the main source of information about defense policies for officials elsewhere in government, at the Board of Trade or the Ministry of Health, for example. The basic impressions conveyed by the quality papers may be of consequence when defense policies or budgets are considered by the cabinet. Third, the press is the major source of information for the articulate public of politicians, writers, and commentators who engage in public debate and criticism of policy. It thus indirectly influences the responsible officials who contribute to the government's rebuttal. Finally, the public reaction to policies comes to the attention of responsible officials largely through the press. Although public opinion polls are of increasing importance in this regard, press reporting undoubtedly precedes and shapes public attitudes. Unfavorable reports may lead to a more active effort by a government to explain and justify its position, even if that position is not changed.

The press has an editorial role in addition to its reportorial function, and it is the vehicle through which the articulate public attempts to influence policy-makers. Since Members of Parliament comprise a large share of that part of the intellectual community interested in foreign and military policy issues, the press is thus an additional outlet for Parliamentary opinion. Commentary from the articulate public is about equally split between the daily and Sunday papers, on the one hand, and the weekly journals, on the other. Press commentary has become increasingly critical in recent years—in contrast to the generally favorable attitudes of the early and middle 1950's—and only the *Daily Telegraph* has consistently and firmly supported the Conservative government's policies.

Press commentary suffers from several deficiencies that serve to weaken its impact on policy-makers. First of all, it is sporadic and occurs mainly after decisions are announced, not while policies are being formulated. As an example, serious questioning of the decision to end conscription occurred after the government had announced its plan in 1957. Second, a good share of press commentary in the quality journals is written by back-bench and opposition politicians, and as a consequence it displays the polemical character of Parliamentary debate. Finally, as Mr. Macmillan, the Minister of Defense in 1955, explained in the defense debate of that year:

Of course, all our critics do not agree with us, but the trouble is that they do not agree with each other. At any rate, during my first few months as Minister of Defence I have not suffered from lack of advice. A great deal has been said and written in speeches and pamphlets during the last few weeks, as well as said in this debate. I have had all these carefully collated. The trouble is that they nearly all cancel each other out.[16]

There are two additional aspects of the role of the press that deserve brief mention. First, a constant theme in press commentary of the past decade has been the concern over the organization for, and method of, policy-making in the military departments.[17] While criticism of the process of policy formulation stems partly from disagreement with the substance of policy, there is nevertheless a genuine concern over the apparatus of policy-making. Almost without exception government defense-reorganization proposals have been acclaimed, mainly because commentators have viewed defense organization as one of the more serious impediments to effective national policies. Interservice rivalry, an object of persistent criticism, has been viewed as both a symptom and a cause of failure: a symptom of the failure to exercise firmer, more centralized control over the military departments on the part of political leaders; the main cause of the inability to formulate a viable national strategy. The second development is the growing agreement among commentators that it is no longer desirable for Britain to maintain an independent strategic nuclear force. Some of the substantive bases for this opinion have already been noted, as have the most frequently advanced alternatives; an element of some consequence in its growth is the Institute of Strategic Studies.

The Institute of Strategic Studies was established in 1958. The initiative for its formation came from several senior American officials in the Department of State and the Department of Defense, who also helped arrange financial support from the Ford Foundation.[18] Membership is limited to individuals "who have something useful to offer to discussions of security problems"; [19] many of its present four-hundred-odd members are Europeans or Americans. Because of its financial arrangements and mixed membership, the I.S.S. has given no direct attention to British security problems. It has instead concentrated on more general security issues; NATO strategy and arms control are two areas of special interest to its Director, the Hon. Alastair Buchan.

The direct influence of the I.S.S. on British defense policy may be negligible; it has, however, made an important contribution to the activities of the articulate public. I.S.S. conferences and meetings link the articulate public in Britain with their counterparts in the United States and Europe and thereby promote the circulation of ideas on security problems. *Survival*, the bimonthly publication of the institute, reprints articles on defense problems drawn from a wide variety of journals and periodicals, both communist and Western. With a circulation of about fifteen hundred copies, *Survival* also facilitates the exchange of ideas within the articulate public. Finally, the I.S.S. has been a major stimulus to research on security problems in Britain: a large majority of the books and monographs published since 1960 have been products of I.S.S. study groups.

In light of the foregoing, what conclusions can be reached about the influence of the articulate public on defense policies? The press is of obvious importance as a source of information, but it is unlikely that commentary and editorial opinion have had much impact on the substance of policy. Press commentary is to some degree an extension and repetition of criticism already voiced in Parliament. Before 1956 or 1957 the volume of commentary was not great or, for that matter, unanimous in its view of policy. Further, the impact of much commentary is lost because of its lack of objectivity, an inevitable result of the political commitments of its authors.

Several writers have suggested that in recent years the articulate public has made a more extensive contribution to defense policies, that

a small but influential group of civilian intellectuals, experts on strategy, has appeared; and these men have been welcomed by the services as allies and experts, the association finding expression now in the recently established Institute of Strategic Studies that specializes in high-level confidential discussion of policy issues between senior soldiers, top civil servants, and other highly qualified civilians.[20]

This appears to overstate the case; the influence of the articulate public seems rather insignificant in substantive policy choices. The reasons are rather compelling. First, any government is somewhat reluctant to seek the services of outside experts. There is in British government an amateur ethic whose symptom is the persistent complaint of misuse and lack of status on the part of specialists within the civil service. More important, a surprising share of the functions of government have been delegated to experts—the civil servants—but experts of known quality and over whom there is firm and explicit control. To utilize outside experts may weaken a politician's relations with his staff of officials, while it also creates uncertainty about the use of advice by ministers.

Other reasons for the ineffectiveness of the articulate public lie in the size and composition of the group itself. The articulate public is very small. One reason for its limited size is that postwar governments have not encouraged or supported the formation of independent research institutions, and a corps of analysts has thus not developed. Parliament's lack of interest in defense-policy issues has been a further contributing factor. Finally, despite "the concern with the arms race which is so evident in the senior and junior common rooms," [21] British universities have demonstrated but little genuine interest in security problems, with the result that there are few faculty members in the country qualified to contribute to discussions of security issues.

A final reason that helps explain the minimal influence of the articulate public is that policy-makers do not want their advice.[22] While it is true that senior officials and military officers have attended a number of conferences with members of the articulate public, it may be suspected that the reasons for their attention are more to articulate and explain policies than to hear suggested alternatives or criticism.[23] There is, in fact, considerable justification for the view that outside advice is not useful. With but few exceptions there are no "experts" outside the government; the articulate public is dilettantist in character, and for most of its members defense policies are only one of several interests demanding their attention. It does not possess unusual skills or knowledge that make its comments valuable to the policy-maker. There are few mathematicians, economists, engineers, or scientists among its membership.

Instructive in this regard are two books that have attracted extensive interest among British officials in recent years: *The Economics of Defense in the Nuclear Age*,[24] by Charles J. Hitch (currently the Department of Defense Comptroller) and Roland N. McKean, and *The Weapons Acquisition Process*,[25] by Professors Merton J. Peck and Frederic M. Scherer of the Harvard Business School. The American authors of these books, economists and management specialists, deal theoretically with problems that are very much the everyday concern of British officials: What is the economic cost of various programs—weapons systems, deployments, movements, facilities? What techniques are useful in cost analysis and budget programming when uncertainties are involved? How can benefits and costs be compared when there are incommensurables? In short, the expert advice that the government needs to make policies does not always concern strategy and basic assumptions; whether policies are good or bad depends on what they cost and the benefits they return. These tedious and technical problems of calculation have failed to attract the interest of critics—much less a recognition that they present intractable difficulties in which major errors are virtually impossible to avoid. The preliminary skills required for the solution of these problems, it should be added, have been developed "in house," within the civil service itself.

The failure of the larger intellectual community to make more than a negligible contribution to the substance of postwar defense policies has been summarized by one of its members as follows:

As commentators and experts we have no direct impact on policy. We are, however, of some importance. Our general criticism of British strategic policies have joined with those of many American analysts. These, in turn, seem to have had an important effect on the Kennedy Administration, to the extent even of leading to a better balance among various capabilities. And as a result of new American policies, the U.S. has recently pressed on the British, without, I regret, much effect on the government thus far, policies which we think should have been adopted long ago. Our influence and channels through which it operates, then, are rather round about.[26]

The exception to this trend is the criticism of the policy process where the effect has been to intensify those characteristics of the decision-making process most deplored by the critics.

1. See Peter G. Richards, *Honourable Member: A Study of the British Backbencher* (London: Faber and Faber, 1959), pp. 90–142, and I. Bulmer-Thomas, *The Party System in Great Britain* (London: Phoenix House, 1953), pp. 119–132.

2. I do not mean to imply that backbenchers do not speak or "lobby" for outside groups—they do. As an example, the present chairman of the Conservative Defense Committee, Air Commodore Sir A. V. Harvey, represents the aircraft industry in the House of Commons.

3. I am advised that several of the articles on defense policy published by Conservative backbenchers have been edited by a Labor member.

4. Richard Goold-Adams (Rapporteur), *The British Army in the Nuclear Age* (Barnet, Herts.: Stellar Press, 1959), p. 5.

5. The relationship between the Research Center and the back bench is strengthened by the CRC's growing importance as a source of Conservative Parliamentary candidates. The importance of the CRC and Central Office in another area of public policy is detailed in H. H. Wilson, *Pressure Group: The Campaign for Commercial Television* (London: Secker and Warburg, 1961).

6. Interviews. The Bow Group, *Stability and Survival* (Crawley, Sussex: Burridge and Co., 1961).

7. Interviews.

8. *The Times*, June 27, 1960.

9. In 1947 two members of the Labor party were caught selling reports of the activities at party meetings to the press. One was expelled from the House; the other was reprimanded for his misconduct (see Bulmer-Thomas, *The Party System in Great Britain*, pp. 122–23).

10. Approaches to the "care and management" of backbenchers are noted by Hugh Dalton in *High Tide and After: Memoirs, 1945–1960* (London: Frederick Muller, 1962), pp. 22–23.

11. Examples of critical comments are those of Sir A. Spearman (670 H. C. Deb. 1003–8) and Mr. Brian Harrison (*ibid.*, 1044–48). For the speeches of Sir A. V. Harvey and Sir John Maitland, see *ibid.*, 1061–74, 1209–15.

12. Reported in *The Times*, January 2, 1963.

13. See, for example, the remarks by Sir Richard Glyn (673 H. C. Deb. 82–93) and Mr. John Eden (*ibid.*, 137–43). Both speakers occupy prominent positions in the Conservative back-bench defense organization.

14. See Alastair Buchan, "Strategic Studies in the Universities," *The Times*, June 5, 1963. Two seminars are conducted at the University of London, one by Mr. Michael Howard, the other by Mr. Hedley Bull; one tutorial is given at Oxford by Professor Norman Gibbs; and there is a lectureship in strategic studies at Aberystwyth.

15. *Encounter* and the *Listener* have also carried some useful commentary, and the *Financial Times* normally has some coverage of the critical issues. There have also been several contributions from British authors to American journals, namely, *World Politics, Foreign Affairs,* and *Orbis.*

16. 537 H. C. Deb. 2178.

17. The implications of this criticism are developed in Chapter VIII.

18. Alastair Buchan, "The Institute for Strategic Studies," in H. G. Thursfield (ed.), *Brassey's Annual, 1959* (New York: Macmillan, 1959), pp. 16–17.

19. Interview.

20. Philip Abrams, "Democracy, Technology, and the Retired British Officer," in Samuel P. Huntington (ed.), *Changing Patterns of Military Politics* (New York: Free Press of Glencoe, 1962), p. 161. This same view is expressed in Laurence W. Martin, "The Market for Strategic Ideas in Britain: The 'Sandys Era,'" *American Political Science Review*, LVI, No. 1 (1962), 23–41.

21. Buchan, "Strategic Studies in the Universities."

22. Interviews.

23. Interviews.

24. A RAND Corporation publication (R-346, March, 1960), it was also published by the Harvard University Press in 1961.

25. Boston: Division of Research, Graduate School of Business Administration, Harvard University, 1962.

26. Interview. In his *New Dimensions in Foreign Policy: A Study in British Administrative Experience, 1947–59* (New York: Macmillan, 1961), p. 182, Max Beloff accurately notes that the importance for government policy of the Institute of Strategic Studies is likely to be considerably greater in the future.

5/ Pressure Groups and Defense Policies

PRESSURE GROUPS and their role in the policy process are a part of British politics which has attracted considerable attention from political scientists in recent years. Studies suggest that there is extensive and continuous pressure-group activity in most areas of public policy; defense is no exception. There are numerous organizations and groups outside the formal structure of government that attempt in various ways to influence defense policies—so many, in fact, that it is difficult to describe their activities. This chapter is concerned with the operations of some of these groups, particularly those of industrial firms which produce defense goods and whose activities are extensive, complex, and more consequential for defense policy than most.

It will be useful as a preliminary to provide some general comments on pressure-group activity in Britain.[1] The extent of pressure-group activity is in most instances a function of current policies. The Navy League, for example, is normally relatively dormant and inactive. It becomes active and attempts to influence defense policies when there is a decision or rumor of a decision affecting the navy. There are, very broadly, three different ways in which a group may seek to influence policy. It may: (1) attempt to create public attitudes favorable to the group's interests in the expectation that political leaders will eventually respond to (or be deterred by) them; (2) lobby in Parliament, hoping the group's position will become known to ministers through the action of friendly MP's; and (3) consult directly with ministers and officials of the various departments within the government.[2] Most pressure groups, of course, utilize all of these avenues in their efforts to influence policy, but in almost every instance groups tend to concentrate on one target. The quickest and most effective method of influencing policy is to consult with officials and ministers in the government departments— where effective power is concentrated. But a group's ability to operate in this manner depends largely on the characteristics of the group itself: if it commands expertise, controls its members, and possesses information, it is likely that the group will have easy access to the government departments. The reason for this is that the government needs the group's information and expertise in formulating policies, while successful execution of policies is facilitated if the co-operation of those affected–the group's members–can be secured.[3] To the extent that these characteristics are absent, a group must press its case indirectly by attempting to influence Parliament or the public. Since both are several stages removed from effective decision-making power, representation in Parliament and public opinion campaigns are inefficient and slow methods of influencing policy decisions.

PRESSURE GROUPS AND PUBLIC OPINION

The two most publicly active groups concerned with defense policies in Great Britain are the Campaign for Nuclear Disarmament and its splinter offspring, the Committee of 100. Despite the great public interest these two groups have aroused, they have had virtually no impact on defense policies. There is also little reason to believe that their significance will increase in the future.

The Campaign for Nuclear Disarmament was formed in 1958. It counts as members such well-known personalities as Bertrand Russell, Canon John Collins of St. Paul's Cathedral, authors E. M. Forster and J. B. Priestley, A. J. P. Taylor, the Oxford historian, and, until recently, Michael Foot of the Labor party. The bulk of the movement, however, consists "mainly of people under twenty-five, in many cases under eighteen." [4] "The campaign also attracted from the outset a high proportion of a potentially important political group in Britain. This comprises teachers, scientists, and technical workers. . . . Well-educated, hungry for advancement, working for low wages, they feel themselves outsiders in the complacent, prosperous, materialist Britain of today." [5] Except for its Organizing Secretary, Mrs. Peggy Duff, it seems to have little in the way of a permanent staff.

There are many different attitudes commingled in British unilateralism. The movement is a protest in the British radical tradition; a reaction against Britain's loss of international power and prestige; an expression of anti-Germanism and anti-Americanism; and a form of "Little Englandism." The CND's unifying focus—the only bond among its members besides the common sense of exclusion and frustration—is nuclear weapons: its goals relate only to this issue. It advocates that Britain: (1) unilaterally renounce nuclear weapons; and (2) withdraw from all alliances (i.e., NATO) that envisage the use of nuclear weapons. Many of its members believe that unilateral renunciation of nuclear weapons would allow Britain to assume a position of world leadership at the head of a "third force," a role all the more attractive because it is unencumbered by the moral complexities attendant upon the possession of nuclear weapons.[6]

The CND's efforts have been directed mainly towards influencing public attitudes on nuclear weapons. It has held numerous protest meetings and public rallies, but its most spectacular effort is the fifty-four-mile Easter march from the nuclear weapons laboratory at Aldermaston to Trafalgar Square in London. Held annually since 1958, the march suggests strong public support and sympathy for unilateralism. Even more aggressive action has been undertaken by the Committee of 100. In December, 1961, it conducted what might be described as a semiviolent resistance campaign, including sitdown strikes and marches at various military airfields used by the Royal Air Force and the U.S. Air Force.

The poll data presented in Chapter III indicate the CND has not been successful in building public attitudes favorable to the renunciation of nuclear weapons.[7] Public sympathy for unilateralism has not increased since 1955—and for the reasons already noted the tactics used by these groups are viewed unfavorably by much of the public. Moreover, there is a suspicion that the CND, like the earlier British Peace Committee, is infiltrated by Communists and communist sympathizers. Mass demonstrations by the CND and the Committee of 100 at the Houses of Parliament have also made a poor impression, and S. E. Finer's general "rule" that "fuss, noise, mass lobbying and similar demonstrations are often an indication of the failure . . . to achieve effective Parliamentary relations"[8] would seem to apply in this case. Finally, unilateralist arguments have had no influence on government defense policies; nuclear weapons have formed an integral part of postwar defense policies, and there is little evidence to suggest a change of policies by the present government.

PRESSURE GROUPS AND PARLIAMENT

The groups interested in defense policies that are active mainly in Parliament include the Navy League, the Army League, the Royal Air Force Association, and the Air League of the British Empire. Their activities are both less conspicuous and less extensive than those of the unilateralist groups. Their influence is more significant, however, although in no event is it absolutely very great.

The service associations are composed of active and retired servicemen and civilian members with a special interest in, or sentiment for, a particular service. Control is usually vested in an executive committee or council whose membership includes retired senior-service officers, political leaders interested in the particular service, and occasionally a commentator or university don.[9] Day-to-day administrative matters are normally handled by a permanent secretary.

While the objective of a service association is to promote the interests of the respective service, there are serious limitations on the influence which each can bring to bear. The most important of these is that government does not need the consent of an association to insure the proper execution of policies. Unlike many pressure groups whose control over members is sufficiently strong to affect the execution of policy, the membership of a service association is either outside the channels of policy implementation or subject to military discipline and authority. Second, the associations lack information. Much of the information they do possess (at least those members who are not on active service) is furnished by the military department itself. As an Admiralty official put it: "We keep the Navy League informed of those issues which we think they ought to know about." [10] Third, the expertise of the members of an association is not usually of value to the government. Military skills, in particular, are already available to the government. Finally, the participation and membership of active-duty officers limits the extent of the political activity that can be undertaken by the service associations. The associations, in sum, can offer the government neither expert assistance nor control of membership: they have nothing to bargain with.

In the face of these limitations, what is the significance of the service associations? In terms of specific policy decisions, it is not great. But because Members of Parliament are active in the associations, they provide a vehicle by which a military department can generate support for its programs among backbench MP's. The service association is a nexus between the department and Parliament, and it contributes to the flow of attitudes through the party structure into, and from, the higher ministerial circles. In the second place, the associations perform a public-relations function for the departments. Thus, the associations attempt to create public sympathies for the services by their sponsorship of, and participation in, patriotic activities; for example, the annual Battle of Britain celebration. The associations also publicize service problems. The Army League is particularly active in this way, and it has sponsored the publication of a series of pamphlets on army problems. To a series of discussions in 1961 and 1962, for example, it brought representatives of the active army, the reserve forces, the universities, Parliament, and the public schools to consider the difficulties of officer recruitment. Not only were these groups alerted to a problem, but the League's report was eventually circulated to a wider audience.[11] Finally, the service associations play an important if unofficial part in shaping and in articulating the attitudes and opinions of the individual members of the forces. Put in other terms, the service associations are leaders and spokesmen for a relatively weak and incoherent pressure group, the members of a uniformed service.

GROUP CONSULTATION WITH THE GOVERNMENT DEPARTMENT

As already indicated, there is extensive contact between officials in government departments and representatives of outside groups. Some of these relationships are quite formal; for example, representatives of the Trades Union Congress are members of some sixty government committees. Less formal arrangements are even more important as channels of department–pressure group intercourse:

Yet, numerous as they are, the official channels do not nearly suffice to convey the swelling tide of the Lobby's problems, notions and grievances. Beyond and around them flows a veritable Atlantic of informal to-ings and fro-ings. This contact is close, pervasive and continuous.[12]

These exchanges are generally conceded to be mutually beneficial; groups feel they have a legitimate interest in the content of policies, while the government benefits from the group's advice and its help in administering policy.

Many aspects of defense policy have been influenced by pressure groups which operate by consulting with the departments concerned. One area so affected is service pay and pensions. The Royal Air Force Association; the Soldiers, Sailors, and Airmen's Family Association; the British Limbless Ex-Servicemen's Association; and the British Legion are among the groups that have negotiated with government departments over pay and benefits for active and retired military personnel. The Retired Officers' Association and the Officers' Pensions Society have been particularly active in efforts to increase the pensions of service widows and retired officers, arguing that inadequate pensions constitute a major deterrent to regular recruiting. Representation by these groups is reputed to have had an important influence on the government's decisions to increase pensions in 1958, 1960, and 1961.[13]

The organization and size of reserve forces have also been affected by pressure-group activity. The bulk (85 per cent) of all reserve forces are army reserves, grouped mainly in the Territorial Army and the Army Emergency Reserve (the "Ever-Readies"). Since the organization of the active army is so heavily conditioned by local and regional differences, and also because training considerations make it necessary to organize reserve units geographically, local notables, local government units, and representatives of the Territorial and Auxiliary Forces Association played an important part in the reorganization of reserve forces in 1961.[14]

Other aspects of defense policy involve still other outside groups. Following the decision in 1957 to reduce the size of the forces, the National Association for Employment of Regular Sailors, Soldiers, and Airmen worked closely with the service departments and the Ministry of Labor and National Service in the resettlement of discharged and prematurely retired servicemen.[15]

The shortage of junior officers in the army has led the War Office and the Ministry of Defense to seek the advice of various educational associations. These organizations, in turn, have contributed a number of recommendations designed to improve the attractiveness of service careers and to increase the flow of officers into the services.[16]

While the outside groups mentioned above are both interesting and important, industrial firms engage in more extensive activity and exert a greater influence on government policies. Preliminary to discussing the patterns of relationships that exist between industrial firms and government departments, however, it is necessary to indicate something of the general shape of the industrial lobby and to describe briefly the sequence by which decisions relating to the production of military equipment are taken.

The Structure of the Industrial Lobby [17]

A great number of individual companies are involved in the production of equipment for the defense establishment. The bulk of the representation by industry comes from one or two industrial groupings, however, and the trend in recent years has been concentration of representation to relatively few individual firms.

The important targets for representational activity by industrial groupings is indicated by the division of defense-procurement expenditures by type of equipment. This breakdown, at three different intervals since the end of World War II, is shown in Table 4 below. While the averages in Table 4 are only a rough guide to the amount of procurement money subject to pressure from industrial lobbies, some refinements are possible. In the first place, guns, armor, and ammunition are produced mainly in government-owned Royal Ordnance Factories. Since they are managed by the War Office, the Royal Ordnance Factories do not need representation in the departments. Second, motor transport production for the military departments has constituted only a very small share— about 10 per cent—of the output of the British motor car and truck industry. Because it has often been unable to meet civilian demand since the end of World War II, this industry has not been especially aggressive in attempting to sell to the defense establishment.[18] Until 1957 much the same situa-

TABLE 4

BRITISH DEFENSE EXPENDITURES ON PRODUCTION, BY PERCENTAGES
IN INDUSTRIAL SECTORS *

Year	Aircraft and Equipment	Electronics	Guns, Armor, and Ammunition	Motor Transport	Shipbuilding and Ship Repair
1949–50	57	‡	6	19	18
1954–55	44	8	18	16	14
1959–60 †	44	12	16	7	21
Average	48	7	13	14	18

* Source: Calculated from D. C. Paige, "Defense Expenditure," *Economic Review*, No. 10, (1960), p. 32.
† Estimates.
‡ Included under other categories.

tion existed in the shipbuilding industry. Output was at record levels, and the industry enjoyed a large backlog of commercial orders. In the face of growing competition from highly efficient Japanese, German, and Scandinavian yards, British shipbuilders have been hard pressed in recent years to find sufficient new orders to keep their yards fully engaged. They have therefore become more interested in defense production, and it is reported that the industry has pressed the government to acquire additional fleet-supply and support vessels.[19]

The two remaining categories, aircraft and electronics, account for over one-half of all defense equipment and weapons expenditures. Military sales also constitute a large percentage of the output of the industries which manufacture these goods —about three-quarters in the case of the aircraft industry. Electronics and aircraft thus account for a somewhat greater share of the total representation to the defense establishment; with shipbuilding, these industries comprise the defense industrial lobby.

The bulk of the lobbying undertaken by industrial firms is directed at the Ministry of Aviation, the Admiralty, and the Air Ministry. The latter two departments are the main users, of course, while the Ministry of Aviation (as its predecessor, the Ministry of Supply) has constitutional responsibility for procuring all aircraft, guided weapons, and electronics equipment used by the service departments. (The Admiralty procures all naval vessels and is the target of representation by the shipbuilding industry.) In contrast to the situation before 1959, when eight engine firms and a dozen airframe contractors competed for contracts, representation by the aircraft industry is now largely the effort of two large consortia—British Aircraft Corporation and Hawker Siddeley Group—which were established in 1959 at the government's urging. (There is a third group, Westlands, which specializes in helicopters.) [20] Each consortia is about the same size, and since each is capable of producing aircraft, guided missiles, or engines, both normally compete for a wide range of defense contracts. However, there are some differences in their operations. British Aircraft Corporation, which usually acts as the "systems manager" for its contracts, co-ordinates the activities of its member firms and subcontractors and undertakes most of the representation to government agencies. Hawker Siddeley prefers that its member firms assume responsibility (usually assisted by the Ministry of Aviation) for co-ordinating the efforts of subcontractors. It also allows subcontractors to do their own representation at the Ministry of Aviation.[21]

The Sequence in Research, Development, and Production Decisions

The relations of industrial firms with the defense establishment are conditioned by the preliminary planning and analysis that precedes decisions to develop and produce major items of military equipment. In most weapons projects there is a relatively standard sequence in which the various aspects of a proposal are considered prior to a final decision to produce the item. This sequence is as follows: [22] (1) An "operational requirement" is formulated by the service department that will ultimately use the equipment. An operational requirement may be based on a new technical idea, a new development in the enemy's force structure, or some combination of these two. (2) Once an operational requirement is established and approved by the Chiefs of Staff Committee, a "feasibility study" is undertaken. It seeks general information on technical feasibility, time required, and cost of the project. A feasibility study may be contracted to industry or, depending on the type of equipment, undertaken by one of the supply agencies —the Ministry of Aviation, the War Office, or the Admiralty. (3) If feasibility studies indicate that the project deserves further consideration, a "project study" is then initiated. Project studies examine in greater detail than previously the technical, time, and cost implications of the proposed development.[23] In theory at least, a completed project study provides the information on which the Defense Research Policy Committee and responsible officials in the Ministry of Defense, the Treasury, and cabinet base their final decision on whether to proceed with the proposed development. (4) If the decision is to proceed, individual firms are invited to submit detailed proposals that are then reviewed by the appropriate supply agency before final production contracts are awarded.

The Types of Industry—Government Negotiations

The contacts between government departments and industrial firms are frequent and at a variety of levels. These contacts are of four general types. Not every industrial firm selling military equipment to the government engages in all four types, but the activities of the two major consortia appear to conform generally to the "model" outlined below.

(1) Contacts with government research establishments. Approximately one-half of all basic research, applied research, and development in Great Britain is supported by government funds, and over three-quarters of the total government effort goes for defense research and development.[24] One-fifth to one-quarter of the defense research and development effort, in turn, is allocated to basic and applied research.[25] These funds support government laboratories and research establishments maintained by the Admiralty, the War Office, and the Ministry of Aviation. There is extensive and continuous contact between the scientists and engineers employed by industrial firms and the staff members of these research facilities. The frequency of contacts bears little relationship to the sequence of research and development decisions. These contacts are mainly to exchange scientific and technical information, although representatives of an industrial firm may from time to time suggest to officials at government establishments that certain types of research be undertaken.[26] The relationship, in essence, is among scientists and technicians: it propagates the results of research and stimulates the exchange of ideas within the scientific and technical communities.

(2) Industry as salesman and innovator.[27] The military departments are large consumers of economic goods and services, and there is a customer-seller relationship between the departments and various industries. There are two aspects to this relationship. First, industrial firms will encourage military departments to procure additional quantities of equipment already on order; firms may also urge the services to make an initial purchase of an item of equipment being produced by the industry. An industry may be asked by the services to urge these purchases on the Ministry of Aviation

and the Ministry of Defense; alternatively, the civil air corporations (B.O.A.C. and B.E.A.) and the Ministry of Aviation may have the industry suggest a purchase to the services.

The second aspect of this relationship concerns future sales. The services' future equipment needs are often unknown—in any case they are imprecisely defined—and the representatives of industrial firms therefore maintain close contact with officials and military officers to understand the problems that face the military departments. Based on their knowledge of future trends and problems, the firms attempt to devise new equipment and processes which will be useful to the services. The firms' proposals, in turn, often enable the military departments to state their needs in explicit and concrete terms. Since the operational requirement is closely related to a specific design, and provided the proposal survives the subsequent feasibility and design studies, the firm has an advantage in the competition for a production contract. The process is of benefit both to the customer and to the supplier.

This type of contact takes place continuously. Its frequency tends to increase when the military departments begin to purchase less of an industry's output. If, for example, military purchases of aircraft are declining, representatives of the major consortia visit the departments more often. During these visits they propose possible new uses for equipment already in production and suggest new products which the services might use in the future. The purpose is plainly to increase sales. The service departments, especially the Air Ministry and Admiralty, are the main focus of lobbying of this type, primarily because these departments have the responsibility for stating operational requirements. Industrial representatives are frequently encouraged by the service departments to undertake representation of this type. A number of important technical innovations are credited to this process, to include VTOL-STOL (Vertical-Short Takeoff and Landing) aircraft; the Canberra light bomber was proposed to the RAF in this manner.[28]

(3) The industrial firm as adviser or technical consultant. In contrast to the continuous exchanges between government and industry described above, the third type of relationship is a sporadic one. It takes place when the government has decided (or is seriously considering) to develop a new weapons system or item of equipment. This phase normally takes place after feasibility studies and project studies have indicated that the project is possible technically and that its cost lies within budgetary constraints. This type of industrial-government relations may, of course, be the result of earlier activities (see above, type 2) by the industry—for example, if industry were able to convince one of the service departments that a particular project would meet some future requirement. But it does not necessarily result from or follow the activities described above.

The problem facing the government at this juncture is to select the "best" proposal from among several competing designs offered by suppliers. In order to make such a choice, it is necessary to examine the alternative proposals in great detail. While the criteria change from proposal to proposal, the procuring agency is usually concerned with five questions: (1) Is the design technically possible, i.e., can it in fact be built? (2) What is the project likely to cost? (3) How much time will be required? (4) Which of the proposals best provides the performance characteristics desired by the user? (5) Do the competing firms have the productive capability and resources to undertake production? While the first three questions have already been considered in feasibility and project studies, they usually have not been analyzed in terms of specific designs.

Accurate cost estimation is particularly difficult. Industry estimates are normally (and understandably) on the optimistic side; those of the Ministry of Aviation are usually more pessimistic.[29] Although it might be possible for Ministry of Aviation officials to analyze the cost and technical characteristics of competing designs without the assistance of the technicians and designers responsible for each proposal, the quality of the answers is greatly improved by their participation. Moreover, government officials cannot easily answer question 5 without detailed information on the firms' production capabilities and plant resources. This data must be provided by industry representatives.

After these questions, particularly 1 through 4, have been considered, there is then sufficient data for officials to make comparisons among the competing proposals. The decision as to which is "best," however, does not normally require explicit or lengthy consideration: the choice normally is defined during the process of determining technical feasibility, costs, and performance characteristics. All that remains is contractual legitimation and announcement by the minister. In an important sense, industry is a part of the decision-making system during these deliberations, and representatives of competing firms are fully aware of the criteria used to make the selection. The firm whose project is accepted knows in what particular ways its proposal was superior. Among the representatives of unsuccessful firms there is an equally explicit understanding of the criteria for the decision and the satisfying knowledge that their proposal was given a fair examination. As one official put it:

The unsuccessful firms are never happy about the outcome, but they are never bad losers either. They know why they lost. I shudder to think what their reaction would be if they did not participate and did not know our grounds for selection.[30]

Throughout the negotiations each firm has encouraged the government to accept its proposal; yet the government is actually relatively free of pressures and can establish its own criteria. Indeed, the procuring agency must use relevant criteria; to do otherwise is to become highly vulnerable to criticism from the unsuccessful competitors. The guarantee against irregular or irrelevant procedures is the representation of competing firms during the selection process. Moreover, that pressure which firms can apply tends to be contradictory and self-canceling, so departments are allowed a relatively free choice. For both these reasons representation by competing industrial firms improves the basis of selection.

An apparent exception to this situation occurs when the Ministry of Aviation cancels a project already under development. Negotiations of the same character occur, except that now only one firm is involved. The pressures it is able to apply are not balanced by those of some other firm, although there are normally countervailing demands from the other defense departments for the financial resources released by the cancellation. One official explained the consequences of this situation as follows:

> The Ministry is somewhat more vulnerable during cancellation proceedings than when a new contract is being negotiated. Yet in every case with which I am familiar, we have eventually cancelled the project. As a result of the industry's protests, our decision to cancel is arrived at very carefully and a project is not dropped as quickly as it might otherwise have been without the industry's lobbying.[31]

The rather frequent cancellations of major weapons projects in recent years seem to substantiate this view.

(4) Industry in an advertising role. While discussions between government and industry on the details of proposals are going forward, industrial firms tend to restrict their representation to the supply agency with constitutional responsibility for purchasing the equipment under consideration. There is, of course, limited contact with the service departments or even the Ministry of Defense, but only the procuring agency is able to consider the details of technical design, costs, and performance characteristics. Further, if an industry lobbies for its project with one of the service departments while simultaneously discussing the proposal with officials at the Ministry of Aviation, it may appear as an effort to circumvent the latter organization.

In stage 4, however, industrial firms expand the scope of their activities. Broadened representation often begins *before* the Ministry officially announces its selection and *before* a formal contract award is announced. This stage nevertheless depends upon what amounts to a decision—a consensus among officials as to the "best" proposal. After the supply agency has completed its examination of the alternative proposals, further representation at that department is of little value: efforts are directed elsewhere. Representatives of the unsuccessful firms call on the service departments and the Ministry of Defense. The Chairmen of the various firms seek appointments with the Minister of Aviation, the Minister of Defense, and other senior political leaders. Other board members call on the service's chief of staff and on the permanent undersecretaries of the relevant departments. There may even be an attempt to discuss the matter with the Prime Minister. And when the government announces its decision, especially if it is a major contract award, lobbying becomes particularly intensive and public in scope. The MP representing the districts in which the unsuccessful firms are located seeks to raise the matter in Parliament. Union officials comment on the number of workers who will become unemployed as a result of the decision. Industry trade groups may note other consequences of the decision; for example, the breakup of skilled design teams.

This extensive and intensive lobbying, contrary to what might be expected, is not necessarily to change or reverse the selection. The firms have already participated in the selection, and, even if they do not agree with the choice, they at least understand the reasons why their proposal was unsuccessful. Rather, lobbying at this stage has quite different purposes: it advertises an unsuccessful firm's capabilities and consequent availability for future projects. After having been unsuccessful the firm's immediate concern is to prevent a similar failure on the next project—just as a baseball player or manager will protest a decision in the hope that the umpire will favor him the next time. Explaining itself to interested government agencies is a way to keep its name and capabilities before responsible officials and ministers who will make future choices.

Another objective of this representation, after the industry-department negotiations on technical feasibility, cost, and performance characteristics, is to influence the production arrangements. In complex weapons systems there are a great number of subsystems and components that can be produced by any number of individual firms and later assembled by the prime contractor. Although an individual firm may have been unsuccessful with its major proposal, it may still hope to get a contract to produce components or subassemblies. To do so, a firm emphasizes its technical capacities and points out what will happen if it does not get part of the contract. These consequences—local unemployment, the breakup of design teams, the loss of skills that may be needed in future production, and the implications for civil aviation—may also be emphasized by MP's in Parliament, by local union spokesmen, by groups of workers lobbying in Westminister, or even by trade associations.

Contract awards and production decisions are frequently influenced by considerations other than military requirements and the capacities of competing industrial firms. Thus, the two nationalized civil air corporations, British Overseas Airways Corporation and British European Airways, are often consulted during decisions on military aircraft, transport aircraft in particular. If the Ministry of Aviation can reconcile the needs of both the civil air corporations and the services, the number of aircraft produced will be about twice as great as would be the case if a separate design were ordered for each. Production in quantity achieves the economies associated with mass production, and the aircraft is more attractive to foreign customers because of its lower per-unit cost. For this reason the support of the civil air corporations may be decisive in a decision on military aircraft. Moreover, the purchase of military transports is one of the most important ways in which the R.A.F.'s demands support civil development, for they guarantee a certain, if small, market for production aircraft at a stage when civil customers may still be unwilling to place orders. The order of Comet II's for the R.A.F. sustained the continuation of Comet production and development after the disaster with the Comet I. Without this support the whole venture might easily have collapsed.[32]

Another consideration in production decisions is the government's desire to ameliorate the impact on localities of shifts in defense-procurement contracts. This has grown in importance since the mid-1950's, when the aircraft industry began to contract in size. The government also recognizes that defense contracts may be a useful way to stimulate economic activity in areas with high rates of unemployment: "If there is no discernible difference in cost or performance characteristics between two competing proposals, we would give the contract to the firm located in the 'developing area.' "[33]

The types of contact between industrial firms and government departments also explain the special role of other nonofficial groups. While negotiations during stage 3 normally involve several firms, they are a set of relatively independent discussions between individual firms and the government. Since several firms are competing for the contract, industrial trade groups cannot easily participate. Thus, the Federation of British Industries, the National Union of Manufacturers, the Society of British Aircraft Constructors, the Shipbuilder's Conference, the Radio Industry Council, the Trades Union Congress, and the Association of British Chambers of Commerce are not usually involved in negotiations of this type. Each of these groups is an organization of individual firms, productive units, or different unions; unless they want several discontented members, these associations must restrict their activities to more general policy issues.

The activities of the Society of British Aerospace Companies, probably the most interested in defense policies of all of these associations, suggest the general pattern: In 1956 and 1957 SBAC representatives served on a government committee, the Transport Aircraft Requirement Committee.[34] Subsequently, the SBAC pressed vigorously for an increase in the airlift capability for RAF Transport Command.[35] In 1959 the society engaged in extensive consultations with the government on the plans for the reorganization of the Ministry of Supply.[36] Finally, the SBAC has repeatedly urged greater government expenditures on research and development.[37] It has not, however, taken a position on individual contract awards. Other associations are in a similar position; their representation with the government must not affect their individual members in any discriminatory way.

The relationship between industrial firms and the defense establishment is viewed by some as an undesirable one. There are two criticisms. On the one hand, it is argued that political or economic considerations are irrelevant to decisions on weapons-system and equipment contracts. On the other hand, there is a fear that the industry with a vested interest is able to exert sufficient influence to prevent the adoption of appropriate policies which have implications unfavorable to that industry.

The criticism that economic or political considerations are irrelevant to awards of large-scale defense contracts implies that military requirements are absolute, that the design characteristics and production schedules stated by the services in their operational requirements cannot and should not be varied under any circumstances. There is little to recommend such a view. While the performance characteristics requested by the services are undoubtedly important, it may well be desirable to modify performance characteristics or alter production schedules to gain some other benefit: foreign sales, the needs of civil air carriers, or even the nature of the social and economic impact of defense expenditures are all legitimate concerns. The representation by firms and other forms of lobbying provide a mechanism through which the wider consequences of defense decisions can be brought to the attention of responsible political leaders and officials. Representation, in short, broadens the basis of decision-making and enables the government, if it desires, to ameliorate the impact of its choices.

There is a grain of truth in the second criticism: the defense industries represent a vested interest which may prevent the adoption of appropriate policies and hinder rapid policy shifts. To the extent that a government is responsive to industry pressures—especially demands to procure additional or new equipment—policy changes may be inhibited; but, unlike the ordinary commercial firm, a government cannot disregard the social or economic consequences of its decisions. It is expected to be more responsive than other customers to the position of its suppliers. A large defense sector with close ties to the government has an important influence on policies, but it is only one influence among many that are relevant to policy decisions. It does not necessarily coincide with, or reinforce that of, other agencies.

Some of the major consequences for defense policies of industrial lobbying are thus relatively clear. Industry performs an innovating function. Based on its understanding of service problems, industry attempts to devise new products that will meet the future requirements of the service departments. Second, industrial lobbying provides the government with expert advice which is of assistance in selecting a specific project from among several proposals, and by so doing the government is able to make better choices. Third, industrial lobbying provides the government with much of the information on which final production awards are based. Finally, industry spokesmen, assisted by interested MP's, trade-association leaders, and union representatives, emphasize the consequences of decisions. As a result, responsible officials are able to select with care and discrimination the best production arrangements and schedules for large-scale defense projects, and thereby achieve the desired impact on local communities and industries. Because of the extent of its participation in the decision-making process, it should also be apparent that industry's influence on defense policies is widespread and virtually impossible to detail with any precision. Industry is one activity among many which contribute to policy decisions, and its influence may run counter to, or reinforce that of, other activities. In short, as with pressure groups generally, industry representation to influence defense research, development, and procurement decisions is a part—and by no means an inimical part—of sound policy decisions by government officials.

1. Two useful references on British pressure groups are S. E. Finer, *Anonymous Empire* (London: Pall Mall, 1958), and, for a theoretical analysis, Harry Eckstein, *Pressure Group Politics: The Case of the British Medical Association* (Stanford: Stanford University Press, 1960).

2. Finer, *Anonymous Empire*, pp. 28–93.

3. *Ibid.*, pp. 28–38.

4. Norman Birnbaum, "The Campaign for Nuclear Disarmament," in Robert Theobald (ed.), *Britain in the Sixties* (New York: H. W. Wilson, 1961), p. 144.

5. Drew Middleton, "The Deeper Meaning of British Neutralism," in *ibid.*, pp. 148–49.

6. See the excellent article by Hedley Bull, "The Many Sides of British Unilateralism," *The Reporter*, March 16, 1961, pp. 35–37.

7. For some additional comments on the significance of the Campaign for Nuclear Disarmament, see Constantine FitzGibbons, "Politics and the Novel: A Letter to Patrick O'Donovan," *Encounter*, (June, 1961), pp. 71–73, and H. A. DeWeerd, "British Unilateralism: A Critical View," *Yale Review*, LI, No. 4 (1962), 574–88.

8. Finer, *Anonymous Empire*, p. 54.

9. The Executive Committee of the Army League, for example, includes six retired officers and four politicians, two from each major political party.

10. Interview.

11. See the Army League, *A Challenge to Leadership: An Examination of the Problem of Officer Recruitment for the British Army* (Barnet, Herts.: Stellar Press, 1962). The League's earlier publications include *The Army in the Nuclear Age* (Stellar Press, 1955) and *The British Army in the Nuclear Age* (Stellar Press, 1959).

12. Finer, *Anonymous Empire*, p. 34.

13. Interviews.

14. Interviews.

15. See Cmd. 231, "Compensation for Premature Retirement from the Armed Forces," and Cmd. 545, "Report of the Advisory Committee on Recruiting," p. 12.

16. See note 11, above.

17. A detailed description of the defense sector is contained in the Economist Intelligence Unit, *The Economic Effects of Disarmament* (London: Economist Intelligence Unit, for the United World Trust, 1963). See also Duncan Burn (ed.), *The Structure of British Industry* (2 vols.; Cambridge: Cambridge University Press, 1958), especially those chapters dealing with aircraft, electronics, and shipbuilding.

18. Interviews.

19. Interview.

20. The current organization of the industry is described in Douglas Robinson, "The Vacillating Paymaster," *Statist*, January 19, 1962, p. 196.

21. Interviews.

22. The process is described in more detail in Office of the Minister for Science, *Report of the Committee on the Management and Control of Research and Development* (London: H. M. Stationery Office, 1961), pp. 57–66.

23. Other questions that may be considered at this time include the export-sales prospects, the implications for civil industry, and the possibilities of purchasing the item abroad.

24. *Ibid.*, pp. 20–21. The terms are defined in *ibid.*, pp. 6–8.

25. *Ibid.*, pp. 20–21.

26. Interviews.

27. The information in this and the following paragraphs was obtained in interviews.

28. Ely Dvons, "The Aircraft Industry," in Burn, *The Structure of British Industry*, II, n. 82.

29. Merton J. Peck and Frederic M. Scherer, in their important book *The Weapons Acquisition Process: An Economic Analysis* (Boston: Division of Research, Graduate School of Business Administration, Harvard University, 1962), discuss the general magnitude of error in project-cost estimates. In twelve American projects the average actual cost was 3.2 times the initial estimate (p. 22). There are two conditions which suggest that British cost estimation, while often far off the mark, is on average considerably better than that done in the United States. First, in the U.K. costing is the primary responsibility of the procuring agency, for most projects, the Ministry of Aviation. There is no incentive to underestimate costs, as is the case in the United States, where the service departments do most of their own cost estimation and procurement. Second, the civil servants who examine most of the estimates in Britain probably are more experienced in cost estimation, because they rotate jobs less frequently, than their counterparts in the United States. There is little relevant theory to guide the practitioner, and experience is the most useful guide to accuracy.

30. Interview.

31. Interview.

32. Devons, "The Aircraft Industry," p. 74.

33. Interview.

34. See the statement of the Minister of Supply, 579 H. C. Deb. 136.

35. For example, the remarks by Sir George Edwards, a director of Vickers (reported in *Flight*, March 22, 1957, p. 355).

36. Interview.

37. See the statement by Mr. Edward Bowyer, Director of the Society of British Aerospace Companies (reported in *Flight*, April 12, 1957, p. 462).

6/ The Policy Elites

DEFENSE POLICIES are the special responsibility of the three service departments, the Ministry of Aviation,[1] and the Ministry of Defense. Three separate professional groups—political leaders, civil servants, and military officers—staff these departments. This chapter is concerned with these policy elites, mainly their educational backgrounds, professional careers, and their respective roles in the policy process.[2]

THE POLITICAL LEADERS

In British government the departments of state are headed by politicians selected from among the members of the governing or majority party who sit in either the House of Lords or the House of Commons. Constitutionally, the political leaders or ministers assume responsibility for all that is done or not done by their departments; moreover, departments speak and act publicly with but a single voice, that of their minister. This institutionalized loyalty down the departmental hierarchy guarantees anonymity to the minister's advisers. In return, advisers are expected to provide ministers with frank and forthright advice and also to accept and support ministerial decisions as if these decisions were their own. The minister is responsible to his political superiors, the cabinet and the prime minister; they, in turn, assume responsibility before Parliament for the decisions and activities of the minister and his department.

In the service departments, relations between political leaders and military officers are essentially the same as those between civil servants and ministers.[3] Except for isolated periods effective political control of the armed forces in Great Britain has not been a serious problem since Cromwell's day. The long-standing tradition of civil control is reinforced by the essential similarity of social background among political leaders and military officers. The maintenance of civil control is also aided by the opportunities available to senior military professionals to enter other elite groups, even the political elite. In short, military officers tend to view themselves as permanent professional servants of the Crown, subordinate to the political leaders of the day. Like civil servants, they expect both to give advice and to remain anonymous in the process.[4]

Functioning within this constitutional framework, then, are the political leaders. In the period August, 1945—December, 1962, thirty-six politicians held one or more appointments as minister of defense, minister of aviation, or as secretary of state (the first lord in the admiralty) of a service department. Of these ministerial positions only the minister of defense has regularly been a member of the cabinet;[5] most observers feel that he ranks between four and six in the strata of ministerial importance. Appointees to this post have tended to be older and to have greater political experience than the parliamentarians heading the service departments or Ministry of Aviation. If one excludes Prime Ministers Attlee and Churchill, both of whom combined for short periods the duties of prime minister and minister of defense,[6] the ten postwar ministers of defense have averaged fifty-seven years of age on appointment. Labor appointees averaged somewhat older (sixty-four) than their Tory counterparts. In recent years there has been a trend toward youth: the last four ministers have been about fifty years of age upon appointment.

Appointees had an average of fifteen years' political experience in Parliament, although Labor ministers had significantly more service than most of their Tory successors. With but one exception all ministers of defense previously headed another department of state. The exception was Viscount Alexander, Sir Winston's first minister of defense, who was a retired general officer and a former governor general of Canada. Five of the ten had earlier held a cabinet position, and seven of the ten had previously served in one of the service departments or the Ministry of Aviation. Previous experience in another department varied greatly, however, and ranged from a year or less (two cases) to over five years (three cases).

The lesser importance and non-cabinet status of the service departments and the Ministry of Aviation are evident in the appointments of these ministries. In both parties an appointment to one of these departments was normally an individual's initial appointment to a ministerial post. Tory appointees tended to be significantly younger than Labor selections, forty-five as compared to fifty-seven. Previous experience assisting a minister as his parliamentary private secretary was normal—indeed, almost a requisite—for appointment to these offices: nearly two-thirds of the ministers of service departments had had this preliminary experience in one of the departments concerned with defense policy. Although there are some differences in the patterns in the three uniformed departments—the first lord of the Admiralty was or became a peer—these do not seem to favor in any way one service over another. The minister of aviation, however, has normally been younger than his colleagues in the service ministries, and occupancy of that office has led in several instances to a subsequent appointment as minister of defense.

As a rule, ministers in the three service departments have enjoyed somewhat longer periods in office than ministers of defense. Excluding the incumbent at the end of 1962, the service ministers' average time in office was approximately twenty-seven months. In contrast, only four ministers of defense were in office this long, and the average of all appointments was eighteen months. Four Conservative ministers of defense, all serving in succession, held office for an average of only six months each; since 1951, Tory ministers of aviation have also changed rather frequently—every twenty-one months.

In considering the relations among political and administrative leaders, it is important to remember that formal education at the university level is limited to a relatively small group in Great Britain—10 per cent of the school population. Further, formal education provides something more than the factual knowledge and intellectual skills that are requisites for responsible positions, however important these may be. The English school system is a special acculturating process: public-school attendance followed by three years at one of the great universities—Oxford or Cambridge—inculcates the social attitudes and manner common among British political leaders and in upper-class British society generally. The homogeneity of the political elite is partly due to this common educational background, which likewise provides elements of cohesion among civil servants, military officers, and political leaders whose sharply different posteducational professional careers would otherwise divide them.

The twenty-two Conservative politicians who have held political office in one or more of the relevant departments have a highly uniform educational background. All had attended a public school; thirteen of the group had attended the same school—Eton. Almost all were university graduates: Oxford and Cambridge accounted for thirteen of the fifteen university degrees, and London for the other two. Five had attended one of the service academies; only two listed no university experience. In the university group four had achieved first-class honors.

Among Labor politicians there are two divergent patterns: Half the Labor politicians had educational backgrounds essentially the same as those in the Conservative party. The main characteristic of the remaining half is the virtual absence of formal education. In the first group four of the six had attended public schools, two at Eton, and had then gone to either Oxford or Cambridge. The remaining two had attended the University of London. Four of the six had won academic honors as undergraduates. The other six Labor ministers had little in the way of formal education, often no more than a few years of grade school. While the lack of a formal education may have been a source of some personal insecurity, it has had little discernible effect on policy or policy positions. Emanuel Shinwell, the secretary of state for war between 1947 and 1950 and the minister of defense in 1950 and 1951, has written of his initial concern over his relations with his senior military advisers. Yet at the conclusion of his service at the Ministry of Defense, he spoke glowingly of the loyalty, ability, and friendliness of the senior military officers with whom he had worked.[7]

The sample of Conservative leaders reveals relatively high social origins: of the twenty whose parents are listed, fifteen seem to spring from the aristocracy or upper-middle classes. Club membership, which indicates current social position as well as a link to other elites, includes virtually all the Conservative sample. While those Labor members who had attended a university appear to have slightly more diverse family backgrounds than the Conservative sample, similarity between these two groups is much greater than within the Labor party. The Labor politicians without formal educations were all from working-class families: several had been coal miners who subsequently rose through the trade-union structure to political office. Unlike their Labor colleagues who had attended public schools and the universities, none of this group belonged to clubs.

THE CIVIL SERVANTS

If we ignore for the moment the minor differences among various departments, we see that Administrative Class officials in the defense departments are responsible for financial planning and control, general administration, and departmental research and development programs. The senior civil servant in a service department—the permanent undersecretary of state (in the Admiralty, the permanent secretary)— is a member of the departmental policy committee—for example, the Army Council (now the Army Board of the Defense Council)—which also includes the political head of the department, the chief of staff, and other senior military officers. Although outnumbered on the Council by uniformed officers, the permanent undersecretary is, within the department itself, equal in importance to the service chief of staff. While the relationships between these groups will be discussed in more detail below, Administrative Class officials lower in the departmental hierarchy normally enjoy the confidence and respect of their military colleagues and maintain the relative equality that exists between the permanent undersecretary and the chief of staff.

The Administrative Class of the British Civil Service has traditionally enjoyed high social status and its corollary, a comfortable economic position. Present-day civil servants in the defense establishment reflect the long-standing attractions of a career of public service to the newly graduated university student—as well as the limited opportunities for promotion to the Administrative Class made available to Clerical or Executive Class employees.[8] In a sample of forty-five senior civil servants, nine from each of the five departments in the defense establishment, thirty-two were university graduates; over half—twenty-six—had attended Oxford or Cambridge, while five were graduates of the University of London. Those with university degrees had impressive academic records: thirteen of the group won first-class honors, and nine listed double firsts. Of the non-university group, four were service-academy graduates. The nine without university training in most cases entered the Clerical or Executive Class of the civil service at an early age. Public-school attendance was limited to roughly the group which had received university and service-academy educations.

The family backgrounds of most civil servants varies slightly from that of the university-trained political leaders. Civil servants with university degrees attended a wide range of public schools, which suggests more diverse family backgrounds than those of the Conservative political leaders. About the same percentage of lower-middle or working-class backgrounds appears in the Administrative Class as in the over-all political group. Some nine or ten civil servants, about one-fifth of the sample, entered the civil service as Executive or Clerical Class employees, while two Administrative Class entrants had attended local high schools. Some two-thirds of all civil servants belong to clubs, a somewhat lower percentage than that of the political leadership group.[9] In sum, the senior civil service is relatively homogeneous in terms of the social backgrounds and educational experiences of its members. Like the political group, it contains a small number of officials who have risen from humble family backgrounds.

Excluding the non-Administrative Class service of Executive or Clerical Class entrants, the average length of government service is approximately twenty-five years; in almost all instances this service was confined to the same department. Of the twenty-seven officials in the service departments, only five had occupied positions elsewhere in Whitehall, usually with another department or agency in the defense establishment. Two of the five were scientists, one of whom entered government service during World War II. Two more held permanent-undersecretary rank which indicates that non-departmental service is a requisite for the top posts. Patterns of experience in the Ministry of Defense and the Ministry of Aviation were more diversified. Unlike the service departments the Ministry of Defense does not recruit civil servants but instead draws from the service departments promising mid-career officials as needed. The civil servants in the Ministry of Aviation also have varied backgrounds, primarily because of the varied functions that are now included in this department.

The general picture of senior civil servants that emerges is thus one of a tightly knit group with long experience in Whitehall, usually experience confined to a single department. In the style of his predecessors, the civil servant is trained to bring to policy-making a "sense of [the] complexity of human affairs" and "enthusiasm for moderation and prudence." [10] Following the pattern of their political masters, civil servants have a network of old-school ties, common civil-service entry dates, and club affiliations that weaves across and within departmental lines, thus reinforcing the cohesive effect of the multiplicity of committees that cut across the formal boundaries of departmental organization.

MILITARY OFFICERS [11]

The senior professional officers serving in the defense establishment are usually on their second or third London assignment, each assignment being normally three years; their average age is fifty-four, virtually the same as that of senior civil servants.

Military officers have less formal education than most civil servants or political leaders. Only three of the sample had attended a university. Service-academy attendance was the rule except for RAF officers, fewer than half of whom were graduates of the RAF college at Cranwell.[12] Most army and air force officers attended a public school prior to entering one of the service academies. Naval officers missed the traditional public-school experience, since at the time they entered service midshipman training usually began at twelve or thirteen. A full description of the educational backgrounds of service officers would have to include reference to the military schools attended, particularly the Imperial Defense College. Unfortunately, data are not complete; however, it would be reasonable to assume that the description above may understate somewhat the educational qualifications of senior officers.[13]

In the eighteenth and nineteenth centuries the younger sons of the land-owning aristocracy normally entered the professions, and the regular army and navy were especially attractive careers.[14] Remnants of this pattern were still evident in the 1920's, when most of the sample entered the service. But, in most cases, officers seem to come from upper-middle or middle-class backgrounds, the same social strata that provides the bulk of the political leaders and the civil servants. Nearly half of the total within the three services were sons of service officers, but this percentage conceals differences between the services: two-thirds of the army officers came from service backgrounds, but only one-third of the naval and air force officers did. A further indication of the middle- and upper-middle-class backgrounds of service officers is the pattern of public-school attendance. Almost all of the sample had attended day schools rather than the more socially prominent and expensive boarding schools (Eton, for example).

Club membership of service officers strikes a different pattern from those of the other groups. Officers are more "clubable" than most civil servants, and only a very small percentage do not belong to a London club. The officers of each service tend to belong to a single club—the army to the Army and Navy Club, the navy to United Services, and the air force officers to the RAF Club. The clustering of officers of each service in a single club is perhaps explained by the autonomy of the three services after World War I, when most of the sample entered the service. Yet senior officers are not an isolated social group; their duties bring them into contact with a wide variety of individuals, and representatives of other occupations and political orientations are found even in the clubs in which service officers concentrate.

Certain factors have acted to raise the general caliber of Britain's senior military professionals. Most senior officers had extensive combat service during (and after) World War II. They have also been subjected to a rigorous selection process over the last decade: as the armed forces have been reduced in size, the officer corps of each service has undergone a similar reduction in members. The regular officer strength of the army fell from 18,698 at the end of 1957 to 15,170 at the end of 1962, a decline of nearly 20 per cent.[15] Reductions of similar magnitude took place in the Royal Navy and the Royal Air Force. Officers adjudged less qualified were, as part of this reduction, "selected out" or retired. This process affected in particular the grades between lieutenant colonel and brigadier (and their equivalents in the Royal Navy and RAF), ranks held by a large share of the incumbents in crucial staff positions in the service departments and the Ministry of Defense.

Do the different patterns of experience in the three services lead to sharply different intellectual skills or outlooks among officers of the three services? To examine this question thoroughly would be a major task in itself. As a first approximation, however, there would not seem to be any noticeable variation. While naval officers are often thought to be more "conservative," the tradition of innovation attached to the Admiralty and the Royal Navy and recent shifts in naval policy make such a claim difficult to substantiate. RAF officers are called "doctrinaire" by their critics because of their commitment to a deterrent concept. Few critics, however, can match the imaginative thinking of Sir John Slessor, a former Chief of Air Staff and author of the "massive retaliation" doctrine.

But in several areas it does seem safe to think some differences exist. Officers of the Royal Navy and Royal Air Force very probably bring to policy-making more comprehension and understanding of the interrelation of science, technology, and policy than do most senior army officers. To use the navy as an example, most of the navy leadership sample entered the service before 1920, when the Nelson tradition of combining seamanship and fighting skills was very much alive. A naval officer was encouraged to specialize in some field—signals, torpedos, navigation—and could do so without prejudicing his future opportunities for high-level command. One-quarter of the navy sample listed specialties from their early naval careers in *Who's Who*. Even for the non-specialist, the very nature of naval armaments, ship propulsion, and navigation demanded some comprehension of technical equipment and a modicum of engineering knowledge. One naval officer, lamenting the decline of this tradition, commented as follows:

At the moment we have at the Admiralty and at sea Flag Officers who have the technical knowledge and experience which enables them to talk the same language as the specialist officers, the designers, constructors, and even the scientists, so that invention, design and utility can go hand in hand; but if the user officer is not to know more about the workings of his ship and of its intricate mechanism than which button to press, how is he going to play his part in evolving new requirements which will stand the test of battle? Or where, we may well ask, are we going to find our future D.N.O.s and D.U.W.s and even Controllers of the Navy? [16]

The background of the army officer failed to give him comparable expertise. Upon joining the army, an officer entered a regiment or branch of service on the basis of his own and the unit's social status: cavalry and horses ranked over tanks; the "teeth" or combat arms, that part of the army from which most senior officers were drawn, over the technical services.[17] The benefits of working with complex equipment and highly technical processes that accrued to both navy and air force officers did not fall to army officers, who were concerned on the whole with relatively simple equipment and the welfare of their men. As a senior civil servant put it: "The Army has always been able, so to speak, to get along on its own two feet; the Navy and RAF have always found it impossible to do so without the scientist and engineer." [18] If the army officer has done without the scientist and engineer, he also has been slow to understand what they can contribute.

The army officer's lack of technical and scientific experience, a deficiency currently being remedied by the courses conducted by the Royal Military College of Science at Schrivenhan,[19] is somewhat balanced by other qualities. Most observers would probably agree that army officers as a group possess a breadth of experience and a political awareness not usually found in officers of the other two services. Army service is less isolating than sea duty or flying service. The present generation of senior army officers, in particular, has extensive experience in dealing with administrative and political problems in the overseas areas. Certainly the large number of retired army officers in Parliament—approximately twice the total number of retired navy and air force officers—suggests a greater interest in politics and public affairs.

THE IMPORTANCE OF CIVIL SERVANTS IN THE POLICY PROCESS

There is a division of labor within the departments between military officers and civil servants. The former are the experts on training, equipping, and using military forces; the latter specialize in the accounting, costing, and administrative functions within the department and the uniformed services. At the higher echelons of policy-making, however, this division of function tends to be blurred. Many, if not most, problems do not fall neatly within the exclusive purview of civil servants or military officers: they involve both. Finally, decisions with relatively broad implications must receive the attention of the minister. In short, major decisions normally involve civil servants, military officers, and political leaders.

Common backgrounds and values help break down the barriers between these groups. This is evidenced in Britain by the lack of explicit concern (as in the United States) over the problem of civilian control and the "military mind." The circulation among the groups, the most common manifestation of which is the entry of military officers into the political elite, is yet another indication of the general lack of group distinctiveness. Yet one of the groups—the civil service—is distinctive, and it plays a particularly crucial role in policy formulation.

Final responsibility and authority in a department rest with its political chief, and, in theory at least, the minister can accept, qualify, or reject the recommendations presented to him by his staff. But unlike the United States, where appointed political leaders occupy a large share of the key policy posts, a British department has relatively fewer political leaders, normally only a single minister.[20] There is, in a word, only a thin veneer of political leadership at the top. This layer of political leadership is limited in its impact on policy. It is not a question of whether a minister has the legal or political authority to overrule his advisers; he does, of course, and his power of decision is carefully respected by his senior officials. But there are important constraints on political leaders which limit their contribution to policy. Since the end of World War II the position of ministers of defense has been particularly weak vis-à-vis their civil and military advisers. Prime Ministers Attlee and Churchill, however experienced and competent, were part-time ministers of defense. The average period in office of the remaining ten ministers of defense has been eighteen months. This rapid turnover has necessarily limited the contribution of political leaders to policy, if only because each new appointee has required a few months to settle into the job.

There is also reason to believe that a minister will regard as highly sanctioned the recommendations of his senior advisers. The permanent staff, civil and military, is experienced, able, and numerous. It is also well-connected elsewhere in government. To reject its advice is to risk a poor decision; to disregard repeatedly the views of senior advisers may cause resentment, a lack of candor on subsequent issues, or even lowered department morale and efficiency.

The final, but most important, limitation on the minister's contribution to policy is his time. Except for those few who are peers, ministers are elected politicians. Even though most have a "safe seat," i.e., they are elected in a constituency in which their party enjoys a large and consistent majority in general elections, there are a number of time-consuming constituency duties which must be performed. It is, in fact, not unusual for a minister to spend many Friday evenings and Saturdays in his constituency. The minister also has duties to perform in Parliament. Besides attending the debates relating to his department's activities, there are the further requirements of voting at divisions, of attending party meetings, and of appearing at the weekly question period. These Parliamentary and constituency demands reduce the time that a political leader can spend on departmental duties.

With an important policy role concentrated below the level of the political leader, it is useful to speculate on the relative contributions of civil servants and military officers. Relations between the two groups are not normally competitive—civil versus military. Civil servants and military officers work side by side in many offices and branches of the service departments, and the two groups enjoy close and harmonious relations. But the civil servant is likely to be more influential than his professional military colleague. As one observer put it: "Although the Service officers' influence may be more in evidence, it is more fleeting and in the long run only secondary." [21]

In addition to his established areas of responsibility and competence, the civil servant's skill as a negotiator and coordinator make him indispensable to his military colleagues. The military officer, like his political chief, is a "bird of passage." His experience in the department and in London is limited. The civil servant, in contrast, has an average of twenty-five years of continuous service in Whitehall, most of it in the same department. Besides an intimate knowledge of his own department, he has an understanding of the intricacies of other ministries and the political environment in which defense policies are formulated. This knowledge is invaluable when policies must be co-ordinated with, or approved by, other departments. For these reasons military officers depend heavily on the advice and comments of civil servants, a condition that contributes greatly to the influence of the latter group in the policy process. The complexity of modern technology and its increasing significance to military policies also underlines the importance of scientists in the civil service. Similarly, the growing interrelation of economic and political factors and military policies has injected a new dimension into policy-making.[22] With few exceptions, departmental expertise on these important matters lies with senior civil servants.

British defense policy is the product of a small sector of the British elite. Compared with the personnel who perform similar duties in other countries, British decision-makers are both experienced and highly homogeneous in background and outlook. Because of long service in the department, senior civil servants occupy an especially important position in the defense establishment. Their presence adds stability and continuity to the policy process; at the same time, permanence in office probably enhances the opportunities for policy innovation. Finally, civil servants, uniformed officers, and political leadership are bound together by a multiplicity of personal and informal ties that fracture the formal barriers of departmental organization and group membership, thus facilitating the conduct of Her Majesty's affairs.

1. The service departments and the Ministry of Defense were formally combined into a single ministry in mid-1963. "Department" thus refers to the legally separate organizations which existed until 1963.
Aviation is used here to refer to the department responsible for mili-

tary research, development, and procurement. Before 1959 these activities were centered in the Ministry of Supply, and immediately after World War II they were split between two ministries—Supply and Aircraft Production. These changes are described in the next two chapters.

2. The remarks and observations in this chapter are based on personal impressions, comments by other observers, and the use of such incomplete biographical data as appears in *Who's Who*. Although there are numerous studies of the civil service and the political elite, analyses of the professional officer corps are less numerous. One of the best to date is Philip Abrams, "Democracy, Technology, and the Retired British Officer," in Samuel P. Huntington (ed.), *Changing Patterns of Military Politics* (New York: Free Press of Glencoe, 1962), pp. 150–89. Simon Raven's "Perish by the Sword," in Hugh Thomas (ed.), *The Establishment* (New York: Potter, 1959), pp. 49–79, is a social equalitarian's impressions of the profession. Interesting and perceptive comments on the process of change in British strategic thinking are contained in a thesis entitled "The Changing Strategy of British Bases" (Princeton, 1959), by Colonel DeWitt C. Armstrong. D. W. Brogan's *The English People* (New York: Knopf, 1943) is one of the best single sources on English national character.

3. The service chiefs of staff are, of course, somewhat more in the public eye. Officers in command of large wartime forces or operations tend to be responsible mainly to the cabinet and prime minister, rather than to the political heads of their departments.

4. The British seldom think of civilian control as a "problem." At a time when the issue of General Walker and "muzzling" of the military were highly publicized aspects of American security policies, for example, British officers and politicians were thoroughly puzzled by the issues involved. Some aspects of civil-military relations are discussed by Robert Blake, "Great Britain: The Crimean War to the First World War," in Michael Howard (ed.), *Soldiers and Governments* (London: Eyre and Spottiswoode, 1957), pp. 27–50. Cecil Woodham Smith's classic, *The Reason Why* (New York: Dutton, 1960), contributes greatly to an understanding of the basic reasons for a tradition of effective civil control of the armed forces.

5. With the establishment of the Ministry of Aviation late in 1959, the Minister of Aviation was added to the cabinet. He was dropped from the cabinet in mid-1962. See Chapter VII.

6. Lord Attlee combined the duties of minister of defense with those of prime minister during the period July, 1945—January, 1947, and Sir Winston held both offices between October, 1951, and January, 1952. All biographical data in this and subsequent sections is from *Who's Who, 1959* (London: Adam and Charles Black, 1959).

7. Emanuel Shinwell, *Conflict without Malice* (London: Odhams, 1955), pp. 193–94, 211–13.

8. These comments are based on a sample of senior civil servants working in the service departments, the Ministry of Defense, and the Ministry of Supply in 1957. The sample includes each department's senior scientist.

9. Clubs are less useful to civil servants than to politicians. Departmental dining rooms are more convenient, especially for personnel assigned to departments away from Whitehall, e.g., the Ministry of Aviation.

10. H. E. Dale, *The Higher Civil Service of Great Britain* (London: Oxford University Press, 1941), pp. 93, 94.

11. The remarks below are based on a sample of forty-five officers of general, air, and flag rank. Each uniformed service is represented by fifteen officers selected from among those serving in the service departments in 1957. Each service sample contains the chief of staff, the members of the departmental policy council (the Army Council, for example), and flag-rank officers elsewhere in the headquarters, including officers heading technical branches (for example, the army's Signals Officer-in-Chief). I do not claim that these small samples mirror perfectly the flag ranks serving either in the headquarters or elsewhere in the service.

12. The British service academies are more narrowly trade schools than the service academies in the U.S. The course at Sandhurst lasts eighteen months, and a cadet's time is divided about equally between military and academic subjects. West Point, in contrast, is primarily academic, lasts four years, and its graduates are awarded a B.S. degree.

13. In recent years about forty British officers have attended the annual course. These include ten from each service, normally lieutenant colonels or junior brigadiers (or equivalents in the navy and RAF), and ten Administrative Class officials usually from the Treasury, Foreign Office, Ministry of Aviation, and Ministry of Defense.

14. Roy Lewis and Angus Maude, *The English Middle Classes* (New York: Knopf, 1950), p. 45.

15. Cmd. 1936, "Statement on Defence, 1963," p. 60, and Cmd. 372, "Memorandum of the Secretary of State for War relating to the Army Estimates, 1958–59," p. 14.

16. Captain E. Altham, RN, in the discussion of a lecture by Vice-Admiral Sir Denys Ford entitled "The Technical Training of the Naval Officer of To-day," *Journal: Royal United Service Institution*, XCV, No. 579 (1950), 390. Compare this article with the one by Major General W. J. Eldridge, "The Technical Training of Army Officers" in the same issue of the *Journal*.

17. See, for example, the comments by Correlli Barnett, *The Desert Generals* (New York: Viking, 1961), pp. 99–103.

18. Interview.

19. See *The Times*, February 10, 1959, and the *Guardian*, February 14, 1959.

20. The one or two parliamentary private secretaries in each department are quite limited in authority and are explicitly outside the department hierarchy.

21. E. J. Kingston-McCloughry, *Global Strategy* (New York: Praeger, 1957), p. 168.

22. Several examples of specific decisions taken by senior civil servants are noted in Laurence W. Martin, "The Market for Strategic Ideas in Britain: The 'Sandys Era,' " *American Political Science Review*, LVI, No. 1 (1962), 25 n., 26 n.

7/ The Service Departments [1]

DEFENSE-POLICY FORMULATION is concentrated mainly in five departments—the Admiralty, the War Office, the Air Ministry, the Ministry of Aviation, and the department which co-ordinates the activities of all of these, the Ministry of Defense.[2] This chapter is concerned with the four subordinate departments, in particular, with the functions, procedures, and goals that are peculiar to each. It attempts also to assess the ability of a department, operating as one part of a competitive and interdependent system, to achieve its organizational goals. It is, of course, impossible to discuss fully an organization as complicated as one of the service departments in a few pages; these are but short sketches, designed to suggest the conflicting goals and relative strengths of each department. Implicit is a political, as opposed to an intellectual, view of the policy process. Such a view assumes that policy is partly a function of the strength and tactics of the participants. This is not to say that ideas or analysis are unimportant, but simply to argue that an organization's political strength also matters. This view of the policy process is considered in a subsequent chapter.

THE ADMIRALTY AND THE ROYAL NAVY

It is not by chance that the Admiralty is the first organization considered in this chapter: The Admiralty occupies a special position among the service departments. It is the oldest of the three and has occupied the same building on Whitehall continuously since 1695.[3] Both the Admiralty's age and the permanence of its residency in Whitehall symbolize its durability and pre-eminence among the service departments.

There is little doubt that the Admiralty is the most effective of the three service headquarters. It is described as an "absolutely first-class organization, in a class by itself." [4] In any discussion of the three services, the Admiralty is invariably the first mentioned and always first in any comparative ranking.[5] A number of features help account for the Admiralty's excellence. Most often mentioned is its internal cohesion—its ability to work out a position without evidence of internal conflicts—which enables the Admiralty to speak with a single voice to all outside departments. The Admiralty's informational network—its ability to know what other departments are doing—and exceptional skill in presenting policies and programs whose implications have been carefully considered also contribute to the Admiralty's reputation for toughness and excellence.

Aside from the comments of officials associated with the defense establishment, there is naturally little public evidence available of the Admiralty's relative competence.[6] An example, therefore, may be suggestive. Following the publication of the 1957 Defense White Paper, the Admiralty sponsored a one-day orientation conference at Greenwich. There was in the background a conviction in some quarters of the Ministry of Defense that the navy had only limited usefulness in the nuclear age. Indeed, the 1957 white paper itself had indicated that "large ships will be restricted to the minimum," and that it would be necessary "to rely on a reduced number of more modern ships." [7] As reported in a letter written to *The Times*

by three industrialists in attendance, the "Fairlead" conference was "a brilliant survey of the complicated problems of
defense as they relate to the Royal Navy in cold war, partial
war, and global war." Continuing, they said:

We think it beyond doubt that all present would deny any suggestion
that the Royal Navy is preparing for the last war. We believe that on
the contrary the Admiralty is thinking ahead on sound and imaginative
lines.[8]

Except for this letter the conference attracted little or no
public attention; the Admiralty succeeded in presenting its
case to a selected audience without evoking criticism or concern over the propriety of service-sponsored public-relations
activities.

About a year later the RAF held a similar affair, this one
called the "Prospect" conference. Somewhat more elaborate
than Fairlead, it was staged in the style of an American
Congressional hearing—with Royal Air Force officers acting
as congressmen, listening to testimony from service officers.
Unlike Fairlead, which avoided the adverse reaction normally
associated with service public-relations efforts, Prospect drew
extensive press and Parliamentary comment. It "was at the
boundaries of propriety insofar as service participation in
politics is concerned; some thought it had exceeded them and
others felt it stayed just short." [9] While the Admiralty's competence and political skill are surely not confirmed by a single
conference, this evidence does strengthen the case for its
superiority.

What are the sources of the Admiralty's strength? What
gives it the relatively monolithic quality that enables "their
Lordships to speak with but a single voice"? Fundamentally,
the Admiralty's excellence and toughness derive from the civil
servants who have a very important part in running it. Indeed,
the navy is sometimes humorously referred to as the only
service department run by civilians. Within the Admiralty

there are no separate and distinct civil and military hierarchies, as is largely the case in the War Office. Instead, civil servants and naval officers are carefully integrated and layered in each separate branch of the Admiralty. As a result, there is constant consultation between civil servants and naval officers, and from the inception of any project alternate views and expertise are brought to bear on problems.

The success of the integrated staff depends mainly on exceptionally close relations between the Admiralty's civil and naval personnel. There is a very high degree of confidence and trust between the two; internal personnel procedures are studiously designed to this end. Newly recruited Administrative Class officials are carefully schooled and indoctrinated at the Admiralty. They develop the same fierce pride in the Royal Navy that characterizes British naval officers and maintain with equal passion that naval service, by virtue of its intensive training and early opportunities for independent responsibilities, develops officers who are superior in every respect to those produced in the other services.[10] Furthermore, Admiralty civil servants act on the assumption that the naval officer is *the expert* on the navy.[11] As E. J. Kingston-McCloughry explains it: ". . . *The Admirals are to some extent in control,* and the civil servants work with them as servants in great mutual trust and confidence." [12] As far as possible, assignment policies bring to the Admiralty officers with recent service at sea. An officer's up-to-date knowledge of problems in the fleet enables him to act as an innovator or catalyst, continually confronting his civil-servant colleague with the new problems that need attention. The role of the civil servant is that of critic and manager, improving and refining the proposal and engineering its approval in the Admiralty or the defense establishment generally.[13]

A second basis of the Admiralty's excellence is Britain's great naval tradition, which continues to be a source of strength to the Admiralty and Royal Navy in their relations with other services and civil groups:

It is not merely that Britain is an island, that the sea is all around and near at hand, that no one lives more than thirty or forty miles from tidal water or that there are few fields that have never seen a sea-gull. It may be because these are basic facts that the devotion to the Royal Navy is so deep and wide, but that devotion is now a thing in itself.[14]

But the tradition is also a spur and incentive to the Admiralty itself. Britain's naval history is "a picture of endless victories, won often against formal odds, but won by skill, by energy, by initiative." [15] Naval officers and Admiralty civil servants could not imagine it otherwise. As a senior civil servant put it: "We think we are good, and we work hard at both being and staying good." [16] The Admiralty thus enjoys the support of a great tradition and the strength of great age and has, as well, powerful incentives to retain the excellence and quality always assumed of the "Senior Service."

The fleet, important as a national symbol, is also a source of strength to the Admiralty: it unifies the navy and gives the Admiralty a single object of attention, a single criterion against which to judge new programs and projects. And because the Royal Navy has been over the years so intimately connected with the national fortunes, the Admiralty presupposes that what benefits the fleet benefits Britain. This also explains the emphasis the navy places on the peacetime benefits of naval forces. In fact, the navy has a tradition of "paying its keep even in peacetime." [17] As an example, the navy estimates in 1957 noted the following: clearance of the Suez Canal, participation in International Geophysical Year activities, fishing-fleet protection, emergency assistance to the Lofoten Islanders, and, of course, numerous diplomatic visits abroad.[18] The other services, incidentally, have only recently begun to publicize their activities.

Alone among the service departments the Admiralty has retained control of its research and development and supply functions (except in aircraft and missiles). While there are some advantages when these activities are centered in a separate organization, such as the Ministry of Aviation, the navy's control has probably added to its strength. Administration is simplified by reducing the amount of co-ordination that is needed among the user, researcher, and manufacturer. A particular service doctrine or possible future role may, in a sense, be brought about because research can be directed to provide the equipment and techniques necessary to support a particular concept, rather than doctrine adjusted to scientific and technological advances.

Despite a period of stagnation in the early fifties, the Royal Navy has been perhaps the most successful of the three services in adjusting to the new conditions of the postwar period. The comparative absence of manpower problems and operational responsibilities undoubtedly facilitated this adjustment. Yet there was the same shortage of financial resources in the navy as in the other services, and some of its less useful activities had to be jettisoned. A second problem was more concrete: What should be done about overseas bases? It was not so much that bases had been lost, as that the ancient and secure assumption that they would be available in the future began to erode after World War II. Because of these bases the Royal Navy was traditionally "short-legged." That is to say, naval vessels tended to have a relatively short operating radius. The transition to "long legs," i.e., an extended operating range for naval vessels, was eased by a shift in naval doctrine and by such technological advances as improvements in ship propulsion systems, greater range in carrier-based aircraft, and improved communication equipment. Today the Admiralty seems reasonably satisfied with the combination of fewer bases and greater action radii in the operational fleet.

The final problem was the most critical, and it went to the heart of the navy's future. Until World War II the capital ship was the battleship; the wartime effort provided clear evidence that it was obsolete. There was, however, less guidance as to its replacement. The choice was between the submarine and the aircraft carrier. After a long discussion the navy had settled by 1955 on the carrier and thus continued

the "cavalry" tradition of the big surface ship. Rejection of the
submarine and the limited resources available subsequently
ruled out easy evolution into a Polaris-type strategic-force
system. The bulk of the navy believed, in addition, that a
strategic nuclear force would require a sharp downgrading
of other valued parts of the service. The American experience
also suggested that a force of the Polaris type would require
an elite group within the officer corps, an idea contrary to
the tight unity that characterizes the Royal Navy. Thus the
navy was not particularly disappointed when it was unable to
develop its own strategic force. In fact, the Macmillan government's decision to build a Polaris nuclear submarine force was
greeted with the rather cool statement that "the Admiralty
are confident that the Royal Navy will be able to meet the
challenge offered by the formidable problems entailed in . . .
this task." [19] After the Nassau Agreement the navy argued
that the financial vote for the Polaris submarine force should
be listed separately from the naval vote, reflecting the Admiralty's fears that expenditures on the strategic force would
cut deeply into other naval programs.[20]

Thus, it may be seen that the Royal Navy is, and apparently
hopes to remain, a "small, general purpose navy." [21] It possesses
a diverse spectrum of capabilities—conventional naval capabilities deployed in the Atlantic, the Persian Gulf, and the
Indian Ocean; limited strategic capability from carriers; and
small internal-security forces for use in the overseas areas.
This spread of capabilities, coupled with the navy's strong
tradition of technical innovation, would seem to insure its
ability to adjust easily and rapidly to Britain's future naval
needs.

THE WAR OFFICE AND THE BRITISH ARMY

Britain's military tradition "is one of victory, but of victory
by muddling through, of success won mainly by toughness,
of not knowing when you are beaten and of applying horse

sense." [22] For this reason alone it would be naive to expect from the War Office the same qualities of excellence and adaptability which are found at the Admiralty. That these characteristics have historically been absent at the War Office is suggested by the pattern of reform in the army. Britain's two great Liberal ministers of war, Cardwell (1868–74) and Haldane (1905–12), imposed their reforms on the army. In both instances the level of professional skill in Continental armies was significantly higher, and there was evidence of "rampant" waste

. . . the beneficiaries . . . [of which] were nearly all stout Tories to whom the Army was something not to be administered in any narrow functional sense, but something as wrapped up in a sacred ritual as cricket or the hunting field. So it was easy for a Liberal government to lay radical and sacrilegious hands on those parts of the military establishment . . . least relevant to military efficiency. And such economies could be accompanied by reform since reform, again, took the form of stressing the professional as against the ornamental and conservative. . . . [23]

The tradition of administrative incompetence and the deep-set conservatism of the past have largely disappeared. But even today the War Office is considered the least effective of the service departments: "The War Office never wins a battle." "The Admiralty has a strategy; the Air Ministry has tactics; the Army has neither." [24]

There are a number of reasons that help to explain the weaknesses of the War Office. First, it tends to be split internally into two separate hierarchies, one civil and one military:

The War Office is today well provided with a strong team of highly efficient staff officers who do not have civil service counterparts at various levels like their colleagues in the other two service Ministries. It is the Army officers alone, therefore, who are concerned with the whole range of War Office responsibilities up to a high level. Thus, civil service supervision in the War Office is concentrated mainly at Council level. [25]

Interesting consequences follow. Since military officers are responsible for an autonomous sector of army business, the War Office frequently is represented at interdepartmental conferences by officers. However well trained these officers may be for military duties, they lack the Whitehall experience which would enable them to meet as equals the civil servants representing other departments.[26] In addition, War Office "style" is frequently claimed to be defective. The officer's traditional concern for the welfare of his men, intensified by the difficult manpower problems of the postwar years, has led the War Office to concentrate heavily on personnel matters. In the opinion of many observers, equally legitimate needs for new equipment received too little attention. Coupled with this imbalance between personnel and equipment needs, the War Office is characterized as "too aggressive." The inability of the War Office to win support for army requirements appears to have caused many army officers to feel that "the War Office is not pushing hard enough," that more "aggressiveness" is needed; an already deficient style was further weakened. It is generally agreed, however, that the War Office is becoming a more formidable opponent. The lost battles of the fifties helped toughen it, and under Sir Richard Way and General Sir Richard Hull there were a number of organizational changes directed toward achieving a better integration of civil and military staffs.[27]

The separation of civil and military hierarchies is not the only source of the War Office's weakness. Fundamental also is the internal fragmentation of the British Army. The army is a congeries: few institutions in Britain mirror so faithfully the regional and social differences within British society. The basic combat unit is the regiment, and, in theory at least, recruiting for each regiment has been tied to a geographic locale.[28] Although the tactical efficiency and morale of army units depend in no small measure on these geographic groupings, the regimental system permits, if it does not intensify, social cleavages in British society to persist in the officer corps.

The organization of the service elements and specialized tactical branches of the army contributes to the same end. The army is divided into separate corps—the Royal Engineers and the Royal Army Service Corps, for example. Each corps has a separate administrative hierarchy that runs from field units to the War Office. Service in these corps has traditionally been less prestigious for an officer than service in a regiment. Multiple fragmentation, present at every level, makes it difficult for the War Office ever to arrive at an agreed internal position. Each branch has its own requirements; there is no central focus, no fleet, against which alternatives may be judged.

The organizational fragmentation has been intensified by the diverse missions assigned the army since the end of World War II. On the one hand, there is the British Army of the Rhine, assigned to NATO forces in central Europe. The type of war envisaged in Europe—whatever its probability—requires mobile units, armored if possible, with extensive artillery and engineer support. On the other hand, consider the army's mission in Malaya, Kenya, and Cyprus, where the requirement has been for internal-security forces. Such forces utilize different organizations, different tactics, and different equipment than are necessary in Europe. A very broad range of equipment is necessary, but the quantity needed of any particular item—except for personal equipment such as rifles or helmets—is often very small. Large fixed costs, research and development expenditures and the expense of establishing production lines, can be spread over only a relatively small number of production items. Unit costs are, therefore, high, while the savings that normally result from improvements in production techniques when large quantities are produced ("the learning curve") are seldom realized.[29]

Equivalent difficulties are evident in the army's research and development program. From just before World War II until late 1959, research, development, and procurement of army equipment was the responsibility of the Ministry of

Supply. One of the reasons that these functions were transferred to another agency was that army research and development services atrophied in the period between the two world wars.

The Army has always been the bottom service and in the inter-war period it tended to get a smaller share of the available resources than the other services. Because of the lack of scientific and technical experience on the part of senior officers, it was easy to misjudge the significance of scientific research and the War Office scientific service was therefore an easy target for economies. Repeated cuts soon snowballed—by the mid-30's the service was not only small but of relatively low calibre as well. Interestingly, many of the better people who left the War Office joined the scientific service at the Admiralty.[30]

Army research, development, and procurement since 1945 have required extensive co-ordination and co-operation with the Ministry of Supply. For the same reason that the army's research and development program declined in the interwar period, the problem of liaison with the supporting research and procurement agency has never been adequately solved.[31] While hardly sufficient to account for the relatively unsatisfactory equipment status of the British Army, this explanation does place in perspective one major postwar problem.

A final problem must be given special emphasis. Since the end of World War II much more has been asked of the army than of the other services. Tactical operations have been in progress during much of this period, and supply, personnel policies, and the evacuation of overseas bases have provided acute administrative and logistical problems. The press of operational and administrative activities has given the War Office little time to reflect on the service's current situation and future role. For example, the army hoped to end its dependence on National Service and return to all-regular forces. An all-regular army would not only ease training problems and lead to improved morale throughout the service but would also reduce the administrative burden on the War Office, particularly the constant transfer of short-service personnel to and from distant overseas areas. But by 1957, when the defense white paper announced the end of conscription, the army had given little serious thought to the problems of *getting* an all-regular force. The army's recruiting service was weak; it had not examined the possibilities of various methods of recruitment, as, for example, through television advertising. It also had done little to explore alternative periods of service.[32]

For the army, divided between overseas areas and Europe, resources have been inadequate to do as much in either locale as it would have liked. This has been particularly true since 1957, and the allocation of forces and supplies between the two missions has become a delicate process. This very shortage of resources is probably the major reason why the army considers the present level of British forces in Europe—British Army of the Rhine—generally sufficient. It is difficult for the War Office to envisage a small war's taking place in Europe: even admitting the possibility of a border incident or civil disturbance, it expects that this would soon develop into a very large-scale operation. Yet BAOR is inadequately prepared for large-scale operations on the Continent. It is small (fifty to fifty-five thousand); its stocks of ammunition and supplies are limited; its mobility and fire support are less than it would like; and it controls no tactical nuclear weapons of its own. Because it assesses the probability of success as being low, the army finds it difficult to accept the alternative advanced by the U.S.—large conventional forces with sufficient capability to effect what is commonly called "the pause," i.e., the stopping of Soviet forces temporarily with conventional forces and without nuclear weapons. The best bet in the army's view is to hope that strategic nuclear forces will prevent the outbreak of hostilities; if war occurs, the larger Soviet ground forces can be stopped only by employing nuclear weapons. Allied ground forces, therefore, need not be large but only of a size sufficient to identify an attacking force and to cause it to deploy. The present level of NATO forces is viewed adequate for this purpose; in fact, the War Office argues, an increase in the size of NATO's conventional forces would be provocative, lead to increased tensions between the Soviet Union and western Europe, and make war more probable.[33]

A small ground force commitment to NATO is desirable for other reasons. Service in western Europe is unpopular with British soldiers, and there have on occasion been morale and disciplinary problems in the British Army of the Rhine. Because there is a shortage of housing and other facilities in Germany, if BAOR strength rises above about fifty thousand, difficult living conditions will be created for junior officers and soldiers. A small commitment to NATO, moreover, allows a larger effort in the overseas areas, and overseas security is still viewed as an important mission. It is a traditional role—the British Army has for centuries been fighting small-scale "brushfire" wars in out-of-the-way places. Small-scale war is also *possible* for the army, and events since 1945 have demonstrated the importance of this type of conflict. The overseas-security role, finally, has the attractiveness inherent in any independent mission: it is solely a British responsibility. The lack of enthusiasm for a larger effort in NATO is thus balanced by a genuine concern for the overseas-security mission. This ordering of priorities may be changing; it will be reversed, one observer concluded, only when "the War Office gets a few years in which to sort itself out." [34]

THE AIR MINISTRY AND THE ROYAL AIR FORCE

The Royal Air Force, the youngest of the services, was formed in January, 1918, by combining the aviation elements the army and navy had organized earlier in World War I. The first chief of the air staff was Major General Hugh Trenchard. Although he resigned this office in late 1918, Trenchard was reappointed in 1919 and held this important position until 1929. A man of great ability, Trenchard was dedicated to the goal of an independent air force performing an independent strategic mission. Viscount Templewood (Sir Samuel Hoare), the secretary of state for air during most of this early period, has described Trenchard's stature and hopes for the Royal Air Force:

Whilst Trenchard spoke, I felt myself in the presence of a major prophet. In his mind there were none of the doubts that Bonar Law has expressed about the continued existence of the Air Force. The very suggestion of dividing the service between the Navy and the Army was, in his eyes, a sin against the light. The air was one and indivisible, the airman, an altogether new type of humanity, distinct and original, thinking and acting in a separate element, living apart from the old world, needing a very special training for the new tactics and strategy. . . .

. . . .
The gift that the new man brought was the new mobility, that could break the deadlock of the old wars, . . . strike direct at the enemy's heart, . . . destroy the moral resistance of his people . . . control wide territories without the need of many local garrisons and long campaigns, mobility, however, that needed to be used by those who had been trained to understand its power.[35]

Trenchard's aspirations were contingent on the continued existence of the RAF as a separate service. Before this was assured, however, the RAF engaged in two bitter struggles, one with the army, the second with the navy. In 1921 Trenchard proposed that the RAF be given responsibility for "the maintenance of law and order in Iraq." Sir Winston Churchill, then the secretary of state for air, undertook this experiment against the "violent opposition" of Sir Henry Wilson, then chief of the Imperial General Staff.[36] The RAF's success and the resulting doctrine of "air control" permitted some financial savings and strengthened the RAF's claim to independent responsibilities. A second and more important battle occurred the following year. At issue were the aircraft and flying personnel attached to the Royal Navy. The Royal Navy, of course, wanted control of these elements. Trenchard believed—and he was undoubtedly correct—that, if this sizeable element were transferred to the navy, what would be left of the RAF would soon be absorbed by the other two services.[37] Although these interservice conflicts were fought out largely by the political leadership, much was at stake for the air force: service morale demanded a separate service, and the capabilities of air power could only be demonstrated and developed by a separate service. These two interservice contests and the recriminations and maneuverings that persisted until World War II are of great importance in the Royal Air Force tradition. Senior commanders of the postwar period were then junior officers. Their deification of Lord Trenchard and belief that air power is a separate and somehow special instrument of strategic policy spring partly from the experiences of the twenties.

The Air Ministry's organizational procedures and its reputation for excellence also date from this period. Although officers from both the army and navy were transferred to the RAF, there were few mid-career or senior officers. With an immature and inexperienced staff and under pressure from the other services, the RAF placed great reliance on the civil servants recently recruited to the department. The close co-operation of civil and military staffs led quickly and easily to an integration of the two, and Air Ministry organization and style are thus more like those of the Admiralty than those of the War Office.[38]

For a number of reasons, however, the Air Ministry is not credited with quite the same degree of strength and excellence as the Admiralty. As Marshal of the Royal Air Force Sir John Slessor explains, the RAF lacks the age and tradition of the other services:

There is salt water in the veins of us all. Sea-power has made us what we are. And the older Services, with their centuries of glorious tradition, are inevitably still more part of the warp and weft of our nation than the Royal Air Force. No one will deny that the youngest Service saved our country, and perhaps the world in 1940. But there is not yet among our people an inborn knowledge and instinctive feeling comparable to that which was such a force behind the Navy League in the "We want eight and won't wait" agitation of Dreadnought days.[39]

Second, to the considerable discomfiture of the Air Ministry, research, development, and procurement functions for the air force are the responsibility of the Ministry of Aviation. These services were developed by the RAF during Trenchard's tour as chief of the air staff and remained with the Air Ministry until early in World War II. In 1940, however, they were transferred to Lord Beaverbrook's Ministry of Aircraft Production and have been carried out by some other agency since that time. Co-ordination between the Air Ministry and supporting supply departments has been very good—undoubtedly more effective than in the War Office. The Air Ministry nevertheless believes that this system complicates its administration and, more important, circumscribes the autonomy and freedom of the RAF to plan its own future. The lack of direct experience and responsibility in research, development, and production matters has contributed to other difficulties:

. . . At the time the Korean War began we had spent so much time chasing the better instead of putting the good into production that the Royal Air Force was not equipped to as good a standard as it could have been had we accepted many of the aircraft that had appeared and put them into production.[40]

More than either of the other services, the Royal Air Force has been concerned with a single strategic concept—strategic nuclear deterrence. Evolving from Trenchard's ideas of the independent role of air power and strongly reinforced by the heavy-bombing experiences of World War II, since the end of the Korean War the RAF has viewed the strategic nuclear force as the keystone of British security policy. Reputed to cost between 10 and 15 per cent of the total defense budget, the strategic nuclear force consumes about one-third of the annual air force budget. This somewhat understates the centrality of the strategic mission in the air force, for the V-bomber force has played a role in the RAF comparable to that of the fleet in the navy. Enhancing the prestige of Bomber

Command and operating to maintain its primacy is the concentration of bomber enthusiasts in the top circles of the air force. Bomber Command has always been the most prestigious RAF assignment—more so even than Fighter Command—and many of the more ambitious officers have advanced to high command through this assignment.

Although the strategic nuclear force has been dominant in the Royal Air Force, the service has other important interests as well: the RAF is closely involved in the NATO commitment generally. The employment of the strategic nuclear force would most likely occur in connection with a major conflict in Europe; until the completion in 1963 of the Flyingdales Ballistic Missile Warning Station, the early-warning and control facilities for Bomber Command were located in Euope. Moreover, the Second Allied Tactical Air Force, a NATO command held by the British, includes a sizeable share of the RAF's total capability in the nuclear-armed Canberra and Valiant bombers. There are also important responsibilities for the RAF in the overseas areas. It provides the air transport for the army's strategic reserve and furnishes, if possible, the tactical air support needed by the army in ground operations.

After a decade as the central service, the Royal Air Force is currently in the process of evolving a new relationship with the other services. A rapidly changing technology which makes manned aircraft obsolescent, even useless, for many missions lies in the background. Of more immediate importance, a limited resource base and the availability of Skybolt led to the cancellation of Blue Streak, the weapon that was expected to replace the V-bombers in the mid-1960's. Following the American cancellation of Skybolt, expected by the RAF in 1964 or 1965, President Kennedy agreed to provide Polaris missiles and technical data so that Britain could replace its bombers with a Polaris submarine force. Since this new force will be developed by the navy, the RAF will be responsible for Britain's strategic nuclear force for only a few more years, probably until 1968 or 1970. The air force is currently attempting to improve the range and performance of both its V-series aircraft and Blue Steel, an air-launched missile dropped a hundred miles from the target, so that the present bombers will remain a credible force until the Polaris submarine fleet is available for service. The RAF also hopes that the TSR2, an aircraft due to enter service in 1966 or 1967, will be suitable for the strategic mission. Although its range is limited, this aircraft will be able to penetrate the outer ring of enemy air defenses at low altitude; if it can be equipped with Blue Steel, the TSR2 would not need to fly above the more heavily defended areas close to enemy targets.

In addition to the shift of responsibility for the strategic nuclear force to the Royal Navy, there have been other changes which have affected the Royal Air Force. The first was the cancellation in mid-1962 of the army's short-range tactical missile system, Blue Water. Without a short-range missile system the army must depend on the air force for battlefield fire and interdiction support. If it is to provide this support, the RAF will need to devote a greater share of its effort to the tactical air support mission than it has in the recent past. This requirement may be offset by a decline in the air force commitment in the overseas areas where carrier-based strike aircraft are expected to provide more of the tactical air support for army operations. The current emphasis on tactical and strategic mobility also suggests a greater emphasis on RAF Transport Command than has been the case in the past.

While these policy shifts have been important, there are a number of decisions that will probably be made in the relatively near future which have major implications for the Royal Air Force. All concern NATO policy, and all depend further on the decisions of Britain's allies. If it is decided to proceed with the Mixed-Manned Nuclear Force proposed by the U.S., will it then be desirable to maintain Bomber Command in its present status until it is obsolescent in 1968–70? Or should it be converted into a tactical force with only a conventional capability? Or should Britain, as an alternative, propose to its

European allies that Bomber Command be used as the nucleus of a joint European strategic force?[41] Finally, if a Labor government is returned (in the general election which must occur before November, 1964) and subsequently decides not to continue with the development of the Polaris submarine force, what should be done with Bomber Command?[42]

Because its most important mission may disappear at virtually any time in the near future, the RAF is in the midst of a difficult transition. Its existence as a separate service is not at stake; an end to Bomber Command will mean that the Royal Air Force will become more a supporting service, assisting the navy and army in their operations but having fewer independent responsibilities than in the past. The adjustment has already begun. Transport Command, for example, has been strengthened in recent years, and there is growing interest in the strike-reconnaissance mission. The youngest of the services is confident, however, both that it can adjust to its new relationship with the older services and that it will continue to have important missions to perform. As a senior air force officer explains in late 1961:

If the Government decided not to continue with an independent strategic force or for other reasons shifts operational control of the force to the Navy, it would be a blow to the RAF. But the service would recover—it would need only two years to readjust. And loss of the deterrent mission would seem to imply a larger Air Force since the RAF would then need more aircraft to maintain a comparable level of capability.[43]

THE MINISTRY OF AVIATION

The fourth agency in the defense establishment performs functions rather different from those of the service departments: it is concerned primarily with research, development, and supply, as opposed to administering military forces and operations. The Ministry of Aviation was created in late 1959, replacing the Ministry of Supply that was formed after World War II. Its lineage traces to the Ministry of Munitions, a department thrown up to meet the shell shortages of 1915. Centralized supply was discontinued soon after World War I, although a few items were procured under a "common manager" system whereby one department—the army, for example—purchased items for all the services. In addition, a subcommittee of the Committee of Imperial Defense acted to co-ordinate supply matters between the three services.[44] In 1939 a new Ministry of Supply was established, responsible largely for War Office procurement. After Mr. Churchill's return to government in 1940, he directed Lord Beaverbrook to organize a Ministry of Aircraft Production, using as a nucleus the Air Ministry's supply section. A third department, the Ministry of Production, was established in 1942.

Shortly after World War II the two ministries, Supply and Aircraft Production, were merged into a single department, the Ministry of Supply. This new department was responsible for all research, development, and procurement for the army and air force, and for research, development, and procurement of aircraft, electronics, and guided weapons for the navy. Initially, control of some critical raw materials, atomic energy, and supervisory powers over certain industries—notably, iron and steel—were also vested with it. Except for the development of atomic weapons, most of these additional functions have since been transferred to other agencies.[45]

To meet the research, development, and procurement responsibilities of the service departments, the Ministry of Supply was divided into several major sections: the Controller of Munitions, concerned largely with the development of equipment for the army; the Controller of Aircraft, responsible for aircraft development and supply for the navy and RAF; the Directorate-General of Atomic Weapons; and finally, the Controller of Guided Weapons and Electronics. Research and development laboratories (such as the Royal Aircraft Establishment at Farnborough) were assigned to the section appropriate to their specialization. The ministry was loosely knit, with each major section operating autonomously.[46]

A major reorganization of the Ministry of Supply was undertaken in 1959. The Controller of Munitions and subsidiary research establishments (some twenty-eight hundred personnel) were transferred from the Ministry of Supply to the War Office. Responsibility for civil aviation, previously the concern of the Ministry of Transport and Civil Aviation, was added to the remaining functions of the Ministry of Supply. The department was thereupon designated the Ministry of Aviation; it inherited from the Ministry of Supply the activities of research, development, and procurement of military aircraft, electronic equipment, guided weapons, and nuclear munitions, and, from Transport and Civil Aviation, responsibility for civil aviation. The War Office now conducts most of its own development and supply and serves as a common manager, procuring for the other services the equipment in which it specializes. The position of the Admiralty is much the same; it has retained responsibility for procuring for itself and the other services ships and associated equipment and has continued to depend on the Ministry of Aviation for those items mentioned above. The Air Ministry, in contrast, does virtually no research or procurement of its own.

This change has had only limited significance for defense research, development, and supply. Despite the extension of the common-manager system, a separate agency remains responsible for those items in which user-manufacturer liaison is most difficult—aircraft guided weapons, and electronic equipment. User-manufacturer liaison had been the object of some criticism, both inside and outside the government; the RAF, for example, had long desired to conduct its own research, development, and procurement activities. It argued that a separate agency increased the difficulties of interdepartmental co-ordination and served as a barrier to effective research and development programs. These functions, the air force felt, should be performed by the individual services. Essentially the same procedures were retained after the reorganization, however, because the Ministry of Defense and the Ministry of Supply felt that concentrating most of the research, development, and procurement activity in a single agency would help to avoid excessive duplication of research effort. A second reason for continuing this arrangement was the belief that control over roughly half the defense research and development effort was too great a concentration of power over the national resources in scientists and laboratories for the Air Ministry.[47]

Another reason for the reorganization was suggested by the newly appointed Minister of Aviation, Mr. Duncan Sandys, when he described to the House of Commons the details of the change. Said Mr. Sandys:

> The principal reason for creating the Ministry of Aviation is to enable the interrelated problems of the aircraft industry and the airlines to be tackled together by a single Minister.[48]

The problems to which Mr. Sandys referred concerned a large industry faced with declining orders from its most important customer, the Royal Air Force, and a demand by Britain's government-owned civil air corporations for jet passenger aircraft comparable to those available in the United States. In other words, the aircraft industry was faced with the problem of contracting output and, simultaneously, shifting from largely military to largely civil production. A second problem was that separate civil and military air-traffic control systems needed integration to provide safe flying conditions in crowded domestic airways.

The final reason, while less important than the other two, is of greater interest here: the reorganization was designed to broaden the outlook of the Ministry of Supply. Elements in the ministry had to some extent become allied with the Air Ministry. More often than not, the views of the Ministry of Supply coincided with, and reinforced those of, the Air Ministry. Before 1956 this is reported to have derived largely from a common interest in equipment; after this time it appears to have been an attempt to further the strategic views held by the air force.[49]

There are a number of factors which help account for the orientation of the Ministry of Supply or at least major elements in that organization. Research and development work for the RAF was on the order of four to six times as expensive as that for the War Office.[50] In 1957–58, for example, the net estimates for the ministry amounted to £230 million. Of this amount nearly £158 million was expended for "Research and Development Work by Industry," the great bulk going to the British aircraft industry. Because research and development work for the War Office was undertaken by research agencies integral to the ministry rather than by private firms, expenditures for this work were largely contained in the remainder of the Ministry of Supply budget. In terms of procurement activities the pattern was similar. In 1957–58 the Ministry of Supply's estimated procurements for the service departments were as follows: Admiralty, £42 million (largely aircraft and electronic equipment); War Office, £77 million; Air Ministry, £236 million. The activities in research and development establishments under the Ministry of Supply also favored the air force: aircraft and electronics activities were in aggregate larger than the other sections. While the breakdown by type of research conducted or division of civil staff is not available, some indication of the concentration of activities is suggested by the number of service officers attached to them. Of the 764 officers on duty with the Ministry of Supply in 1957–58, 107 were navy, 439 were air force, and 218 were army. Research establishments concerned with aircraft and electronics activities are also reputed to have been staffed by civilian personnel, who, if not more highly qualified, were at least more pressing in their demands on the ministry.[51] For these reasons the interests of the Ministry of Supply were often the same as those of the Air Ministry.

In light of its specialized functions, the orientation of the Ministry of Supply was not particularly unusual. But the grouping of these services in a single agency served to institutionalize in the defense establishment the interests of the industrial sector most associated with defense production. Certainly a department whose "function . . . [was] to act as a link between the Services and the [aircraft] industry and not as a barrier" was acutely aware of the problems and needs of British aircraft firms.[52] As a link between the services and the industry, the Ministry of Supply had a dual responsibility. To perform properly its research, development, and procurement responsibilities to the service department, the ministry had to be concerned with the state of the industry. To insure the future of the industry and to maintain development and production capabilities in certain specialized fields, it was necessary to influence the content of defense policies. The reorganization in 1959 enabled the Ministry of Aviation to link the industry with both civil and military consumers, and therefore it spread industrial considerations across a wider sector of governmental activity.

The specific impact of the Ministry of Supply on defense-policy decisions is very difficult to discern: the consequences of the department-industry relationship were compounded by several factors. First, the influence of the industry was enhanced because the ministry failed "to exercise adequate control"; "[the] attitude [of the ministry] to service requirements. . . [was] that, provided the Services firmly state a demand and 'the powers that be agree they must have that'. . . , the Ministry of Supply cannot do otherwise than make arrangements for the project to proceed."[53] Second, industry-department relations have not always been harmonious, especially since 1956. Finally, on many (probably most) research and development decisions, the ministry is judged to have maintained a strict neutrality, doing no more than assessing the technical feasibility of the project.[54]

A reasonable judgment would be that the Ministry of Supply compensated for any disadvantages in bargaining power that the RAF suffered as compared to the navy. However, it added little to the position of the War Office. To paraphrase one senior official:

The War Office and the army are in a difficult position. Only a small part of the Ministry of Supply's activities were related to the army, and practically none of the Ministry of Aviation's duties involve the War Office. Much of the army's equipment is produced in Royal Ordnance Factories [run by the War Office]. As a result, the War Office lacks the back-up and support, both of industry and of another government agency, that the navy and air force enjoy. It seems to me that this situation puts the army in a weaker political position than either of the other services.[55]

There is wide agreement as to the relative abilities of the departments in achieving their organizational goals. The Admiralty is the most effective; the War Office, the least. The position of the air force and, in some degree, the navy, has been reinforced by the Ministry of Supply. Each department, aside from its valued goal of organizational autonomy, has multiple strategic interests. The efforts of the army and navy are split between NATO and the overseas areas. The nature of naval forces, however, enables the Royal Navy to shift the balance between these two commitments more easily than the other services. Although air force interest has centered on the strategic nuclear force, a mission that is expected to be assumed in a few years by the navy, the RAF also has responsibilities in NATO and the overseas-security mission.

The goals of organizational autonomy and the multiple strategic interests of each service raise the problem of control and resource allocation. How are resources allocated among the three major programs? What is the importance of contrasting styles and differences in political power? It is to these questions that we now turn.

1. Much of the material in this chapter was obtained in interviews. British views on the importance of the organizational features discussed here varied somewhat. A few were convinced that they counted for less than the school ties worn by one's colleagues. Most seemed to

think them well worth discussing, while several, usually those not in one of the three uniformed departments, stressed their special importance. The organization and operation of a number of the individual government departments have been described in the "New Whitehall Series" published by Allen and Unwin. These include the Colonial, Home, Foreign, and Scottish offices, the ministries of Works, Transport and Civil Aviation, and Pensions and National Service. It is hoped that the Ministry of Defense will be considered in a subsequent issue.

2. In July, 1963, the Macmillan government announced plans to consolidate the Admiralty, the War Office, the Air Ministry, and the Ministry of Defense into a single department, which will be known as the Ministry of Defense. The details of the change are explained in Chapter VIII. Even though the departments will lose their separate legal status, the differences among them will continue to influence policy-making and policy choices.

3. C. F. James, "The Admiralty Buildings, 1695–1723," *Mariners Mirror*, XXVI, No. 4 (1940), 356. All of the service departments except the RAF will move in 1964 and will occupy jointly the office building in Whitehall Gardens now shared by the Board of Trade and the Air Ministry.

4. Interview.

5. Interviews.

6. On the contrary! The Admiralty was one of the "models" for C. Northcote Parkinson's humorous polemic on the proliferation and growth of bureaucracies. See *Parkinson's Law and Other Studies in Administration* (Cambridge: Riverside Press, 1962), pp. 2–13.

7. Cmd. 124, "Defence: Outline of Future Policy," p. 6.

8. *The Times*, May 22, 1957.

9. DeWitt C. Armstrong III, "The Changing Strategy of British Bases" (Ph.D. Dissertation, Princeton University, 1960), p. 119.

10. Interviews.

11. Interviews.

12. E. J. Kingston-McCloughry, *Defense: Policy and Strategy* (New York: Praeger, 1960), p. 118. (Italics mine.)

13. Interviews.

14. D. W. Brogan, *The English People: Impressions and Observations* (New York: Knopf, 1943), p. 246.

15. *Ibid.*

16. Interview.

17. E. J. Kingston-McCloughry, *Global Strategy* (New York: Praeger, 1957), p. 169. See also Admiral Earl Mountbatten of Burma, "The Role of the Royal Navy," in H. G. Thursfield (ed.), *Brassey's Annual, 1954* (New York: Macmillan, 1954), pp. 29–34.

18. Cmd. 151, "Explanatory Statement on the Navy Estimates, 1957–58," pp. 20–24.

19. Cmd. 1936, "Statement on Defence 1963," p. 15.

20. See the letter to *The Times* from Sir Frederick Brundrett, the former chief scientist at the Admiralty and, later, at the Ministry of Defense, on January 15, 1963.

21. Interview.

22. Brogan, *The English People*, p. 246.

23. *Ibid.*, p. 238.

24. Interviews. These are the opinions of observers outside the service departments. Without exception the three departments are ranked in the same order: Admiralty, Air Ministry, and War Office. However, there are differences among observers in how much better one department is than another.

25. Kingston-McCloughry, *Defense*, p. 119. Because of their competence, War Office staff officers perhaps feel less need for the civil servant and thus perpetuate the cleavage. Some observers feel staff officers stay at the War Office too long and thereby fail to make a contribution because they lack an awareness of current army problems.

26. At the same time this experience contributes to the greater political awareness which, more than among officers of the other services, characterizes the senior army professional.

27. Interviews.

28. Recent changes in tactical organization may help to overcome some of the negative features of the regimental system.

29. Ely Devons has furnished an excellent example from the aircraft industry: " . . . the total development expenditure on an aircraft such as the Britannia may amount to £10 million.

. . . .

Suppose one takes the direct production cost. . . , including engines, to be of the order of £500,000. Then if the research and development expenditure is spread over an order for twenty aircraft, the average total cost would be £1.2 million; if spread over an order of forty, the average total cost would be £850,000; and if spread over an order of 100, the average cost would be £640,000." See Ely Devons, "The Aircraft Industry," in Duncan Burn (ed.), *The Structure of British Industry*, II (Cambridge: Cambridge University Press, 1958), 75.

30. Interview. See above, Chapter VI, p. 99.

31. Interview.

32. Interviews. The Advisory Committee on Recruiting, headed by Sir James Grigg, was not convened by the Minister of Defense until December, 1957, and did not submit its report until October, 1958. See Cmd. 545, "Report of the Advisory Committee on Recruiting," especially pp. 30–32, 49–56.

33. There are some elements in the War Office who prefer the U.S. alternative, i.e., larger conventional forces in Europe. They feel, however, that there is little possibility of an increase in army resources, either manpower or financial, and have no option but to accept the basic position outlined above.

34. Interview.

35. Viscount Templewood (Sir Samuel Hoare), *Empire of the Air: The Advent of the Air Age, 1922–1929* (London: Collins, 1957), p. 41.

36. Sir John Slessor, *The Central Blue: The Autobiography of Sir John Slessor, Marshal of the RAF* (New York: Praeger, 1957), p. 52.

37. Responsibility for shipborne aviation was returned to the Royal Navy in 1937. The land-based, over-water, anti-submarine patrol mission has remained with the air force in Coastal Command. Because this mission has been a contentious issue, Coastal Command has always been a prestigious assignment for senior RAF officers.

38. Interviews.

39. Slessor, *The Central Blue*, p. xi. The air force is less than fifty years old and except for the Battle of Britain has little in the way of tradition.

40. The Select Committee on Estimates, *The Supply of Military Aircraft* (London: H. M. Stationery Office, 1956), paragraph 666.

41. The French have already made such a proposal to the British and the Germans.

42. According to a recent statement by the Labor spokesman on defense, Mr. Denis Healey, the decision would hinge on whether there was an "alliance requirement for a British Polaris component" (690 H. C. Deb. 480).

43. Interview.

44. See Lord Ismay (Hastings Lionel Ismay), *The Memoirs of General Lord Ismay* (New York: Viking, 1960), pp. 53–55.

45. An excellent short history of the supply organization is contained in D. N. Chester and F. M. G. Willson (eds.), *The Organisation of British Central Government 1914–1956* (A Survey by a Study Group of the Royal Institute of Public Administration), (London: Allen and Unwin, 1957), pp. 215–39.

46. Interviews.

47. Interview.

48. 613 H. C. Deb. 673.

49. Interview.

50. The data in the paragraph are from "Class VI, Trade, Labour and Supply," *1957–1958, Civil Estimates* (London: H. M. Stationery Office, 1957), pp. 77–113.

51. Interviews.

52. The Select Committee on Estimates, *The Supply of Military Aircraft*, p. xxi.

53. *Ibid.*, p. xx.

54. Interviews.

55. Interview.

8/ The Politics of Decision-Making

On July 2, 1963, the Macmillan governnment announced an important reorganization of the defense establishment.[1] Approved by Parliament on July 31, 1963, the reorganization is greater in scope than any undertaken since the end of World War II. The government's plans are expected to be completed by April 1, 1964.

The most prominent feature in the government's white paper on defense reorganization is the announcement that the three service departments and the Ministry of Defense are merged into a single new department known as the Ministry of Defense and housed in a single building in Whitehall Gardens. Political control of the services, until now divided among the minister of defense, the first lord of the Admiralty, and the secretaries of state for war and air, is assumed by a single official, the secretary of state for defense. It is intended that the secretary of state for defense be assisted by three "ministers of state for defense," each responsible for one of the services. A second intended change is the consolidation of the service-department councils—the Board of Admiralty and the Army and Air councils—into a single "Defence Council." The Defense Council, with the secretary of state as chairman and the three ministers of state as vice-chairmen, is divided into three "boards" that will "execute policy on behalf of the Secretary of State in respect of a designated Service. . . ." [2] The effect is that the service boards, each headed by a minister of state, replace the existing departmental councils. Included as members of each board are the service's senior civil servant, chief scientist, chief of staff, and those senior officers heading major staff sections. Finally, the Defense Committee, formed in 1946, is replaced by a "Committee on Defense and Overseas Policy." The prime minister serves as chairman; other members include the first secretary of state, the foreign secretary, the chancellor of the Exchequer, the home secretary, the secretary of state for Commonwealth relations and colonies, and the secretary of state for defense. The members of the Chiefs of Staff Committee are expected to attend the new committee's meetings; other ministers may be invited to sit with it when matters relating to their departments are under consideration.

Despite the loss of departmental status, each service retains its separate identity—and separate uniform. Indeed, there are three essentially individual service organizations within the framework of a single department. The critical change takes place in the central policy-making machinery which, until the reorganization, comprised the Ministry of Defense. This is increased in size and integrated with the top echelons of each of the service organizations. It is intended that this arrangement provide a "greater knowledge of the background problems and currents of opinion within the Services than can be secured with four separate Defence Departments responsible to separate Ministers." [3]

The naval, general, and air staffs lose their separate legal identities and are formed into a single Defense Staff under

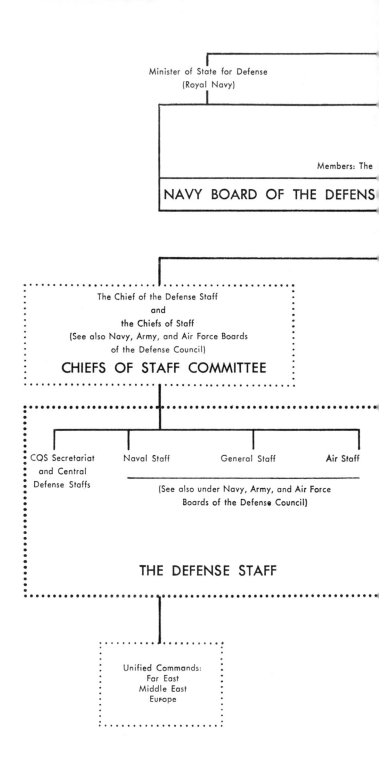

Minister of State for Defense
(Royal Navy)

Members: The

NAVY BOARD OF THE DEFENS

The Chief of the Defense Staff
and
the Chiefs of Staff
(See also Navy, Army, and Air Force Boards
of the Defense Council)

CHIEFS OF STAFF COMMITTEE

CQS Secretariat
and Central
Defense Staffs

Naval Staff   General Staff   Air Staff

(See also under Navy, Army, and Air Force
Boards of the Defense Council)

THE DEFENSE STAFF

Unified Commands:
Far East
Middle East
Europe

the direction of the chief of the Defense Staff and the Chiefs of Staff Committee. (The Chiefs of Staff Committee, established in 1924, is composed of the three service chiefs of staff and, since 1957, the chief of the Defense Staff. Its American counterpart is the Joint Chiefs of Staff. The chief of the Defense Staff, as his American opposite, the chairman of the Joint Chiefs of Staff, is without departmental duties.) The major change in the military organization, however, is the strengthening of the joint staff: it is double its former size, and four new joint staff sections—an Operations Executive, an Operations Requirements Staff, a Signals Staff, and an Intelligence Staff—are formed. The Joint Warfare and Joint Operations staffs, established earlier, continue in existence.

As with the military staffs, the administrative staffs of civil servants (to the extent that these are separate from the service military staffs) retain their autonomy and continue to perform duties associated with each service. The senior civil servant in each service department, the second permanent undersecretary of state, is explicity subordinate to the permanent undersecretary of state, the title assumed by the present permanent undersecretary at the Ministry of Defense. A fourth second permanent undersecretary heads a new body, the Defense Secretariat. Under the direction of the permanent undersecretary and his deputy, the secretariat assumes primary responsibility for co-ordinating the views and activities of the military, scientific, and administrative staffs. A key official in the secretariat is the deputy undersecretary of state for programs and budget, "responsible for the full scope and content of the defence programme and the Defence Budget." [4] Review and analysis activities corresponding to the "systems analysis" done in Deputy Assistant Secretary of Defense Alain Enthoven's section of the U.S. Department of Defense are now centered in this office.

The changes in the Defense Scientific Staff are similar in scope. The position of the chief scientific adviser, a co-equal to the permanent undersecretary of state and the chief of the Defense Staff, is strengthened by the appointment of two new assistants, a deputy for "studies" and one for "projects." It is envisaged that these two officials will co-ordinate and supervise the work of the personnel assigned to the chief scientific adviser. The scientific staff, whose increase in size is proportionally greater than that of the military or administrative staffs, is expected to provide the bulk of the members for two new committees—the Defense Research Committee and the Weapons Development Committee—which replace the present Defense Research Policy Committee. Finally, a Defense Science Secretariat is established, one of whose more important tasks is to provide the deputy undersecretary for programs and budget with accurate long-term estimates of defense research, development, and procurement expenditures.

In sum, the staff directly responsible to the secretary of state for defense is approximately twice as large as the one available to the minister of defense. The increase is expected to improve the quality and detail of its policy recommendations. The proximity and availability of the service staffs also facilitates the flow of information to senior officials. Finally, special emphasis has been given to the two areas in which major difficulties have been encountered in recent years—programs and budgets, and research and development.

Although the 1963 reorganization is more extensive than earlier changes, a single basic force has underlain each modification in the defense organization undertaken since the end of World War II: both policy-makers and commentators outside the government have felt that the defense organization has not provided the unified policy and close interservice coordination that have been desired. One important aspect of the failure has generally been considered inherent in the policy process: conflict among the services has been persistent and often intense, and policy by "compromise" and "bargaining" has been the rule rather than the exception. One of the earliest

critics was Field Marshal Montgomery, chief of the Imperial
General Staff between 1946 and 1948:

> I can recall only one case of real unamimous agreement in the Chiefs
> of Staff Committee and that was when I put forward a proposal in July
> 1948 that we should ask the Prime Minister for a new Minister of
> Defence. But that agreement came to nothing, since my two colleagues
> declined to face the music on the day of battle. In all other cases agree-
> ment was reached only by compromise.[5]

The situation improved somewhat during the period 1950–52
when the chiefs were an unusually compatible group.[6] By the
mid-1950's, however, decision-making by bargaining and compromise had returned, and the policy process again became a
matter of concern. In the 1955 defense debates, for example,
no less than seven speakers commented on policy-making:
"The great military interests are still writing White Papers
and Defence Estimates," argued the late John Strachey, then
Labor's army spokesman.[7] As one symptom of the ailments,
interservice rivalry was especially deplored, and Vice-Admiral
Hughes Hallet, a Conservative backbencher, was one of several
MP's who demanded that the services be unified: "I can see
no other certain way of bringing to an end the interminable
and sterile arguments that have gone on for so many years
between the champions of the Navy and the champions of the
Royal Air Force." [8] At the close of that debate Harold Macmillan, then the minister of defense, felt it necessary to deny that
there was a lack of agreement and co-operation among the
service departments.[9]

Although interservice rivalry has been considered the most
serious weakness in the policy process, it has also been widely
suspected that the defense-budget decisions were taken arbi-
trarily and that many recommendations of the chiefs of staff
were ignored. These suspicions were well founded as Mr.
Shinwell, the minister of defense during 1950 and 1951, confessed in 1958:

[In 1950 the service chiefs] produced a programme which involved the expenditure of £6,000 million, and we toned it down to one of £4,750 million. Who did it? I did it. How was it done? Let us take the War Office as an example. The War Office put in a programme amounting to many hundreds of millions of pounds, including a very large sum for new vehicles. We cut it, just like that, and the War Office had to accept the cut.[10]

An arbitrary ceiling on defense expenditures was also established. It did not, however, prevent the services from fighting for a larger share of the appropriations. Sir Anthony Eden noted "some difficulty in reconciling the Treasury's view of what could be afforded with the Service estimates of what was essential." [11] It was decision by bargaining and compromise.

A common explanation for the bargaining and compromise was the lack of power granted the minister of defense. Under the legislation of October, 1946, which established the Ministry of Defense, the minister's authority was limited to three areas: (1) "administration of inter-Service organisations" (the Joint Intelligence Bureau, for example); (2) "questions of general administration on which a common policy for the three Services is desirable"; and (3) "apportionment, in broad outline, of available resources between the three Services in accordance with the strategic policy laid down by the Defence Committee." [12] In the absence of an agreed strategic policy, the direction of interservice organizations and general administration was insufficient to enable the minister to exercise over-all control. The Ministry of Defense also lacked the information and organizational resources available to each service minister and chief of staff—a situation that contributed further to his inability to control policy. As one commentator explained, the "strength [of the minister of defense] lay in the fact that he was a member of the Cabinet and the Service Ministers were not, and the power he exercised depended in practice on his personality." [13]

Beginning in 1955, a number of steps were taken to increase the authority of the minister of defense. The most important came early in 1957, when the new prime minister, Mr. Harold Macmillan, announced that Mr. Duncan Sandys, his recently appointed minister of defense, would

> . . . have authority to give decisions on all matters of policy affecting the size, shape, organisation and disposition of the Armed Forces, their equipment and supply (including defence research and development) and their pay and conditions of service. He will similarly have power of decision on any matters of Service administration or appointments which, in his opinion, are of special importance.[14]

At the same time the prime minister abolished the position of chairman of the Defense Staff, an office created in 1955, and appointed a chief of the Defense Staff. Dubbed the "Supremo," the chief was without departmental responsibilities, an arrangement that was expected to allow him to act as a "nonpartisan" military adviser to the minister of defense. In July, 1958, it was announced that a "Defence Board," with the minister of defense as chairman, would be established "for the discussion of inter-Service problems." [15] At least one commentator believed this series of changes represented the "transition from a defence organisation based on co-ordination to one based on control." [16]

But whatever the mechanics of organization, the symptoms persisted and even intensified. The establishment of an arbitrary budget limit contrary to the recommendations of the service chiefs found its parallel after 1957 in an arbitrary manpower ceiling. In 1956 a War Office committee under the chairmanship of General Sir Richard Hull (later the army's chief of staff) examined future army manpower requirements.[17] Its recommendation was for a force of "about 220,000 all ranks," an "absolute minimum," assuming "full civilianisation of the tail and a generous supply of transport aircraft." [18] This proposal was rejected by Mr. Sandys; instead, the level was set at 165,000. It is generally conceded that this figure was an "actuarial estimate" of the "numbers we would get" by recruiting.[19] R. H. S. Crossman, the most persuasive of Sandys' many critics, claimed the minister had "fudged." "He accepted as the target," Crossman argued, "not what was required for the defence of this country but what it was hoped to have out of Regular recruiting." [20]

One of the most interesting general comments on the policy process during the initial years of the Macmillan government was made in the 1959 defense debates by Mr. George Brown, then Labor's defense spokesman. There is little reason to doubt the essential accuracy of his description:

Its worst consequences [referring to Mr. Sandys' period in office], . . . was the passionate opposition which the right hon. Gentleman [the minister of defense] aroused to the proposed new central defence planning organisation and direction in his own Ministry of Defence.

. . . .

I believe the aim and desire to have been sensible and valuable, but it foundered on personal antagonisms that were aroused by the right hon. Gentleman's attempted implementation of his own policy.

. . . .

The consequences of all this were that the individual Services fought like mad to protect their own forces and their own projects. By so doing, they prevented the savings which at that time the right hon. Gentleman thought he could make and sought to make. This has led to contradictory decisions since 1957. The right hon. Gentlemen's fight back for his own policy led to a refusal to place orders that should have been placed.

Later in his speech Mr. Brown noted:

In fact, I believe that we are back to the old 1957 position and that this year there has been no central defence policy, which is why the Minister makes no mention of doctrine. We are back to the old days of a straight bargain between the three Services, in which they have each got as much of the money as they could and are putting it to the best use they can for their own purposes. That is the measure of the right hon. Gentleman's failure.

Mr. Brown closed his remarks by proclaiming:

We believe that there is no doubt, as I have attempted to show, that there has been a great lack of coherence in the policy followed by the Government both prior to the right hon. Gentleman's advent to office and since. We believe there is clearly no strategic doctrine now governing the Government's defence policy.[21]

In short, accommodation by compromise and bargaining is one main characteristic of the defense-policy process since World War II. A second attribute is arbitrary decision-making, with the views of the chiefs of staff often ignored and issues resolved on the basis of political or economic factors. Air Vice-Marshal Kingston-McCloughry's observations on the policy process were shared by most observers: " . . . To the informed it is quite plain that all is not well in Whitehall, and that, in respect of Defence at least, this part of the machine creaks audibly." [22] Although organizational changes have not seemed to improve the policy process, each modification has tended to be viewed as an antidote to the ills indicated by the persistent symptoms.

AGREEMENT VERSUS BARGAINING

Those characteristics of the policy process described above are of very great importance. For policy-makers they have been a stimulus to further centralization of power in the Ministry of Defense; for critics and observers they have been an always available and often utilized object of criticism and commentary. But several questions remain: Are these features descriptive of defense policy-making generally or do they pertain to only a limited part of the process? What are the causes of the bargaining and conflict among the service departments? What factors condition the relationships among the various departments? And more importantly, what are the results of this process?

Agreement

The gist of the commentary on the defense policy process is that bargaining and interservice rivalry are abnormal, if not pernicious, ways of making decisions. This view is correct in the sense that many decisions—indeed, a majority—do not generate conflict among the interested departments. The norm is amiable interdepartmental meetings that stress analysis and logical methods of problem-solving and which lead easily and quickly to solutions acceptable to all the participants. According to Sir John Slessor, chief of the Air Staff under both Lord Attlee and Sir Winston Churchill, "[disagreements] seldom become serious, and, in a rather typically British way, an arrangement which contains some anomalies works, by and large, quite well—it is a matter for the exercise of tact and common sense by everyone concerned." [23] This, the more acceptable style of decision-making, has not been limited to minor policies. Many major decisions of the postwar period, to include the adoption of a deterrence strategy, had the support of all service departments and chiefs of staff.[24]

There are many features of British government which facilitate a pattern of this kind. The broad agreement on basic values that exists in Britain is, of course, fundamental. Of relevance for the conduct of governmental affairs, however, is the attitude of officials at all levels: that legitimate opposition soon becomes unwarranted obstructionism. The ethic of an expeditious conduct of business is suggested by the motto "Her Majesty's business must be carried on"; supporting this motto is the sense of unity and cohesion among higher civil servants.[25] In the service departments there is homogeneity of social backgrounds and educational experiences among civil servants, military officers, and political leaders. While there are differences among the groups, these seem relatively less important than, for example, those in the United States. The common ties within the American armed services—service-academy classmates, and to a lesser extent, service-school attendance—are supplemented in the British forces by the public-school tie, relatively common service experiences, club membership, and, very frequently, family ties. These social, educational, professional, and family connections weave together the three occupational groups that participate in decision-making: they provide a vast complex of horizontal links across the formal bureaucratic boundaries and facilitate the negotiations and discussions essential to an ongoing flow of business. The great propensity of the British to form and use committees also attenuates many of the differences that must be overcome to conduct business.[26]

In most organizations budgets are a particularly troublesome aspect of decision-making. Bargaining techniques of problem-solving are almost always required. Not only is an organization's political future at stake, but the allocation of resources often implies preferences for alternative courses of action whose consequences are so uncertain as to make analytic techniques of problem-solving inapplicable. Yet in this particular area the division of functions among decision-makers is of great importance in limiting conflict among the services. Budgeting and finance are the special responsibility of higher civil servants. While officials can no longer be regarded as "outposts of the Treasury" [27]—as Sir Warren Fisher described their outlook prior to 1920—it is nevertheless true that senior civil servants retain an acute sense of the possible. Aside from the corporate character of the senior civil service, the civil servant's permanence in office and contacts at the Ministry of Defense and the Treasury are of considerable importance in moderating departmental financial requests and hence limiting the intensity of budget conflicts.

The basic features that promote agreement and the use of analytic processes of problem-solving are strongly reinforced by the criticism of the policy process. As indicated in Chapter III, defense policies, whether formulated by a Labor or Conservative government, have commanded broad support, particularly among the political elite. Since defense policies have generally been politically acceptable, it has been assumed by many critics that there are no substantial bases for the disagreement among the service departments, and for this reason few aspects of defense policy have drawn more intensive or persistent attention than interservice rivalry. This attention acts as a special incentive to avoid disagreement among senior policy-makers.

Among the groups involved in the policy process, senior military officers are undoubtedly the most sensitive to criticism of interservice rivalry.[28] A senior officer has a special identification with his own service and a concomitant sense of responsibility for its activities. Since service activities are viewed critically, the senior military officer cannot easily avoid feeling personally responsible for what is generally construed to be a failure in policy-making. This incentive to avoid disagreement is strengthened by the institutional relationships in the Ministry of Defense, particularly in the Chiefs of Staff Committee. The chiefs are the principal military advisers to the Minister of Defense. If there are irreconcilable divisions among these advisers, the military aspects of a problem may not be weighed so heavily as the economic or political aspects. The alternative requires that the chiefs speak with a single voice, even if some of them feel that this is the second-best alternative.[29] The criticism of interservice rivalry and the fear that relevant military considerations will be ignored are thus incentives to military officers to avoid disagreement.

Bargaining

The easy agreement on policy choices that forms one end of the continuum is balanced at the other pole by a pattern of disagreement and bargained policies. Bargaining is a relatively common form of decision-making. It takes place in all forms of government, and the amount of bargaining is largely a function of the degree of social pluralism in the society. Contrasting group identifications and orientations prevent initial agreement; yet bargaining implies the prospect of agreement based on shared goals and values. Bargaining also indicates that there is interdependence, with the actions of one group affecting in some degree those of other groups.

Although bargaining may be quantitatively less significant than other forms of decision-making, it deserves particular attention: first, because bargaining is often believed to be infrequent in British government and therefore tends to be viewed as an unusual form of problem-solving; and second, because the issues resolved by bargaining are almost always important. For the reasons already noted, most issues are resolved quite amicably by discussion among the interested departments. When there are differences on values and goals among the participants in the policy process, however, bargaining techniques are substituted for analytic processes. Budget decisions, as suggested by Sir Anthony Eden's comment, are a case in point. They very often engender some degree of conflict simply because budgets prescribe the future of the organizations involved. If resources were unlimited, there would be no problem. But resources are always limited, and in this sense at least, the shortage of resources is one of the basic "causes" of bargaining. The tendency to resort to bargained solutions is increased when analytic techniques of problem-solving are not of great utility, for example, when competing alternatives have incommensurable benefits. A second kind of problem that is often solved by bargaining is the control of new weapons systems or operational forces, "roles and missions" issues.[30] As in the case of budgets, the political future of one or more organizations is at stake in decisions of this kind. There have been a number of these conflicts in Britain: Coastal Command has been the subject of a running controversy between the navy and the RAF; the army and air force have contested for control of various ground-to-air missiles systems; and more recently the air force and navy have engaged in a dispute over which would furnish tactical air support for army operations in the overseas areas.

The actual pattern of interservice conflict since the end of World War II demonstrates the validity of these basic hypotheses concerning the causes of bargaining and conflict. According to Sir John Slessor's testimony, relations among the services were relatively harmonious when he was chief of the air staff during the Korean War. This was a period of rapidly rising defense budgets, however, and the services had sufficient resources for most of their major programs. The period 1957–58 stands in sharp contrast. To judge from the press, there was intense bargaining and conflict. It was also a period in which important changes were taking place. A serious effort was under way to prevent further increases in the level of defense spending, and all of the services were short of financial resources. The authority of the minister of defense and his department was being increased—at the expense of the service departments. Each service was dissatisfied with some aspect of Mr. Sandys' policy: the navy's future role was in doubt; the RAF was ordered to expedite the shift from manned aircraft to ballistic missiles; and the army was faced with the difficulties of a major force reduction. The service departments contested these decisions and, with varying degrees of success, succeeded in reversing parts of them. This intense competition and bargaining was not caused by a lack of positive leadership or control. Mr. Sandys, the minister of defense during this period, has been described by his predecessor, Brigadier Head, as an individual of "great qualities of strength of character and of determination." [31] The evidence points to the conclusion that interservice rivalry and conflict is the result of change and positive control and not necessarily an indication of the need for change or leadership.

Bargaining techniques of decision-making have been prevalent in two institutions, the Chiefs of Staff Committee and the Defense Research Policy Committee.[32] These two committees are the scene of extensive bargaining for quite simple reasons: each is composed of representatives of the three services, individuals with different orientations, perspectives, and values; and each considers major policy choices with important implications for the futures of the separate services. The processes by which differences are resolved in these two committees are also familiar: decisions can be postponed or, as often happens, the problem may be referred for additional study even though the important elements have already been thoroughly canvassed; decisions can be stated in vague and general terms with limited operational significance; and finally, the affected departments can agree by log-rolling, that is, by supporting the proposals of another service in return for its support on a different issue.[33]

It is difficult to avoid comparing the Chiefs of Staff Committee with its American counterpart, the Joint Chiefs of Staff. The composition and responsibilities of the two groups are the same. The issues on which the chiefs disagree are also the same, as are the processes of resolving conflicts. One senior British officer drew the following comparison: "A quite accurate description of the operations of the Chiefs of Staff Committee has been written by General Maxwell Taylor, and appears in his book, *The Uncertain Trumpet.*" [34]

The comparison between the United States and Britain cannot reasonably be carried beyond this point. Bargaining among the American service departments is a fluid and open process, and on many issues the area of decision-making is expanded outside the Joint Chiefs of Staff or even outside the defense establishment. The amount of expansion seems, as a first approximation, largely a matter of the importance of the decision to the departments concerned. The Congress, particularly those committees concerned with military affairs, is normally a participant in this process. On occasion, state and local political institutions and various pressure groups become allies and advocate service-department positions before the Congress or in the Executive. The diffuseness of the process is largely explained by the division of power in American government between the executive and legislative branches and between the federal government and the states.

By contrast, in Britain bargaining and interservice conflict tend to be conducted largely within the Executive. This is partly a matter of tradition, but it is more a function of the concentration of power within the government. There is relatively little to be gained by expanding the area of decision-making simply because there are few centers of power outside the Executive whose support can be decisive. Parliament, for example, is seldom involved. It is unable to change the over-all size of the defense budget or to reallocate resources among the services. Its usefulness to a service department is therefore very limited, as is its value as a forum for lobbying by other pressure groups.

Publicity, a favorite weapon in American interservice battles, is also less useful in Britain. It is normally little used by pressure groups as a technique for influencing government policies.[35] The services, moreover, are under special constraints. To publicize differences openly conflicts with an important norm in British politics—a government governs—and public-relations activity by a service department immediately raises questions of constitutional and political propriety. The articulate public also reacts unfavorably because it associates publicity with service conflict in the U.S., to which it attributes many of the weaknesses of American policies. The adverse publicity from the RAF's Prospect Conference is a case in point; a speech by Major General Sir John Crowley in which he expressed opinions contrary to official policy provides another.[36] Although it was cleared (perhaps undertaken deliberately) by the War Office and clearly labeled as his personal view, Sir John's speech received a cool reception. Though he could have used Sir John's divergent opinions to attack the substance of government policy, Mr. Roy Mason, a Labor MP, instead asked the minister of defense the following questions: "Irrespective of whether the Minister agrees with the contents of the lecture, does he not think this a dangerous practice? Does he not intend to take some steps to try to stamp out this frankness and these blatant remarks by officers of Her Majesty's Forces who are openly declaring opposition to the Government's defence policy?" [37]

To expand the area of decision-making is thus to elicit support of a rather ineffective character and also to run the risk of adverse publicity. On issues of great importance to a service, however, outside support may be considered to be of some value. There are several approaches it may utilize. A service may mobilize its supporters in Parliament to press its position upon the minister of defense through the back-bench defense organization. A service can also encourage outside interests to lobby with other departments, hoping that mutual interests will lead to an alliance within the Executive.[38] If, for example, a decision on naval ship construction was under consideration, the navy might encourage the industry to make representations to the Scottish Office or a Northern Ireland Ministry— shipbuilding is an important industry in both Scotland and Northern Ireland—hoping these representations would subsequently influence the decision.

Illustrative of a number of points made thus far are the tactics employed by the navy in its fight against the 1957 Defense White Paper and the intention of the minister of defense to downgrade the navy. The Admiralty considered the new minister a very serious threat to its future. Aside from its own organizational resources, the Admiralty succeeded in mobilizing in its behalf a considerable measure of support. It enlisted in its cause two senior civil servants, both in key positions in the Ministry of Defense.[39] It stepped outside the boundaries of the Executive and held the Fairlead conference at Greenwich.[40] Except for brief mention in the House of Lords and a letter by Lords Chandos, Godber, and Weeks to *The Times*, the conference received no publicity. Some clues as to the Admiralty's tactics would seem to follow from the positions of these three visitors. All were prominent industrialists. Chandos and Weeks were members of the board of Associated Electrical Industries; both had an interest in the shipbuilding industry—Weeks, through his association with Vickers, Ltd., and Vickers Nuclear Engineering Company, and Chandos, as chairman of the Development Council for Northern Ireland. Lord Godber represented important petroleum interests (Shell Transport and Trading Company, Ltd., and Anglo-Saxon Petroleum). Both Godber and Chandos had active interests in the overseas areas—Godber, as chairman of the Commonwealth Development Finance Company, and Chandos, as a former secretary of state for the colonies. Whether as a result of representations by these three industrialists (and others in attendance) or Admiralty efforts within the Executive, or more likely, because of both of these activities, the Foreign Office and Colonial Office lined up on the navy's side.[41]

It is also probable that the Admiralty informed Commonwealth governments of the plans to reduce the navy. During Mr. Sandys' tour of Asia in the early summer of 1957, he was advised by several of his hosts of the vital role of the Royal Navy in Commonwealth defense.[42] Later, in August, Mr. Macmillan was urged by several of the delegates to the Commonwealth prime ministers' conference to reconsider the government's plans for the navy.[43]

During this same period, the Admiralty attempted to bolster its case by advising "quality" public opinion of the Soviet submarine threat: "For weeks now," the *Observer* reported, "senior members of the silent service have been breaking their silence to remind journalists of the Russian submarine menace and the folly of slashing navies." [44] And in October, 1957, from the sanctuary of a NATO command, Admiral Sir David Eccles reopened the case for "broken-backed" warfare. The Admiralty is "probably glad that the Admiral is unmuzzled," the *Economist* suggested, "and able to say what the Minister of Defence ignores, that there is not enough allied hardware. . . . " [45]

These combined efforts, particularly those within the Executive, evidently were sufficient to give the minister of defense second thoughts. The 1958 Defense White Paper shifted the navy's mission, giving more attention to the area east of Suez, anti-submarine warfare, and a slightly greater share of the defense budget. In an article entitled "Sandys Hoists the Navy with Its Own Petard," Alastair Buchan has suggested that the navy was a victim of its own propaganda on the Soviet submarine threat.[46] Although the anti-submarine role appeared to run counter to the navy's immediate interests—carrier task forces and the Commando—it probably did not do so in the long run, since greater emphasis on the submarine threat generally strengthened the case for the navy.

The Outcome of Decision-Making

Whether policy choices are made by agreement, by bargaining, or by processes somewhere between these two extremes, the resulting choice depends in some degree on the qualities of the participants. In the case of agreement the outcome rests on the logical soundness of the alternative proposals and the skill with which each is presented; in the case of bargaining the outcome hinges on the political power of the participants and the ability of each to develop meaningful support, particularly within the Executive. If the participants possessed equal skill and equal strength, over a period of time the results would not favor one department over another. But the departments are unequal in skill and power, and, for the reasons explained in the last chapter, the Admiralty is considered the strongest, the War Office the weakest, of the three service departments.

The first question that must be answered with regard to this inequality is whether it has any actual significance in policy choices. It is highly probable that it does. The virtually unanimous agreement that the Royal Navy is the strongest of the three services rests on its greater success in getting proposals adopted. Evidence of this success is not limited to the testimony of civil servants who negotiate with all three services. A forceful statement to this effect has come from a former minister of defense, Mr. Shinwell:

It may be that I am prejudiced in the matter, having been Secretary of State for War, but I regard the Army as one of the most efficient ve-

hicles of organisation in this country. We may disagree with the Army
occasionally about policy matters, but in respect of organisation it is
supreme, and, in my judgment, is much better than the Royal Navy.
The trouble with the Navy, the Silent Service, is that it gets away with
murder. I remember when I was Minister of Defence and had to preside
over the Defence Council the Navy hardly said a word. It always got
its own way without saying anything, whereas the Army and the Royal
Air Force had to fight for what they wanted. There the Navy's representatives sat, with all the gold braid at their command. Even the
present supreme authority at the Ministry of Defence, Lord Mountbatten,
never said a word, but the Navy always got what it wanted.

The Navy is like the Russians. It does not have to go to war because
it always gets what it wants without a struggle.[47]

Other evidence suggestive of the Admiralty's strength is
furnished by the allocation of the defense budget among the
services. These data are contained below in Table 5. While the
division of Ministry of Aviation expenditures among the three
services is unknown and may distort this comparison slightly,
it is nevertheless true that the navy has had smooth sailing
throughout the past decade. Changes in the importance of the

TABLE 5

ALLOCATION OF THE BRITISH DEFENSE BUDGET FOR
THE YEARS 1949-50 THROUGH 1962-63, BY PERCENTAGES *

Year	Navy	Army	Air Force	Defense and Aviation
1949-50	25.2	39.2	27.2	8.4
1950-51	24.4	39.8	28.9	6.9
1951-52	24.4	38.0	29.0	8.6
1952-53	23.8	37.0	30.0	9.2
1953-54	23.8	35.7	30.5	10.0
1954-55	24.1	33.2	32.3	10.4
1955-56	24.0	33.0	30.7	12.3
1956-57	22.5	32.7	30.9	13.9
1957-58	24.7	27.1	33.0	15.2
1958-59	25.4	29.6	30.7	14.3
1959-60	24.6	29.0	32.8	13.6
1960-61	24.4	30.3	33.4	11.9
1961-62	24.9	30.6	31.8	12.7
1962-63	24.5	30.4	32.0	13.1

* Sources: Computed from data contained in Central Statistical Office, *Annual Abstract
of Statistics*, No. 96 (London: H. M. Stationery Office, 1959), p. 253, and No. 98 (1961),
p. 259. Computations after 1960-61 are based on service estimates.

navy in the over-all scheme of policy bear little relation to budget figures: expenditures have held closely around 24 per cent of the total defense budget, with the maximum variation only 1½ per cent either way. The army, the weakest of the services, provides a sharp contrast—from a high of nearly 40 per cent in 1950–51 to a low of 27 per cent in 1957–58—and includes a shift of over 5 per cent between 1956–57 and 1957–58. The air force pattern is more like that of the navy than that of the army, but it still lacks the year-to-year stability, through good times and bad, that characterizes the navy.

The pattern of budget allocations also provides a possible answer to a second question: What are the consequences of different departmental strengths? The differences in strength are obviously not so great that the strongest department can, over a period of time, absorb a weaker department; it seems likely, however, that political and administrative strength contributes to departmental stability. Departmental strength serves as an umbrella sheltering the service during periods of rapid change and enabling it to develop in a secure and relatively stable environment new roles and missions to replace those outdated by technological and strategic shifts. The corollary is that a lack of administrative and political strength entails making internal adjustments and innovating new missions while under the pressure of demands for a downward revision in the service budget and role.

CRITICISMS OF THE POLICY PROCESS

The policy process has been persistently criticized in recent years, and interservice rivalry and arbitrary decisions have attracted special attention from responsible political leaders. In large measure, one suspects, these criticisms reflect disagreement with the substance rather than the mechanics of policy-making. But there is a current of genuine concern over "vested interests," interservice rivalry, and, to use Mr. Crossman's word, "fudging." The consequences of these characteristics of the policy process are examined below.

The easiest criticism to deal with is that of "arbitrary" decisions. In the context of security policies there is grave doubt in the public generally, and among elite groups particularly, about the desirability of allowing military officers or civil servants to make decisions of great importance. For this reason politicians are appointed to control the various military departments. Ministers are supposed to make decisions after consulting with their advisers, but the purpose of having political leaders is that they can reject or modify as necessary the recommendations of soldiers or civil servants. Whether a decision is then arbitrary is almost wholly a matter of whether one agrees with it. If it is a pleasing choice, it reflects positive leadership, a "strong and able Minister"; if it is not a pleasing choice, it is, of course, arbitrary. The contention that arbitrary decisions are taken for political or party motives is indeed true. In a democracy most decisions taken by a politician have some political content, otherwise a civil servant could make the choice. But judgments of whether decisions produce political gain are highly uncertain, perhaps as arbitrary as the decisions in question. There is, for example, little evidence to support the contention that either the Conservative party or Mr. Sandys personally benefited in any meaningful way from the decision to end conscription.[48]

Arbitrary decisions are also criticized as highly "irrational." The implication is that rational processes, to include accepting the advice of officials and advisers, are more desirable and give more effective decisions. But defense decisions, important ones at least, present many unusual problems: that the Hull committee recommended a 220,000-man army should not obscure the difficult and tenuous assumptions necessary to derive even this figure. How large must expenditures be to provide Britain with an adequate security position? How can the gains of larger deployments on the Continent be compared with the costs of a larger payments deficit? These questions, to say the very least, are not easily resolved analytically: they are almost infinite in their complexity; the costs and benefits are not easily compared; and, because defense planning often projects five to ten years in the future, there are major uncertainties involved. That advisers do not agree is the best evidence that such problems are not easily resolved by rational processes. Yet such questions must be answered. Arbitrary choice is quick and easy; indeed, it may be one of the more rational ways of deciding these matters.

The second criticism relates to the effect of vested interests in the policy process:

. . . The great military interests are still writing White Papers. . . . I do not want to attack them; in many ways they are perfectly legitimate and natural interests. Anybody who has worked with distinguished generals, admirals and air marshals knows that they are very able men . . . selfless men, and nothing could be more natural than that they should fight to preserve what seems to them to be the interests of their respective Services. That is what has happened, and that is how the present defence programme has been drawn up.
. . . The agonizing reappraisal of the rôle of the Defence Services has not been carried out. I always imagined that it would take a hydrogen bomb to shift the dead weight of military tradition, but we see now that even the hydrogen bomb does not do it.

.   .   .   .

The consequences are that the Government are trying to get something of everything and are succeeding in getting enough of nothing . . . . If we divide up those limited resources fundamentally in such a way that no admiral, general or air air [*sic*] marshal is offended, we shall not get a very happy result.[49]

This speech by the late John Strachey, a former secretary of state for war, reflects quite faithfully the Liberal-Radical critique of the policy process.[50] The extent of disagreement with the substance of policy varies, but the lack of an agreed strategic policy is deplored, and interservice rivalry is alleged to be the cause of policy inadequacies. Conflict and disagreement are symptoms of the lack of control, an abdication of leadership. Organizational remedies apply—with the vested interests of service loyalty, tradition, and reaction removed from the body organizational, differences on strategic policies could be resolved easily.

There is a measure of truth in these descriptions of the policy process. In many cases policy is the product of compromise and bargaining. There is no agreed strategic doctrine, and the service departments may be in some sense "vested interests." But the value of separatism and service independence far outweighs the gains that would result from service integration. Critics who decry the separate services as vested interests perceive them performing only an integrative role. Military forces, in an effort to create highly cohesive groups able to act effectively during periods of maximum individual and group stress, emphasize tradition, loyalty, and discipline. These strands of tradition and loyalty, as well as the administrative and bureaucratic interests inherent in all large organizations, are viewed as a single, integrated, monolithic force directed toward a *particular* and, for the critic, wrong strategic policy. To some extent this description of the services is accurate, but increasingly the pattern of service activity is multiform. The navy is concerned, not with "command of the seas," but with a contribution to limited military operations in the overseas areas, a contribution to NATO, and the strategic nuclear force. The army has a similar division of interests, as does the air force.

As defense programs proliferate, are subjected to shifting technological and political environments, and therefore change in relative importance, the services perform four separate functions. First, the services *moderate* the competition among the different programs. The division of resources among NATO, the strategic nuclear force, and the overseas mission is analytically no easier to resolve than the allocation among the navy, army, and air force. Separation of the services insures that part of the process of allocation between competing programs is carried out within each service staff rather than directly between the services: the intensity of the competition for resources is fragmented and thereby reduced, because the allocation is made at several different levels. It may also be that the division of resources between functions proceeds on a slightly more rational basis within a service than would be the case between functions. Authority patterns in the services facilitate hierarchical control and reduce the bargaining necessary to resolve important issues.

Second, the separate services enhance flexibility, since they ease adjustment between operational programs. These come and go. Although the Coast Artillery lasted 150 years, it was finally abolished. The strategic nuclear force will be shifted from the air force to the navy and in the near future may be subject to further changes. The services tie loyalties and traditions—and the administrative and bureaucratic procedures (e.g., promotions) that somehow must be accomplished—in such a way that they do not strengthen the functional programs.

Third, as holding companies—truly "vested interests"—for service traditions, loyalties, and administration, and less and less as the advocates of particular strategic programs, the services perform a disjunctive function. They provide a means of preventing the alienation of groups that might otherwise be disaffected by changing security needs. While the services focus loyalties and traditions in such a way as to facilitate adjustments among different programs, this also precludes the disaffection of groups as these change. Just as trade unions add strength to a democratic society by integrating interests, moderating their clash, and, in most cases, preventing the alienation of an important social group, so too the services strengthen national-security policies. They integrate policy in the only possible way for a pluralistic society—by multiplication.

Separation serves to moderate conflict, facilitate adjustment to change, and prevent disaffection among service groups. More important than these, however, is that the separate services improve the quality of policy by injecting into the decision-making process a degree of competition and diversity. Competition and diversity improve the quality of policy in at least three ways. First, the separate services provide alternative solutions to common problems. Responsible officials can thus select from among several different approaches to the problem. Second, separatism promotes criticism and discussion within the military establishment. Because the services are competing for the same limited resources, each has a strong incentive to criticize the other's proposals; since each commands the professional expertise and the necessary classified information, the services are also highly competent critics. Finally, the competition among the services is a stimulus to the development of new service roles and missions.[51]

Although most observers would admit that there is a need to devise alternative proposals, to criticize them, and to think up new roles and missions, interservice rivalry is frequently deprecated because it is motivated by the desire to maintain service interests rather than the national interest. But motivation by service self-interest does not invalidate these benefits; indeed, service self-interest seems to insure that criticism is persistent and continuous, rather than perfunctory and contingent on specific issues.

To argue that separatism and interservice rivalry have important benefits is not to say there is no room for organizational modifications. But the essential problems are those of choice and adjustment to change, and shifts in organization must be designed to strengthen those parts of the policy machinery that enhance choice and adjustment to change. With specific reference to British security policies since the end of World War II, interservice rivalry seems especially desirable. The lack of sustained criticism and debate among the articulate public has made it doubly important that conflict and disagreement be an explicit part of the decision-making process. Most would agree that national-security policies are too complicated, too uncertain, and too important to be left to the decision of one man or a few men, however capable. Policies need to be argued, debated, discussed, and on occasion reversed.[52] The conflicting views that exist within the Executive thus seem highly desirable; centers of political power that can effectively resist or modify a decision are a necessary corollary to alternative views. While these conditions preclude an agreed policy, they do no more than recognize the lack of agreement in the society as a whole on the kinds of policies that are necessary. But it is also clear that one of the reasons British policy-makers have meaningful choices in the 1960's is a pluralistic executive and the conflict and lack of agreement over policy, not the Parliament or the articulate public. If the system prevents agreement and ends in compromise, it nevertheless operates to insure against premature choices.

It is difficult to believe that organizational arrangements have contributed in any major way to the weaknesses attributed to recent British security problems. The problem is partly a lack of resources and partly an uncertainty over national goals. In fact, the defense-policy machinery seems as adequate as that in other areas of public policy—probably more so than in most. Its complementary features enhance the capability for producing and modifying policy in a highly complex and rapidly changing environment. It combines civil servants, whose stability in office insures continuity and moderation, and military professionals, whose constant circulation contributes diverse viewpoints and an awareness of current problems. A highly homogeneous decision-making group, a feature that facilitates decision-making on a day-to-day basis, is balanced by the contrasting orientations provided by the separate services. The separate services also moderate conflict, facilitate adjustment to change, and, by their competition, improve the quality of policy. Criticism of the policy process is understandable in the sense that it is simpler and easier to discuss the mechanics than the more difficult and important questions of policy. But to the extent that criticism has limited and reduced conflict among the services on substantive issues, it has contributed to policy weakness, not to better choices.

1. In Cmd. 2097, "Central Organisation for Defence" [1963]. All the data in the following paragraphs are drawn from this source.

2. *Ibid.,* p. 3.

3. *Ibid.,* p. 1.

4. *Ibid.,* p. 10.

5. Viscount Montgomery of Alamein, *The Memoirs of Feld Marshal Montgomery* (New York: World Publishing Co., 1958), p. 438. See also pp. 427–46.

6. Laurence W. Martin, "The Market for Strategic Ideas in Britain: The 'Sandys Era,'" *American Political Science Review,* LVI, No. 1, (1962), 25. See also Sir John Slessor, *The Central Blue: The Autobiography of Sir John Slessor, Marshal of the RAF* (New York: Praeger, 1957), pp. 450–63.

7. 537 H. C. Deb. 2070.

8. *Ibid.,* 1921.

9. *Ibid.,* 2188.

10. 592 H. C. Deb. 1000.

11. Anthony Eden, *Full Circle: The Memoirs of Anthony Eden* (Boston: Houghton Mifflin, 1960), p. 415.

12. Cmd. 6923, "Central Organisation for Defence" [1946], p. 7.

13. Vice-Admiral J. Hughes Hallett, "The Central Organisation for Defence," *Journal: Royal United Services Institution,* CIII, No. 612 (1958), 490.

14. 563 H. C. Deb. 396.

15. Cmd. 476, "Central Organisation for Defence" [1958], p. 5.

16. Michael Howard, "Organisation for Defence in the United Kingdom and the United States, 1945–58, "in H. G. Thursfield (ed.), *Brassey's Annual, 1959,* (London: Macmillan, 1960), p. 74.

17. This account comes from Brigadier Antony Head and was given in the House of Commons on July 28, 1958 (592 H. C. Deb. 986–94). Head was Secretary of State for War until October, 1956, and then served for a few months as Minister of Defense under Prime Minister Eden. He resigned, apparently, because of his unwillingness to carry out the manpower cuts desired by Mr. Macmillan. A slightly fuller account is contained in Martin, "The Market for Strategic Ideas in Britain," pp. 28–29.

18. 592 H. C. Deb. 989–90. "Civilianisation of the tail" refers to replacing soldiers with civilians in the army's supporting supply and service elements.

19. *Ibid.,* 990.

20. *Ibid.,* 1048.

21. 600 H. C. Deb. 1155, 1160–61, 1166. And of course Mr. Sandys delighted in making the same observations on the Labor party and on Mr. Brown's performance as its defense spokesman. Both leaders were forced to operate in pluralistic group and interest situations.

22. E. J. Kingston-McCloughry, *Global Strategy,* (New York: Praeger, 1957), p. 178.

23. Slessor, *The Central Blue,* p. 462.

24. Interviews.

25. On this point, see Samuel H. Beer, *Treasury Control: The Co-ordination of Financial and Economic Policy in Great Britain* (2nd ed.; London: Oxford University Press, 1957), pp. 112–19.

26. The difference is evident even in the arrangement of offices. The style in Britain is to have a small table in the official's office. The American pattern runs more to the conference or briefing room.

27. Sir Edward Bridges, *Treasury Control* (London: Athlone Press, 1950), p. 10.

28. Interviews.

29. Interviews.

30. Interviews.

31. 592 H. C. Deb. 994.

32. Interviews.

33. Interviews.

34. Interviews. New York: Harper & Bros., 1959.

35. See S. E. Finer, *Anonymous Empire* (London: Pall Mall, 1958), pp. 75–93. I have particular reference to "Fire Brigade Campaigns."

36. The speech was delivered to a meeting of the Royal United Services Institution in November, 1959. The lecture ("Future Trends in Warfare") is published in *Journal: Royal United Services Institution,* CV, No. 617 (1960), 4–16.

37. 613 H. C. Deb. 380.

38. My impression is that the penalty for encouraging outside support (being caught, that is) has increased in recent years, mainly because the constant criticism of interservice rivalry has placed a high premium on harmony among the services. It should also be pointed out that a department would almost never approach a member of the opposition for support.

39. Interviews.

40. See above, pp. 124–25.

41. *Observer,* July 28, 1957.

42. *The Times,* July 1, 1957.

43. *Observer Foreign News Service,* August 8, 1958.

44. April 7, 1957.

45. *Economist,* October 5, 1957, p. 24.

46. *Observer,* February 16, 1958.

47. 613 H. C. Deb. 665.

48. Some of Sandys' harshest critics, those who have pressed for a selective service system, also believe that public opposition to conscription has been exaggerated. As one MP explained: "I have represented

a working class district for many years, and there is a streak of radicalism, even Bevanism, in the constituency. For several years I have urged a return to conscription or some form of selective service. I have taken the most careful pains to point out in speeches and the like just what my position is. I have also indicated that a selective service system would be unfair, probably hit them harder than the other economic or social groups. Despite this I have never had a *single protest, question, or letter,* indicating any disagreement or concern with my position."

49. 537 H. C. Deb. 2070–72.

50. See Samuel H. Beer, "The Representation of Interests in British Government: Historical Background," *American Political Science Review*, LI, No. 3 (1957), 628–35, but especially pp. 630 and 633. Other examples of this line of criticism may be found in 537 H. C. Deb. 1921, 1977, 1984–85, and 2001, as well as in the writings of Field Marshal Montgomery and Air Vice-Marshal Kingston-McCloughry, cited above.

51. Interviews. It is of interest to note that one of the most forceful arguments for the maintenance of separate American services came from the RAND Corporation—specifically, Dr. Alain Enthoven and Dr. Henry Rowen, both of whom are now deputy undersecretaries of defense. Enthoven and Rowen emphasize the advantages of service competition, mainly because they feel it improves allocation decisions.

52. It is not my intent to raise here this larger issue of control of policy in a democracy. I think, however, that the content of policy suffers without debate and discussion, whatever the degree of public participation.

9/ The Politics of Defense Spending

IN THE FINAL MOMENTS OF DEBATE on the 1957 Defense White Paper, the new prime minister assured the House of Commons that the highly publicized revision of defense policy was "not intended to weaken us." "It is," Mr. Macmillan continued, "intended to increase our real strength both from the military point of view and from the point of view of the economy, which is the only basis upon which military strength can really ultimately depend." [1] This brief statement exposes what is undoubtedly the fundamental problem of postwar British defense policy: How to divide national resources between defense and domestic programs in an economy that is highly dependent on, and therefore perilously vulnerable to, the larger forces of the world economy.

C. F. Bastable, a student of English public finance, wrote in 1895 that

. . . while strongly insisting on the great advantages that are certain to result from the maintenance of peace, and the reduction of military and naval expenditure, it is quite as essential to assure that so long as present conditions last, a well-organized and effective system of defence is a necessary art of state expenditure. . . . To maintain a due balance between the excessive demands of alarmists and military officials, and the undue reductions in outlay sought by the advocates of economy, is one of the difficult tasks of the statesman.[2]

Bastable's conception of the problem needs but little alteration to serve as a model of the process of allocating resources to defense in the years since World War II. Political leaders continue to weigh the demands of the military establishment for resources against similar claims of the non-military departments. But they simultaneously judge the benefits of all government expenditures against the social, economic, and political advantages of reducing the share of the economy's output that is controlled by the government. Each set of calculations, of course, influences the other.

DEFENSE DEMANDS FOR RESOURCES

From 1890 until World War I defense expenditures averaged about £50 million annually—less than 3 per cent of the Gross National Product—and exceeded £100 million a year only around 1900. This pattern was repeated in the period between the world wars: total defense costs were between £130 and £140 million annually, again something less than 3 per cent of the national income.[3] Manpower levels in the forces were maintained around three hundred thirty thousand—some one hundred thousand in the navy, thirty thousand in the Royal Air Force, and two hundred thousand (plus the colonial troops that served in the overseas areas) in the army. The result was a modest army, well suited for police and "brushfire" operations in the overseas areas and adequate for initial operations in case of war on the Continent. An efficient navy could be maintained with moderate capital expenditures, partly because technological developments were less rapid than at the present time. With the overseas-base system and control of strategic points on the major trade routes, the navy was thus able to protect army deployments abroad and to insure the overseas trade on which Britain's economic life depended. This combination of geography, an overseas empire that furnished cheap manpower and strategic bases, and a favorable technological position provided an inexpensive but effective national-security position.

Britain's security position since World War II bears little resemblance to this traditional posture. The change is strikingly illustrated by the increase in defense expenditures. By 1948 military spending had decreased from its wartime peak of about 50 per cent to about 7 per cent of the Gross National Product. This level was maintained until the Korean War, when defense costs amounted to about 12 per cent of the GNP. After 1952 defense expenditures remained relatively stable, about £1,600 million annually; because of the economy's growth this amount represented but 7 per cent of the Gross National Product in 1960, the percentage level which has been maintained to the present. From a peak of over four and one-half million men at the end of World War II, service manpower had by 1948 fallen to about eight hundred thousand. Although there was a slight increase in force levels during the Korean War, manpower levels declined to four hundred thirty thousand in early 1963 and are expected to be maintained at about that level in the immediate future.[4]

The demand for resources by the military departments—greater, of course, than the resources actually consumed—is largely explained by the perceived "threat" to British security. This has emerged on two levels. In the overseas areas long-term responsibilities diminished but short-term commitments remained very heavy. In the immediate postwar period large numbers of troops were utilized in occupation tasks in the Middle East and Southeast Asia. Although commitments in these areas were reduced fairly rapidly in 1946 and 1947, a series of new obligations developed after 1948—a ten-year guerrilla war in Malaya, the Korean War, and prolonged periods of civil unrest, first in Kenya and later in Cyprus. But the major danger came from the Soviet Union. After 1945 troops remained in Europe on occupation duty; in 1948, the year of the coup in Czechoslovakia and the Berlin Blockade, there was general recognition that the Soviet Union constituted a seemingly permanent danger to European, and therefore British, security. The military contribution to NATO was increased substantially beginning with the outbreak of the Korean War; in 1954, in an effort to secure French approval for a German military commitment to European defense, the Eden government agreed to maintain four army divisions and a tactical air force in Europe. Forces were withdrawn from Europe in 1957 and 1958, and Britain's conventional commitment now numbers about fifty thousand. This level has been temporarily increased during periods of increased East-West tensions such as occurred in late 1961.

Defense demands have also been influenced by recent changes in military technology. Rapid obsolescence is now a prime characteristic of weapons systems, and it is common to replace usable equipment with new items that possess increased capabilities. In addition, the costs of equipment have increased rapidly. A growing portion of equipment cost is incurred in the research and development stage; total costs are further increased by the unusual precision and quality control required in the production of complex items of military hardware.

The choice of strategies also underlies the military's resource requests. The decision to build a strategic nuclear force at a cost of between 10 and 15 per cent of the total defense budget is an obvious example. This force has little if any utility for a broad range of conflicts; its usefulness in a general nuclear war is uncertain and hotly disputed. The decision that Britain cannot be defended against a bomber or missile attack has had the opposite effect on defense resource demands.

THE AVAILABILITY OF RESOURCES

The requests for resources from the military departments are never fully met. They are reduced both because the resources available to the government are limited and because there are numerous claimants for these resources in addition to the armed forces. These complex relationships and their impact on the defense budget are considered below.

Central Governmental Expenditures [5]

The ultimate constraint on governmental expenditures is, of course, the total of national output, the Gross National Product. But this constraint is meaningful only during periods of national emergency. In a major crisis first things come first. Increased needs for defense are matched by a willingness on the part of the public to reorder values and to defer major public and private goals. During the active operations of World War II, for example, the standard rate of income tax was increased to 50 per cent, raw material controls were imposed, and food, clothing, and coal were rationed.[6] The public accepted these restrictions and half the national output was shunted directly into the military establishment. When the external dangers to the society are perceived as less immediate or less severe, "security," while perhaps no less valued, tends to be taken as a given. Alternative goals and values return to their more normal order of rank. Taxation rates drop to levels which political leaders believe the public will accept, levels which compromise between the public's contradictory demands for more public goods and services and a larger personal or disposable income. As a result, the total of governmental revenue falls, and a loosely defined but still meaningful "upper limit" on total government spending is established.

The suggestion that there is a limit on total governmental expenditure is a common-sense judgment. Britain is after all a very stable and highly consensual society, and the attitudes of political leaders on the share of the national output which should be controlled by the government can be expected to change only very slowly. It is not suggested that what is accepted as the proper level of taxation does not change: ideas on the level of taxation evolve slowly, as new social needs are recognized by the leaders of a society. Periods of national emergency, moreover, increase the rapidity of change. Emergencies bring increased governmental obligations and extend the degree of governmental control of the economy. Attitudes undergo a corresponding shift, and what was formerly intolerable becomes normal and accepted. In the wake of crisis expenditure levels fall, but they seldom return to pre-crisis standards. Emergency and the accompanying social disturbances impose permanent new obligations on government. War, for example, creates debt, which requires servicing, and disabled veterans, who need pensions. Thus, crises tend to increase permanently the levels of governmental expenditure, as well as to change the attitudes on taxation.[7]

There is a second element in this equation, however. The consensus of political leaders on the degree of government control of the national output is sufficiently broad in scope for the apparently distinct party attitudes to be significant. On issues such as nationalization of industy, the contrast between the two major political parties is clear. And if political campaigns and literature from recent elections are indicative, it is reasonable to believe that the Conservative party, more than Labor, views lower taxes and decreased levels of governmental expenditure as desirable objectives, in and of themselves. In the 1950 general election, for example, the Tory manifesto (*This Is the Road*) spoke of the "crushing burden of taxation" and demanded that government spending be reduced.[8] Sir Winston Churchill and Sir Anthony Eden both emphasized that a Tory government would lower taxes and cut expenditures.[9] This theme was also prominent in some two-thirds of the Conservative campaign addresses. It had no counterpart in the Labor party.[10]

Much the same pattern emerged in the 1951 general election.

The "Churchill" manifesto promised that " a Conservative Government would cut out all unnecessary expenditure," [11] while Labor indicated that tax cuts would be made when and where possible.[12] About half of the Tory election addresses stressed the need to reduce taxation.[13] If such a doctrine is part of a larger Conservative ethic, the first postwar Tory Chancellor of the Exchequer, Mr. R. A. Butler, would seem to have been fully committed to it: he had been active in revamping the party after 1945 and had served as chairman of the Council of the National Union and Conservative Associations. During his four years at the Treasury, the estimated loss of revenues through personal and corporate income and expenditure tax reductions amounted to £530 million.[14] Reductions by subsequent Conservative chancellors during the five-year period 1956-60 amounted to an estimated £528 million annually.[15] Whether a Labor government would have prescribed similar reductions is an unanswerable but irrelevant question. The Conservative party formed the government, and tax reductions significantly reduced the share of the national output available to the central government.

Governmental spending follows a composite of the two patterns described above. Between 1890 and 1913 expenditures (by both central and local authorities) at current prices roughly doubled; as a percentage of the GNP the increase was less striking—from 8.9 to 12.4 per cent. In the interwar period governmental expenditures at current prices remained very stable—the 1920 level represented 26 per cent of the GNP; the 1938 level, only 30 per cent.[16] Total revenues available to the central government in 1946 were £3,357 million; the sum available increased by 1960 to over £7,000 million.[17] As a percentage of the GNP, however, the share under central governmental control declined. Between 1946 and 1949 the *average* stayed close to 37 per cent; since 1954 the Treasury's income has been very near 29 per cent.[18]

In each instance the share of GNP under governmental control was increased by war. But unlike the earlier periods, governmental expenditure as a fraction of the national output was lower in 1960 than a decade earlier. This change was influenced by the postwar economic crisis which began to ease in 1948 and the relatively prosperous period that began in 1953. The decline between 1950 and 1954 was due to the lower receipts during the economic recession in 1951 and the sharp cuts made in early 1953 under Mr. Butler.

The higher revenue levels of the post–World War II period have been accompanied by taxation increases over prewar rates. The standard rate of income tax in 1938–39 was 5/6 on the pound. Rates increased to 10/0 during World War II, fell to 9/0 in 1947, and remained at this level until Korean rearmament, when a 6*d.* increase was imposed. Rates returned to 9/0 in 1953, fell to 8/6 in 1955, and then fell again to 7/9 in 1959. The effective exemption limit increased by 50 per cent between 1947 and 1955—from £120 to £180—while lower rates in the exemption bands were probably almost offset by their declining width.[19] The average return from income taxes in the period 1946–50 was 18.3 per cent of the GNP; this declined to 15.7 per cent in the period 1951–55, and to 14 per cent in the following five-year period. The receipts from expenditure (sales) taxes also traced a descending course. Taxes on expenditures returned 15.3 per cent of the GNP to the Treasury in the first five years after the war. In the period 1956–60 receipts in this category were slightly under 12 per cent of the national income. The third major source of revenue, National Insurance and Health Contributions, is a bit different: contributions have risen from about 3 per cent of the GNP in the immediate postwar period to just under 4 per cent between 1956–60.[20] Thus, income and expenditure tax reductions largely explain why the total resources available to the central government have grown more slowly than the national product.

The doctrine of the "balanced budget" finds little support in Britain. Even before Keynes, unbalanced budgets were a fairly common occurrence, and the depression of the 1930's dispelled this myth from the intellectual baggage of most British politicians. Writing on the subject in 1939, Macgregor, whose evidence came largely from Parliamentary debates, suggested that "the principle that the Budget should balance every year has come to be described as 'mouldy.' " [21] And postwar chancellors of the Exchequer, Labor or Conservative, have accepted the view that the budget is an instrument of economic control as well as a plan for the government's forthcoming activities.

The amount that governmental expenditures can be increased over the level of receipts has been limited, however: inflationary pressures are generated by this increase, whatever the short-run advantages in economic growth, employment levels, or the size of national output. Following World War II, the British economy was also plagued by sharp inflationary pressures arising from structural imbalances. In the early postwar period there was a great deal of excess purchasing power remaining from the war years. As this was absorbed, it was replaced by new domestic demands for consumption and investment and, later, for rearmament. The shortage of labor and the tendency of many unions to translate all demands into wage increases intensified the pressure on prices.[22] International activity was also inflationary. The balance of payments position, which remained weak through 1958, was an important factor, since the need for large exports limited the amount of goods and services available for domestic use. The cost of imported raw materials increased steadily during the late 1940's and then soared to high levels during 1951; devaluation and rearmament and stockpile purchases, which increased world demand, were the principal causes of these price rises.

The index of consumer prices reflects the severity of the problem. In the ten-year period 1946–55 the consumer price index rose from 88 to 123 (1948 = 100); the increase (on an index 1954 = 100) from 1950 to 1960 was from 83 to 115.[23] It is not surprising, therefore, to note the existence of a "hard money" view. In 1946 Labor's first chancellor of the Exchequer explained: "I have quite deliberately gone slow with tax reduction and with the increase of purchasing power . . . because I was not going to be responsible for landing this country in an inflationary spiral." [24] One of his successors at the Treasury, Harold Macmillan, in presenting one of the few balanced budgets (1956) of the postwar period, argued an equally hard line:

Whatever the temporary difficulties from which we may suffer by trying to run too fast, if we stand still we are lost. Inflation must be curbed, because runaway inflation ends up by being itself restrictionist. But deflation—in the sense of seeking stability by courses which, among other things, would result in an increase in the debt burden in relation to the national income—that is out of the question. We must all be expansionists, but expansionists of real wealth. The problem of inflation cannot be dealt with just by cutting down demand; the other side of the picture is the need for increasing production. [25]

Mr. Peter Thorneycroft, a subsequent chancellor who is currently the minister of defense, saw inflation as the central problem facing Britain. In his first speech in the House of Commons after his resignation from the government in early 1958, he pleaded with his colleagues as follows:

It is not that there is not agreement about the aim. We are all agreed about the aim. Of course we are. Any hon. Member in this House would say he was against inflation, as men say they are against sin. The question is where and when we choose to stand and fight it. [26]

Inflationary pressures and a hard-money philosophy have limited the amount of deficit financing that has been undertaken by the Treasury in the postwar period. During the seven fiscal years from 1951–52 through 1957–58, the average amount financed by borrowing the £400 million per year. [27] The average of annual governmental receipts in the same period was in excess of £5,300 million. The amount by which the total of available revenues has been increased is thus rather small— about 7.5 per cent of the total receipts.

In short, central governmental revenues largely determine expenditures. Revenue levels are based on relatively stable attitudes on taxation and the values of political leaders concerning governmental intervention in the economy. Deficit financing provides only a limited method for increasing expenditures, primarily because of persistent inflationary pressures and the corollary hard-money philosophy of successive chancellors of the Exchequer.

The Competitors for Governmental Revenues

What is the significance for defense policies of the decline in the share of the GNP under governmental control between 1949 and 1954? What is the significance of its stability since?

The programs among which a government may allocate its resources are numerous. All, however—at least during periods of relative international and domestic stability—must be met from a fixed resource base. Defense is but one competitor for this "pie" against major alternative programs like social services, economic services, and debt charges.[28]

In absolute terms social-service expenditures [29] by central and local authorities have increased sharply over the last two generations. In the period 1920–29 social services cost an average of £417 million per year; between 1930 and 1938 the average was £524 million annually. In the period 1950–56 this category of expenditure had increased fourfold to an average of about £2,450 million a year.[30] As a percentage of total central and local governmental expenditure the change is much less dramatic. The share in the three periods is 36.0 per cent, 44.0 per cent, and 43.7 per cent, respectively. A closely related category, economic services,[31] has followed somewhat the same pattern. Costs averaged £143 million a year between 1920 and 1929, £129 million between 1930 and 1938, and £590 million in the period 1950–56. These represent a *declining* share of total governmental expenditures—12.1 per cent, 10.8 per cent, and 10.7 per cent, respectively.

Although central and local authorities' expenditures for social and economic services have declined somewhat, there has been a sharp increase in the share financed by the central government. This change is depicted in Table 6. The inference

TABLE 6

BRITISH SPENDING FOR SOCIAL SERVICES AND ECONOMIC SERVICES, EXPRESSED AS A PERCENTAGE OF TOTAL GOVERNMENTAL EXPENDITURES *

YEAR	SOCIAL SERVICES		ECONOMIC SERVICES		TOTAL	
	Central	Local	Central	Local	Central	Local
1920	15.1	10.9	7.9	4.8	23.0	15.7
1928	19.3	20.3	1.3	9.4	20.6	29.7
1933	25.2	20.4	1.8	8.7	27.0	29.1
1938	18.3	19.2	2.0	7.6	20.3	26.8
Average					22.5	25.1
1950	30.4	15.8	9.6	3.0	40.0	18.8
1952	26.1	16.2	8.0	2.9	34.1	19.1
1955	27.4	17.2	5.5	3.2	32.9	20.5
Average					35.6	19.5

* Source: Alan T. Peacock and Jack Wiseman, *The Growth of Public Expenditure in the United Kingdom* (Princeton: Princeton University Press, 1961), pp. 107, 184–85.

is clear. Responsibility for social and economic services has shifted slowly from local authorities to the central government. The welfare state has replaced the local welfare authority.

The shift of responsibility for social and economic services to the central government, mostly as a result of World War II, has pre-empted a large share of the resources available to the Exchequer. These charges, moreover, tend to remain stable, although some elements in the social-services category—pensions, for example—may require a declining share of revenues during periods of inflation or at full employment (because of the higher receipts brought about by a progressive tax schedule). For this reason other items of the central government budget are often decisive in their short-term effects on revenue outlets such as defense expenditures. Debt charges are an example. Interest on debt, as social or economic services, must be paid out of the total resources available to the central government. At first glance it might be assumed that debt charges have declined: the internal national debt in 1947 was about 2.7 times the national income; by 1959 the ratio of debt to GNP had declined to 1.3.[32] But shifts in the interest-rate structure have been such that debt charges have required a fairly constant share of governmental revenues. These costs are represented in Table 7 below.

TABLE 7

BRITISH DEBT-SERVICING CHARGES, 1946–60 *

Year	Total (000 Omitted)	Percentage of Total Governmental Revenues
1946	486	10.9
1947	519	13.3
1948	509	12.6
1949	507	11.6
1950	407	10.3
1951	550	12.5
1952	609	11.5
1953	639	10.5
1954	637	11.2
1955	708	12.4
1956	725	12.3
1957	707	10.8
1958	783	11.1
1959	777	10.6
1960	869	11.0

*Sources: Central Statistical Office, *National Income and Expenditure, 1956* (London: H. M. Stationery Office, 1956), pp. 34, 35; and Central Statistical Office, *National Income and Expenditure, 1961* (London: H. M. Stationery Office, 1961), pp. 32, 35.

A 1 per cent shift in debt charges is a change on the order of £60 million, and increases of this magnitude occurred in 1950–52 and 1954–58. In both of these periods, incidentally, the government undertook extensive examinations of the size of the defense budget.

There is another element in this problem. The change of governments in 1951 brought an increased reliance on monetary policies, rather than fiscal and physical controls, as a means of controlling the economy as a whole. The interest rate was therefore more important than between 1946 and 1951. It was necessary that the rate change: bank rates jumped from 2 per cent at the beginning of 1951 to 4 per cent in March, 1952. After a decline to 3 per cent in 1953 and 1954, by September, 1957, rates had increased to 7 per cent. Public Works Loan Board Rates and recommended mortgage charges also increased.[33] These increases in the interest rate, which added to the costs of debt-servicing, provoked general concern about the level of domestic capital investment. Increased investment, especially in manufacturing, was one of the most important objectives of government policy. To promote investment, initial (or investment) allowances for capital expenditures in the private sector were re-established in 1953. This action was followed in the mid-1950's by governmental plans to modernize several basic industries: the Coal Board announced a £635 million investment plan; the Transport Commission's railway-modernization scheme was to cost an estimated £1,200 million between 1955 and 1970; and, finally, the nuclear power and electric supply program envisaged expenditures of about £4,250 million.[34] Investment incentives reduced the revenues returned to the Treasury; public-sector investments required a larger slice of the central government "pie."

The years since the end of World War II have thus been characterized by conflicting pressures. On the one hand, the share of the national output available to the central government declined between 1949 and 1954 from 37 per cent of the GNP to about 29 per cent, the approximate level of revenues in the early 1960's. On the other hand, alternative revenue outlets—debt charges and those social and economic services for which responsibility was largely assumed by the national government after World War II—have remained fairly stable. The result has been great pressure for reductions elsewhere in government. This pressure, particularly strong after the Korean War, fell largely on defense, the largest single category of expenditures.

The relationship between defense spending and the size of the central government's budget deserves special emphasis; indeed, the size of the government's budget is the most important decision concerning defense policy in any given year.[35] Governmental expenditures cannot exceed revenue intake and borrowing. Once a budget figure is decided upon, for whatever reason, and the relatively stable charges for domestic programs are deducted, only that amount remaining is available for defense. Even if all the competing programs, whose total always exceeds the desired budget level, are reduced by an equal percentage, the absolute amount given up by defense is greater than in any other program. There is, in addition, a long-standing presumption that defense should take a smaller share of the national output. In the past the Treasury has argued that (1) defense expenditures are unproductive—they slow economic growth in that they limit investment by drawing off the output of the capital goods industry, (2) the balance of payments effects of defense spending are such as to require policies that are deflationary in their effect (i.e., higher exports which limit consumption and investment, or restrictive fiscal and monetary policies, or both), (3) defense outlays contribute to inflation and thereby slow the economy's growth, and (4) lower current defense expenditures are necessary so that a stronger and larger economy can afford defense at some future date. The difference between the amount requested by the Ministry of Defense and the Treasury's view of the allowable limit has reportedly been about £100 million in recent years.[36] The Treasury's position has been strengthened by the arguments of prominent political leaders supporting a strong economy as the first line of an adequate security position. For example, in 1953 Sir Winston Churchill argued that no one . . . could challenge our claim that the effort [then about 12 per cent of GNP] we are making on defence is the absolute maximum of which we are capable, and that any further substantial diversion of our resources from civil to military production would gravely imperil our economic foundations and, with them, our ability to continue with the rearmament programme.[37]

The same argument has been voiced by other leaders—Lord Attlee, Mr. Sandys, Mr. George Brown, and Lord Monckton, to name but a few—throughout the past decade, even when the level of defense spending was significantly lower than in 1953.[38]

For these reasons, the decision on the size of the government budget is a crucial one for the substantive aspects of defense policy. The competition for resources also explains another series of developments—the changes in the budget process. As the fight for resources intensified in the mid-1950's, the service departments reacted by devising new budget procedures and processes. Their motives were relatively straightforward. The departments hoped: (1) to prevent further erosion in the share alloted to defense; (2) to dampen the fluctuations and shifts in the size of the defense budget; and (3) to improve the allocation of resources within the defense establishment itself.[39] The current budget process, which is described below, has evolved since 1955 and incorporates the new procedures that have been developed.

THE DEFENSE-BUDGET PROCESS [40]

The military departments present their annual operating budgets to Parliament early in each calendar year. These set forth expenditure plans for the fiscal year beginning April 1. Shortly after a budget is presented to Parliament, the departments commence preparation of the next year's budget. The cycle is thus a full year in length, and soon after a budget is made public, action on the subsequent budget is initiated.

The most important development in the budget process is

the long-term, or "full forward costing," budgetary system. Since 1958, when this procedure was started, budgets have been projected five years in advance.⁴¹ Put another way, the budget presented to Parliament is supported by estimates of spending for each of the next four fiscal years; the second year in the five-year forecast becomes the starting point for each new budget.

Budgetary projections for the coming fiscal year are revised in accordance with guidelines prepared by the Ministry of Defense. These guidelines reflect policy decisions made since the previous budget was prepared. Known changes in the costs of items being procured and in research and development projects are also the basis for changes in the previous estimates. Concurrently with the preparation of a draft budget for the coming year, the departments revise their projections for the second, third, and fourth years and prepare new initial forecasts for the fifth year.

The draft budgets of each department are usually completed by mid-June and are then forwarded to the Ministry of Defense. There follows an intensive round of negotiations within the ministry to check the accuracy and validity of the budget estimates. While primary consideration is given to the coming fiscal year, the long-term forecasts are also examined. The cost calculations of the services are sometimes compared with independent computations of officials in the Ministry of Defense or the Ministry of Aviation. One side benefit of these discussions is to identify those projects in each department's budget which can be cancelled or postponed.

About August 1—at least this has been the target date in recent years—the Ministry of Defense presents to the Treasury the budgets for the entire military establishment. There follows a brief round of particularly important negotiations between officials of these two departments—negotiations to settle on a total budget figure. At the conclusion of these discussions, there is a meeting of the Defense Committee (and sometimes the cabinet) at which the proposed defense budget for the coming fiscal year is considered. Gaps between the Ministry of Defense and the Treasury can often be resolved only by a major policy decision because the defense request for financial resources represents the aggregate of previously approved programs, while the Treasury's view of what should be allocated to defense is influenced by estimates of revenue inputs in the coming year and demands by the non-military departments.

Every effort is made to resolve the differences between the Ministry of Defense and other agencies before the August Bank Holiday, when most political leaders flee London for their summer vacations. If the Defense Committee makes the necessary decisions, the draft budgets are then returned to the service departments. The agreed expenditure levels are subject to an "escape clause," that is, the Treasury permits increases due to price rises or policy changes subsequent to August 1 to be incorporated into the final budget. The services then begin work on their final budgets and revise their earlier drafts in accordance with the August decisions. This action is expected to be completed in early December. With the completion of the final drafts by the services, there follows a third round of negotiations, again between the Ministry of Defense and other agencies. Final drafts are reviewed first by the Treasury, then sent to the cabinet where, unless there have been major policy changes since August, they receive *pro forma* consideration. After cabinet action the budgets are processed for submission to Parliament. The cycle then begins again. The sequence is remarkably similar to the process in the United States. The major difference is the action by the legislature: action by Congress makes further adjustments and negotiations necessary; Parliament normally does not change the details of a government's budget.

The budget process described above, a pattern which has been followed in the last few years, is somewhat different from that found elsewhere in British government. While the general time sequence is much the same, the procedure in the non-military departments calls for bilateral negotiations between the department and the Treasury.⁴² In the case of the defense budget the Ministry of Defense is an intermediary between the service departments and the Treasury and has become in recent years more and more involved in the process. As a consequence of increased participation by the Ministry of Defense, there has been a change in the kind of control exercised by the Treasury: it is less concerned with detail and tends now to concentrate on the aggregate total requested by the defense establishment.

In the non-military departments the Treasury controls expenditures by means of a system of "prior approval." ⁴³ All proposals involving new expenditures must be submitted to, and approved by, the Treasury before the project can be initiated. Prior approval is still required when a service department initiates a new project. But Treasury control of individual service-department projects has weakened in the last few years. In order for the Ministry of Defense to perform its policy-making and control functions, it too must pass on service projects. For the Treasury to then give the project the same careful scrutiny is redundant and time-consuming. Increasingly, the Treasury has attempted to control military expenditures by influencing over-all financial and manpower levels. The Treasury's prior approval system corresponds somewhat to the "program change proposal" system in the U.S. Department of Defense, which was established by Mr. Charles Hitch, the current comptroller. Program-change proposals are initiated by the service departments and forwarded through the Department of Defense Comptroller (for recommendation) to the secretary of defense (for decision). Proposals are required on all new programs, as well as on changes in approved programs. Unlike Treasury prior approval, program-change proposals do not go outside the Department of Defense.

While prior approval has declined in importance as a mechanism of Treasury control, it has been replaced by a new system of budgetary or management control. This is generally referred to by British officials as "program control," and it is centered in the Ministry of Defense, rather than the Treasury. It is closely related to the long-term forecasting or "full forward costing system," although it came into general use somewhat later.

As explained above, the departments now prepare five-year forecast budgets. These long-term forecasts were obtained initially by projecting the expenditures for each major budgetary component—personnel, operations and maintenance, procurement, and research and development—over a five-year period. Since the initiation of this procedure projects submitted to the Ministry of Defense which involve expenditures have been accompanied by projections of the estimated costs during each fiscal year for five years into the future. (Many projections are for even longer periods of time.) While some categories—personnel, for example—can be projected with great accuracy, procurement estimates and research and development costs are subject to much greater uncertainty. These latter programs are therefore subject to very detailed analysis: [44] both cost and the sequence in which funds are to be expended are explicitly considered. Once a project is authorized, the estimates for each fiscal year are added to the projections of other approved projects.

The long-term budgetary system and program control are important innovations. Program control requires the departments to estimate the costs of individual projects for several years into the future, and the long-term budget provides a suitable framework in which to interrelate projects. Officials and political leaders are thereby provided with an estimate of the *future* financial implications of any particular decision, particularly important in the case of those projects whose initial costs are low but which involve large outlays several years after initiation. It will thus be possible to avoid sharp fluctuations in the over-all budget caused by improper phasing of schedules on weapons systems, and, simultaneously, to reduce the number of projects cancelled because of unanticipated costs.

Another innovation that has proved useful is the budget ceiling. Currently, the ceiling is loosely defined as a percentage of the Gross National Product. The advantage of a ceiling is that service department budget requests are restricted to reasonable levels. In the absence of a ceiling these departments tend to make unusually large requests which must undergo heavy pruning, a process that usually takes place under great pressures of time, in an arbitrary manner, and by officials unfamiliar with the details of the various programs. An arbitrary ceiling also limits the number of new projects proposed by a department. Otherwise, the Ministry of Defense and the Treasury would be swamped with projects, and a great amount of effort would be required to determine the most useful projects if there were no ceiling requiring the departments to give more careful consideration to their proposals. The service departments are, in short, forced to allocate within a constraint, and new proposals are limited because the addition of a project very often means that an existing project must be given up. Finally, if change in the ceiling is allowed, it is relatively simple to select the one or two marginal projects to be dropped or added. Thus, the use of a budget ceiling has improved decision-making by requiring deliberate selection within a department, by facilitating last-minute changes, and by avoiding the unnecessary effort that goes into preparing and examining projects which have little likelihood of being accepted.

To summarize, the size of the defense effort is limited by the total resources under central governmental control and the alternative expenditures which compete with defense for these resources. The revenues available to the central government over the past decade have constituted a fixed share of the national output. The possibilities of increasing government resources by deficit financing have been limited by persistent inflationary pressures in the economy. Expenditures on alternative programs have been relatively stable, because these are established by law and applicable to major social groups; defense demands, in contrast, have been more vulnerable to reductions. One by-product of the intensified competition for government resources has been improvements in the defense-budget process. These include five-year budget forecasts, program control by the Ministry of Defense, and the use of budgetary ceilings.

1. 568 H. C. Deb. 2050.

2. *Public Finance* (London: Macmillan, 1895), cited by Murray L. Weidenbaum, "The Impact of Military Procurement on American Industry," in J. A. Stockfisch (ed.), *Planning and Forecasting in the Defense Industries* (Belmont, Calif.: Wadsworth, 1962), p. 135.

3. The data in this section are drawn from Alan T. Peacock and Jack Wiseman, *The Growth of Public Expenditure in the United Kingdom* (Princeton: Princeton University Press, 1961), pp. 168–69.

4. Cmd. 1936, "Statement on Defence, 1962," p. 7.

5. This discussion draws heavily on Peacock and Wiseman, *The Growth of Public Expenditure in the United Kingdom*, pp. 12–34 and especially pp. 26–27.

6. See A. J. Youngson, *The British Economy, 1927–1957* (Cambridge: Harvard University Press, 1960), pp. 141–57.

7. Peacock and Wiseman, *The Growth of Public Expenditure in the United Kingdom*, pp. 24–30.

8. H. G. Nicholas, *The British General Election of 1950* (London: Macmillan, 1951), p. 117.

9. *Ibid.*, pp. 95, 133.

10. *Ibid.*, p. 219.

11. D. E. Butler, *The British General Election of 1951* (London: Macmillan, 1952), p. 45.

12. *Ibid.*, p. 48.

13. *Ibid.*, p. 56.

14. Calculated from the data in National Institute of Economic and Social Research, "Chronological Tables," *Economic Review*, No. 10 (1960), p. 40.

15. *Ibid.*

16. Peacock and Wiseman, *The Growth of Public Expenditure in the United Kingdom*, p. 166.

17. Central Statistical Office, *National Income and Expenditure, 1956* (London: H. M. Stationery Office, 1956), p. 35, and *National Income and Expenditure, 1961* (London: H. M. Stationery Office, 1961), p. 32. This annual publication is hereafter referred to as *Blue Book, [date]*.

18. Computed from data in *Blue Book, 1956,* pp. 1, 35, and *Blue Book, 1961,* pp. 1, 33.

19. "Chronological Tables," p. 41.

20. Computed from data in *Blue Book, 1956,* pp. 34–35, and *Blue Book, 1961,* pp. 32–33.

21. D. H. Macgregor, *Public Aspects of Finance* (Oxford: Oxford University Press, 1939), p. 95.

22. Cmd. 827, "Committee on the Working of the Monetary System: Report (The Radcliffe Report)," paragraphs 23–26, 401–3.

23. *Blue Book, 1956,* p. 22, and *Blue Book, 1961,* p. 18.

24. Hugh Dalton, *Principles of Public Finance* (4th ed.; New York: Praeger, 1955), p. 233.

25. 551 H. C. Deb. 859.

26. 580 H. C. Deb. 1297.

27. On the difficulties in computing the extent of deficit spending in any given period see Cmd. 827, "The Radcliffe Report," pp. 24 n, 27 n, and 28. These difficulties are the reason why the data are limited to the period indicated.

28. In 1955 all other expenditures by the central government amounted to less than 10 per cent of total governmental expenditures (Peacock and Wiseman, *The Growth of Public Expenditure in the United Kingdom,* p. 187).

29. Included in this category are "education and child care, health services, national insurance (unemployment, sickness benefits, retirement pensions, etc.), national assistance (relief of the poor and family allowances), housing (subsidies and capital expenditure), and food subsidies" (Peacock and Wiseman, *The Growth of Public Expenditure in the United Kingdom,* p. 183).

30. *Ibid.,* pp. 184–87.

31. This category, in general terms, includes expenditures on: (1) "agriculture, forestry, and fishing"; (2) "industry and commerce" and "industrial research"; (3) "transport," i.e., the coast guard, mercantile-marine services, civil-airfield operating expenses, and Air Ministry meteorological services; and (4) "expenditure . . . on employment exchanges, and on . . . industrial services for the disabled" (Peacock and Wiseman, *The Growth of Public Expenditure in the United Kingdom,* p. 183).

32. *Blue Book, 1961,* p. 1; Central Statistical Office, *Annual Abstract of Statistics,* No. 93 (London: H. M. Stationery Office, 1956), pp. 243, 257; and No. 96 (1959), p. 255.

33. "Chronological Tables," p. 44.

34. Youngson, *The British Economy,* pp. 193–95, 203–4.

35. Interviews. This point was repeatedly stressed by officials at the Treasury, who command an excellent view of the over-all budget and allocation process.

36. Interviews.

37. 512 H. C. Deb. 577–78.

38. See, for example, 524 H. C. Deb. 1127, 568 H. C. Deb. 1759, 564 H. C. Deb. 1294 ff, and 549 H. C. Deb. 1018.

39. Interviews.

40. The information on which this section is based was obtained in interviews.

41. The first announcement of the procedure was in the 1961 Defense White Paper (Cmd. 1288, "Report on Defence 1961," p. 7). It is reported that the government delayed announcing the adoption of the system because it anticipated an adverse reaction from Parliament, which is naturally jealous of its control of the purse strings.

42. See S. H. Beer, *Treasury Control: The Co-ordination of Financial and Economic Policy in Great Britain* (2d ed.; Oxford: Oxford University Press, 1957), pp. 13–65, but especially pp. 16–32.

43. *Ibid.*, pp. 16–20.

44. The reorganization of 1963 attempted to ease this problem by creating the Secretariat under the chief scientific adviser and by appointing a deputy undersecretary of state for programs and budgets. See Chapter VIII.

10/ Defense and the Balance of Payments

BRITAIN is a small, crowded, and highly industrialized country. It has few natural resources—the only raw material in
which the United Kingdom could be considered self-sufficient
is coal; the supply of the next most abundant item, low-grade
iron ore, is inadequate to meet the needs of Britain's industries. Britain also imports about half its food, including
"wheat, meat, butter, fodder grains, citrus fruits, tea, tobacco,
[and] wool. . . ."[1] To pay its very large import bill, a correspondingly large share of the national output must be sold
abroad. Moreover, "as many of its exports are made largely
of imported materials, exports must meet the cost of these
imports as well as of those which are retained for consumption
at home."[2]

With such a large share of its domestic economic life dependent on international trade, Britain is highly vulnerable to
changes in economic activity abroad. Shifts in the costs of
imported raw materials cause similar swings in the costs of
British goods. A recession in another country, the United

States, for example, reduces the demand for British exports; conversely, a rapid expansion of activity overseas increases exports. Because of its reliance on imports and exports and vulnerability to changes elsewhere in the world, the balance of payments position is a key indicator of Britain's general economic situation.

Prior to World War II Britain normally ran a sizeable deficit on its merchandise account. It was also a capital exporter, financing a large share of the investment that took place in the colonies and dominions. The deficit resulting from capital outflows and trade imbalance was offset by invisibles—the earnings from services such as banking, shipping, and insurance—and the dividends and income returned to Britain from its extensive foreign investments. The position after World War II was radically changed, however. Wartime disinvestment cut the flow of income from overseas investments. Merchant-fleet losses reduced the invisible earnings that, together with the returns from foreign investment, covered the merchandise deficit before the war. The task immediately after World War II was thus to increase exports by an amount sufficient to fill the gap created by the loss of invisible and interest income.[3] Table 8, below, which compares the current accounts of two prewar years, 1935 and 1936, with those of 1955 and 1956, indicates the extensive changes over this period in the relative importance of imports, invisibles, and, particularly, exports.

The long-run objective of British international financial policy after World War II was to achieve full convertibility of sterling. (Sterling remained convertible within the sterling area.) There were several reasons why convertibility was desired. The most important by far was that a guarantee of full convertibility at some future date was a prerequisite to the acceptance of sterling in payment for raw materials sold to Britain, especially materials imported from countries outside the sterling area. Britain's wartime effort had to some extent been financed by its raw-materials suppliers, and at the

TABLE 8

PREWAR AND POSTWAR CURRENT ACCOUNTS *
OF BRITISH IMPORTS, INVISIBLES, AND EXPORTS †

	1935	1936	1955	1956
Imports as a percentage of GNP	18.4	19.3	20.2	18.9
Visible exports as a percentage of GNP.	10.4	10.8	18.1	18.6
Imports minus visible exports..	8.0	8.5	2.1	0.3
Invisibles as a percentage of GNP.	8.8	8.1	1.67	1.68
Balance of payments (£ millions omitted). ‡	+32	—18	—73	+237

* Excludes capital movements, foreign grants, etc.
† Sources: GNP for 1935 and 1936 is from A. R. Prest, "National Income of the United Kingdom; 1870–1946," *Economic Journal,* LVIII, No. 229 (1948), 58–59. The remainder of the data for 1935 and 1936 is from Central Statistical Office, *Annual Abstract of Statistics,* No. 91 (1954), p. 177. The data for 1955 and 1956 is from *Blue Book, 1960,* p. 1, and from H. M. Treasury, *United Kingdom Balance of Payments, 1946-1957* (London, H. M. Stationery Office, 1959), p. 16.
‡ (+)—added to U.K. monetary balances; (—)—subtracted from U.K. monetary balances.

end of the war the sterling balances of these countries amounted to £3,700 million. About one-third of this sum was outside the sterling area, held by countries whose raw materials were still needed.[4] A second reason for sterling convertibility was that it would facilitate the return to a multilateral free-trade system—from which Britain would be an obvious beneficiary. Finally, convertibility was strongly urged by the United States; in fact, one of the conditions of the U.S. Loan Agreement of 1945 was that sterling would become fully convertible in the summer of 1947.[5]

Convertibility was attempted in mid-1947, as stipulated in the American Loan Agreement, but the balances held by countries outside the sterling area were switched into dollars and gold at such a rapid rate that it was necessary to suspend the privilege.[6] The trial demonstrated clearly the inadequacy of Britain's gold and dollar reserves. The feasibility of convertibility at some future date thus hinged on Britain's ability to increase its reserves of gold and dollars. Larger reserves were also desired to sustain sterling-area commerce through normal trade-cycle fluctuations.

The main source of reserves for both the United Kingdom and the sterling area is the "Rest of the Sterling Area" (RSA), i.e., all the sterling-area countries *except* Britain. As a rule RSA countries run a surplus in trade with the *dollar* area. These dollar earnings are used to balance the *sterling* deficits in the unilateral trade accounts between RSA countries and the United Kingdom, and, when returned to the central bank in London, the dollars become part of the area's reserves. Because the dollar surplus earned by the RSA countries fluctuates with the price and activity changes in the American economy, there is some uncertainty about this source of reserves. However, RSA dollar earnings are particularly important since Britain's merchandise account with the hard-currency areas— the United States and, since the mid-1950's, Europe—is normally in deficit. To this basic deficit must be added the outflow occasioned by the U.K.'s debt repayments. Held mainly by the United States, external debt amounted to £2,500 million in 1949; about £35 million has been repaid each year since then.[7] Debt servicing imposes an additional demand on reserves since the repayment must be made in either gold or dollars.

DEFENSE DEMANDS AND THE BALANCE OF PAYMENTS

The problem in the years immediately after World War II was thus to expand exports to earn sufficient foreign exchange to pay the import bill. The long-term goal—a substantial surplus on the merchandise account—was simply an extension of this interim target. As the balance of payments surpluses accumulated and increased Britain's gold and dollar reserves, sterling convertibility would become possible. These financial objectives, however, conflicting in a number of ways with a large national-security effort.

In 1946 and 1947 the need to improve the balance of payments position was central in the decision to cut back on defense spending. Hugh Dalton, then chancellor of the Exchequer, referred to this period—one of dispute within the Labor government over the financial and manpower costs of defense–as "the Battle of the Balance of Payments." Dalton's position was clear: "Among the payments which, if we were to win, must be cut, hard and quickly, were payments for the Armed Forces and for their supply, particularly for forces stationed overseas." [8] The outcome was a reduction in the 1947–48 defense budget, and since labor was in short supply, a cut in service manpower levels. Later in 1947, in the midst of the financial crisis touched off by the first attempt at convertibility, additional reductions were ordered.

Although the level of defense spending remained below £800 million between mid-1947 and the outbreak of the Korean War, service manpower levels were reduced an additional one hundred thousand in 1948 and 1949 to make more labor available to the export industries. Despite the improvements these reductions allowed in Britain's exports and reserves, the £4,700 million rearmament program was seriously affected by the balance of payments problem. Britain's major goals during this period, as set forth in the "Economic Survey for 1951," were as follows: "First, so far as it lies within our power, the defence programme must be pushed through, in full and without delay. Second, we must at the same time preserve our economic strength and independence." [9] "Economic strength and independence" meant larger exports and a strengthened balance of payments position. Exports were heavily dependent on the output of the metals-engineering industries. Defense production, however, was concentrated in the same sector of the economy.

Prior to World War II over one-quarter of Britain's exports consisted of coal and textiles. After 1945 the sale of these items fell rapidly, and in 1957 they accounted for only one-tenth of the value of exports. Concurrently with the decline in importance of coal and textiles, exports of manufactured products from the engineering and metals industries increased greatly in importance. The far-reaching adjustments in the export sector are suggested by the data in Table 9 below.

TABLE 9

PERCENTAGE OF TOTAL BRITISH EXPORTS BY VALUE *

Industry	1938	1957
Machinery (other than electric)	11	17
Cotton Goods	10	3
Coal	9	†
Iron and Steel	6	6
Chemicals	6	8
Manufactures of metal	5	5
Vehicles and Aircraft	5	12
Miscellaneous textiles	5	3
Electric machinery, apparatus, etc	5	7
Woolen goods	4	3
Petroleum and Petroleum Products	†	3

* Source: Adopted from A. J. Youngson, *The British Economy: 1920–1957* (Cambridge: Harvard University Press, 1960). p. 210.
† Less than 3 per cent.

Between 1946 and 1948, when defense purchases of engineering and metals products were below £100 million per year, the conflict between defense and exports was not severe. Although there was some increase in 1949 and early in 1950, defense-hardware outlays rose sharply following the outbreak of the Korean War. Table 10 below indicates defense purchases by type of product since 1949.

The implications of rearmament for exports and the economy generally were discussed at length in the "Economic Survey for 1951":

The increased claims of defence are not distributed evenly over the economy, but are largely concentrated upon particular sectors—most of all upon the metal-using industries. The great bulk of the output of these industries goes to home investment and exports and only a very small part consists of consumption goods. This makes it much more difficult to shift the main burden of rearmament on to consumption. It is indeed certain that defence orders must to a considerable extent conflict with production of metal goods for export and investment. . . .[10]

TABLE 10

TYPES OF BRITISH DEFENSE PURCHASES,
FOR THE YEARS 1949–50 THROUGH 1960–61 *
(£ Millions Omitted)

YEAR	ARMAMENT AND ENGINEERING PRODUCTS†		SUPPLIES‡		TOTAL
	Amount	Percentage	Amount	Percentage	
1949-50	173	48	186	52	359
1950-51	186	49	196	51	382
1951-52	272	42	376	58	648
1952-53	524	53	458	47	982
1953-54	592	60	388	40	980
1954-55	614	63	366	37	980
1955-56	545	59	373	41	918
1956-57	551	58	392	42	943
1957-58	504	60	334	40	838
1958-59	459	60	306	40	765
1959-60§	508	62	310	38	818
1960-61§	501	61	326	39	827

* Source: Computed from D. C. Paige, "Defense Expenditure," *Economic Review*, No. 10 (1960), p. 32.
† Includes aircraft and equipment, electronics, guns, armor and ammunition, motor transport, and shipbuilding and ship repair.
‡ Includes works and buildings, food, clothing and textiles, petroleum products, and other fuels.
§ Estimated.

It was hoped, nevertheless, that both defense and export demands could be satisfied: with a "moderate increase" in metal-industry output, export losses could be offset by increased output of "other metal products." [11]

The world-wide scramble for raw materials made 1951 a more difficult year than had been anticipated: mainly because of raw material purchases for defense production and stockpiling, the import bill increased by some £1,100 million.[12] Because of the uncertainty of the period and the change-over to defense production, exports increased only slightly. From a surplus of £244 million in 1950, the balance of payments position shifted to a £521 million deficit,[13] and the sterling area's reserves fell about $1 billion.[14] The "Economic Survey for 1952" describes in detail the consequences of the deficit in 1951:

By the end of 1951 good progress had been made with the placing of the necessary [defense] contracts, and about £1,320 of the £2,000 million for production in the original three-year programme had been translated into actual orders. Production had not, however, proceeded as fast as had been hoped, and it was already clear that the original programme could not be completed within the three years. This was partly because of inevitable difficulties over design and production planning and partly because of the shortages of labour, materials, components and machine tools. But in addition, the sharp change in the balance of payments has made it necessary to ease the burden of defence on the metal-using industries so that engineering exports can be expanded more rapidly. Defence demands for building and civil engineering work have also had to be restricted because of the shortage of steel and the recent overloading of the building industry.[15]

During 1952 the economic situation improved greatly. The price of raw material imports declined, and the balance of payments position improved by almost £690 million.[16] The loss of gold and dollar reserves also slowed, then stopped, and in the fourth quarter there was a net gain of £57 million.[17] The competition for metal-industry output between defense and exports continued, however, and the effect was to constrain defense spending:

By the end of 1952 defence production in the metal-using industries, excluding civil defence work, was running at the rate of about £500 million a year. The Government has decided that for the time being no substantial increase above this rate of production would be consistent with proper provision for the expansion of exports of plant and machinery and for the re-equipment and development of home industry, and the defence programme has been adjusted accordingly. Expenditure on works services for defence has risen sharply during the past two years, but no further increase is expected in 1953–54.[18]

This evidence of the limitations imposed on the rearmament program by the competition between exports and defense production is echoed in the defense white papers of the period. The white paper published in 1953, over two years after Prime Minister Attlee first announced the £4,700 million rearmament program to the House of Commons, argued as follows:

. . . It was becoming clear when the . . . [Churchill] Government took office that the [£4,700 million rearmament] plan could not in any event be completed by March 1954. But it was also apparent that the momentum reached in the third year of the plan would have led to a rate of expenditure during that year which would have imposed too great a burden on the economy, particularly on the balance of payments, and to a still higher rate of expenditure in the following year. There was also good reason to doubt whether, even after the plan had been completed, the cost of maintaining the forces which would have by then been built up and of keeping them equipped with the most up-to-date material would have been within the country's resources.

. . . .
Further investigation showed that, even with this spreading forward, the load which the defence production programme would place upon industry was greater than was compatible with the increase in engineering exports to which it is necessary to look for a major contribution to the solution of the balance of payments problem.[19]

One consequence of the intense demands on the metals and engineering industries was an increase in their capacity; it was acknowledged that the output of these industries was sufficient by 1954 to meet the needs of both defense and exports:

. . . Now that more steel is available and the defence load has levelled off, exports of capital goods are no longer being seriously impeded by the pressure of home demand. Indeed, a number of these industries have spare capacity which could be used for increasing exports or home improvement.[20]

A second and perhaps more important reason for the decreased effect of the balance of payments problem on defense spending is the improvement in Britain's reserve position after 1953. Although defense production and stockpiling increased the import bill and thus contributed to the deterioration of the current account in 1950 and 1951, the rearmament program *strengthened* Britain's ability to earn reserves in the years thereafter. There are three reasons. First, the United States initiated a program of defense assistance—primarily because none of the NATO countries had sufficient reserves of gold or dollars to finance rearmament independently. U.S. assistance began in 1952, after the crisis of 1951 had been corrected, and continued through 1956. The total received by the United Kingdom amounted to about $1 billion.[21] Second, Britain earned dollars because of American military deployments. The strength of U.S. Air Force units, first assigned in the United Kingdom in 1948, was increased in 1951 and 1952. Dollar expenditures in support of these units, as well as spending by American and Canadian servicemen stationed in Britain, rose to £90 million in 1957 and averaged £65 million per year between 1951 and 1960.[22] Finally, the Korean War expanded total world demand for military hardware; because of the United Kingdom's rearmament effort, British industry was able to capture part of this market. Through 1959, the value of military exports amounted to £206 million.[23] Some of these sales were financed by the United States through the off-shore procurement program; they thus contributed directly to the sterling area's dollar reserves. Defense spending on military aircraft, which strengthened the competitive position of this industry, was particularly important. Overseas sales of airframes and engines averaged £70 million per year between 1950 and 1960; except for the Viscount turboprop transport, exports consisted largely of items such as the Canberra bomber and the Hunter and P.1 fighters.[24]

Although the indirect contribution of rearmament to reserves was considerable, the size of the defense effort continued to be a concern. In the years immediately after World War II, domestic investment had been restrained in order that more manufactured goods would be available for export. Home investment continued at a low level during the Korean rearmament period, when defense procurement represented an additional burden on the engineering and metals industries. As German, French, and Japanese recovery progressed, however, foreign competition became more intense, even in those overseas markets traditionally tied to the British economy. Thus, investment received a higher priority because of the need to improve the United Kingdom's competitive position abroad. Domestic investment increased in almost all sectors in 1953 and accelerated rapidly through 1954 and 1955. As investment expanded and defense outlays continued above £550 million per year, the pressures on the metals and engineering industries also intensified:

While the basic trouble . . . [in 1955] was the excessive level of total demand, the position was made still more difficult by the growing concentration of demand on the metal using industries. Consumers' expenditure on cars and other durable goods increased relatively more than their total expenditure. Investment in plant, machinery and vehicles increased sharply; and export demand was stronger for metal goods than for other goods. Consequently great pressure was put on the metal-using industries. They absorbed two-thirds of the increase in civil employment and increased their output by 9 per cent., nearly twice as much as industry as a whole. In a word, the structure of the economy changed in the direction of producing relatively more metal goods, but it could not change as fast as the pattern of demand required.[25]

Another aspect of the defense effort that attracted attention in the mid-1950's was the shortage of scientists and engineers. In September, 1956, a lead article in the *Economist* estimated that 60 per cent of "the [human] resources this country can assemble to invest in technological progress" were consumed by the defense effort.[26] The fear was expressed that defense research and development was draining scientific and technical personnel from British industry. The result would be to lower the rate of productivity increases and to slow economic growth, both of which would weaken the competitiveness of British exports abroad. The high quality of British scientists and engineers was appreciated, but compared to the United States and the Soviet Union, relatively fewer were available. Nor was the educational system particularly well designed to produce large numbers. The first official comment on the problem indicates the impact of the shortage of scientific and technically trained manpower: "The claims of defence research must be balanced against the competing claims on our limited resources of scientific manpower." [27]

The interdependence of the defense program and Britain's economic position is clearly indicated by a passage from the 1956 Defense White Paper:

The continued economic strength of the free world is an essential element in our ability to resist Soviet aggression and the burden of defence cannot be allowed to rise to a level which would endanger our economic future. This burden does not consist only in the effect of high defence expenditure on the general level of taxation, important though that is. Defence production falls in the main upon the metal and metal-using industries, which supply about half our exports and are of great importance in the re-equipment of British industry. They thus play a vital role in strengthening our balance of payments. The maintenance of British forces overseas involves a heavy direct charge on the balance of payments. . . . And the size of the forces themselves inevitably affects the manpower available for the tasks of civil industry.[28]

DEFENSE DEPLOYMENTS AND THE BALANCE OF PAYMENTS

A large share of Britain's military forces have been stationed outside the United Kingdom since World War II, either in Europe with NATO forces or in garrisons in Africa, the Middle East, and Asia. These deployments cause a direct outflow of sterling from the domestic economy. The loss takes place in two ways: First, government spending in foreign economies for the goods and services needed to support local installations and their assigned garrisons; and second, spending by military personnel in the purchase of items from local economies for individual consumption. For balance of payments purposes both expenditures are outflows or deficits—the equivalent of imports into the British economy.

TABLE 11

CURRENT ACCOUNTS OF BALANCE OF PAYMENTS AND
BRITISH MILITARY EXPENDITURES ABROAD, 1948–60 *
(£ Millions Omitted)

YEAR	WITH REST OF STERLING AREA		WITH NON-STERLING AREA		WITH OEEC† COUN-TRIES	TOTAL	
	Balance of Payments	Military Expend-itures Abroad‡	Balance of Payments	Military Expend-itures Abroad‡	Balance of Payments	Balance of Payments	Military Expend-itures Abroad‡
1948	+256	75	—249	38	—79	+7	113
1949	+299	69	—261	41	—22	+38	110
1950	+283	65	+14	35	+104	+297	100
1951	+320	78	—734	48	—209	—414	126
1952	+348	92	—121	49	—42	+227	141
1953	+152	90	+27	54	+72	+179	144
1954	+267	99	—56	52	+26	+211	151
1955	+214	105	—287	52	—54	—73	157
1956	+306	127	—48	52	—62	+258	179
1957	+360	114	—131	49	—35	+229	163
1958	+434	109	—89	74	—45	+345	183
1959	+223	117	—84	55	—76	+139	172
1960	+234	136	—164	78	—66	+70	214
Average	+284	98	—168	52	—37	+116	150

* Sources: Data for the period 1948–57 is from H. M. Treasury, *United Kingdom Balance of Payments: 1946–1957* (London: H. M. Stationery Office, 1959), pp. 16–23, 26, 50; data for 1957–60 is from Cmd. 1188, "United Kingdom Balance of Payments 1957 to 1960," pp. 6–9, 11, 17.
† By definition, part of the non-sterling area.
‡ Net costs to the United Kingdom. Contributions by foreign governments such as West Germany have been deducted from total expenditures to arrive at these figures.

Table 11 indicates total military expenditures overseas and the balance on current account since 1948. The average current-account surplus between 1948 and 1960 is £116 million. Over this same period overseas military deployments have caused outflows which amount to about £150 million a year.

The foreign-exchange costs of military deployments abroad thus exceed the average annual surplus earned by the export of British goods and services; it is reasonable to assume that Britain's reserves of gold and hard currency would be much larger had fewer troops been stationed overseas. These direct foreign-exchange outlays—in contrast to the indirect effects of defense procurement on the balance of payments position— have had an important effect on decisions relating to both the size and the deployment of British forces.

The charges that arise from overseas military deployments increase the gap between payments and receipts that must be filled by exports. More resources, labor in particular, are therefore required in the export sector. If military forces are reduced in size, fewer troops are likely to be stationed overseas, thereby lessening the foreign-exchange outflows. More important, the manpower released by a force reduction is available for transfer to the export industries. For these reasons, the armed forces have been a prime target for manpower cuts. As Chancellor of the Exchequer Hugh Dalton explained in a letter to Prime Minister Attlee during the balance of payments crisis of early 1947:

> Much the most important [of the several proposals to reduce the present balance of payments deficit] . . . was for a further cut in the personnel of the Armed Forces and of those making their arms and equipment.
> The reduction which we proposed, would have been brought about by a quicker release of the next age groups—many of whom have now served more than four years. Its great merit was that it would have given us an exceptionally good reinforcement of manpower, containing a large number of strong and skilled men in the prime of life—not children leaving school, nor middle-class young ladies.[29]

Another example of this relationship occurred in 1955. Domestic activity was then at its postwar peak: prices and wages were rising, and labor was in short supply, as demonstrated by an unemployment rate of less than 1 per cent. By mid-summer reserves were falling rapidly as domestic demand reduced the quantity of goods available for export. Sir Anthony Eden, then the prime minister, wrote to his chancellor, Mr. Butler, as follows:

I have been thinking over our talks yesterday. I hope they were useful. They have convinced me that we must put the battle against inflation before anything else. After all, if we win out, the other problems, for example the gold and dollar reserves, will take care of themselves.

Therefore I think we should approach our problem mainly from this angle. With this in mind I will press the Services hard, because to release more men is to fight inflation.[30]

Although cuts in the size of the forces serve to ease the balance of payments position by shifting resources to the export sector, the deficit may be lessened by action of another type: troops deployed overseas can be returned to the United Kingdom. The total sterling outflows are reduced—while the over-all size or costs of the forces remains unchanged. As one example, the British withdrawal from Greece in early 1947 seems to have been influenced heavily by calculations of this kind:

As part of my general campaign to reduce our military overseas expenditures, I had for some months been concentrating attention on our expenditure in Greece; on a British Division stationed in Greece, on the maintenance of the Greek Army and on its equipment. This tussle came to a head in March [1947] and I was successful.[31]

However, overseas military deployments have been influenced in sharply different ways by the balance of payments problem. The effect depends upon the geographic area in question, primarily because different payments arrangements are applicable to the various areas in which troops are stationed. Most British overseas bases and garrisons—Hong Kong, Kenya, Aden, Gibraltar, for example—are located in the sterling area.[32] Monies expended in support of these forces, about two-thirds of all military expenditures overseas, have different balance of payments implications than outlays in the non-sterling areas, especially outlays in the relatively hard-currency countries of NATO. In the short run, expenditures in the sterling area have only minor balance of payments effects: there is a simple bookkeeping transfer of credits and debits by the central bank, in this case London, with no immediate shifts in the sterling area's gold reserves or its position relative to the dollar area. In the long run the consequences are again minimal: military spending in the overseas areas adds to sterling balances which the RSA countries or territories can use to buy British exports. Although the U.K.'s tight trade links with the sterling-area countries have weakened in recent years, a large share of these sterling earnings are normally returned in exchange for British goods. And to the extent that these outflows strengthen local economies and increase the demand for goods available only from non-sterling, hard-currency countries, the Treasury and the Bank of England are usually able to restrain or delay RSA purchases from these sources.

Military expenditures in the non-sterling area pose a more formidable problem. The largest single outflow is caused by the British Army of the Rhine. As Table 11 indicates, exports to the OEEC countries have been on average insufficient to cover the costs of the NATO commitment, the current account deficit amounting to some £37 million annually. This deficit must be financed by *gold or dollars* earned elsewhere—always a difficult task in the postwar period. The NATO commitment has become more of a problem in recent years. Prior to May, 1955, the local expenses incurred by the various national forces assigned to NATO were partially covered by a West German contribution (limited to a total of £600 million per year). Following the restoration of German sovereignty, financial aid in the form of a contribution to support costs was continued.[33] After 1958, however, German assistance was reduced from about £40 million to approximately £12 million annually.[34] In addition to being far short of the foreign-exchange costs of the British Army of the Rhine, this contribution was to continue only through 1960. Despite the reductions in the size of BAOR in 1957 and 1958—a decision in which the balance of payments problem figured heavily—the foreign-exchange costs of British forces in Europe have increased from £50 million to about £75 million annually.

The differential balance of payments effects of overseas deployments are important in explaining the division of military effort between NATO and the overseas areas. A civil servant in the War Office argued in these terms:

If a soldier in Singapore wants a new car, he will probably go and get a Morris. If he is in Germany he will buy a Volkswagen. In the first case it all comes back to us. In the second, no. And since we already buy a large range of items from the Germans, the situation is already difficult. Our present overseas deployments reflect these different circumstances.[35]

Another official's comment was representative of several on the central problem posed by the NATO commitment: "The difficulties are not those of our overall budget but rather those of the balance [of payments]." [36] The payments arrangements, in short, are such that troop deployments in the overseas areas have only limited balance of payments implications; NATO deployments, in contrast, cause a direct outflow of scarce gold or hard currency.

The different balance of payments effects of the currency exchange arrangements are strengthened by several related factors. Military deployments abroad, especially in the colonial areas, give rise to many local problems. A base may become the focus of local nationalist discontent. Generally symbolic of imperialism, past or present, a garrison may effectively shorten the occupant's tenure and even reduce his influence in the host country. But overseas bases have many indirect benefits. They provide an organizational structure through which to support moderate elements in an emerging political system. They are almost always important in the host economy and concurrently provide a means of acquiring the foreign exchange that is vital for economic development. Finally, bases can be used to channel technical or administrative assistance into a developing nation. It is not that bases are necessarily the most effective way, politically or economically, of accomplishing these tasks, but bases offer these returns *in addition to* their military value. For many British decision-makers these secondary benefits are a decisive reason for maintaining the remaining overseas bases. One civil servant, for example, argued in these terms in late 1961:

> The situation in Singapore is bad—the Communists there are pressing at the door. Our naval base is important in maintaining a degree of stability in the area. It is the most important single factor in the economy. One of the major secondary reasons for the base is that it is a convenient way to channel assistance to the area. If we didn't do it this way we would have to do it through one of our technical missions. A naval base in Darwin would be cheaper but it cannot perform this secondary function. This general argument is applicable to Malta and Aden and only slightly less important in the case of Gibraltar and Cyprus.[37]

"Without the base at Malta there would be a considerable number of problems which would have to be handled by some other agency," another official suggested. "We prefer to meet the situation by giving the Maltese laborer a pay packet from the dockyard every Friday." [38]

The secondary effects of troop deployments in the NATO area are somewhat different. For the host country, in this case West Germany, expenditures for local goods and services are the equivalent of exports—but without the effort commonly associated with overseas sales. In the case of West Germany the gain in gold and dollar reserves is viewed as a windfall: "The Germans have spent relatively less on defense than we have," one official commented, "but they have reaped enormous benefits, both from the United States and Great Britain." [39]

Britain has attempted in recent years to offset the foreign exchange outflows of the NATO commitment by increasing its sales of military equipment on the Continent. Unfortunately, it has enjoyed little success. Its main competitor, the United States, enjoys the advantages conferred by a larger defense sector offering a much greater variety of equipment and the sales leverage that inheres in its position as the leader of the Atlantic Community.

Britain's inability to compete with the U.S. in the export of military equipment has also influenced other aspects of military policy. Research and development on the Blue Water, a medium-range tactical missile system, was stopped in mid-1962 partly because none could be sold to the NATO countries. In the absence of export sales the costs of producing Blue Water were too great, given the relatively small number needed by the British themselves. The British believed that the Blue Water was greatly superior to any comparable American missile— which explains the prevailing sentiment in London at the time the project was cancelled: "The energy and persistency— occasionally to be classed as lack of scruple—of American businessmen have played their part," complained a correspondent in the *Illustrated London News*. "Time after time, when we have had good prospects of exporting up-to-date weapons, they have with the support of their Government brushed our agents aside." [40]

Because of its reliance on international trade and its need to accumulate reserves to insure sterling convertibility, a balance of payments surplus was a primary goal of British policy after World War II. This goal required a high volume of exports, which were increasingly composed of metal and engineering industry products. Since defense production was concentrated in these same industries, the balance of payments problem constrained the level of defense spending. After the completion of the Korean rearmament program, the competition between defense and exports became a three-way fight for metals-engineering output among defense, exports, and domestic investment. Higher domestic investment, necessary to insure the long-term competitive position of British industry, and the shortage of engineers and scientists became the major constraints on defense in the mid-1950's.

Although the size of the forces has been reduced to transfer resources to the export sector, the most important effect of military expenditures abroad has been to condition overseas deployments. Spending in the sterling area has relatively limited balance of payments consequences; the secondary consequences of these expenditures are viewed as desirable and necessary—an easy substitute for more direct forms of economic or technical assistance. Deployments in the NATO area, in contrast, have a direct impact on Britain's reserves of gold and hard currencies. Efforts to offset these outflows to West Germany by the sale of military equipment have been largely unsuccessful because of the intense competition from the United States—an ally with a more recent, but equally severe, balance of payments problem. Aside from strategic arguments on the division of forces between the overseas areas and NATO, deployments in the former areas have favorable economic implications; in the latter areas, inimical economic implications.

1. Central Office of Information, *Britain: An Official Handbook* (1962 ed.; London: Central Office of Information, 1962), p. 247.

2. G. D. H. Cole, *The Post-War Condition of Britain* (New York: Praeger, 1956), p. 175.

3. For an account of British economic problems and policies after 1945, see Sir Roy Harrod, *The British Economy* (London: McGraw-Hill, 1963), pp. 27–35, 117–51.

4. *Ibid.*, pp. 117–51, and especially 121–22.

5. The loan, which was agreed to in December, 1945, and approved by Congress in mid-1946, amounted to $3.75 billion. An additional $650 million in Lend-Lease credits was also granted, for a total of $4.4 billion. Canada provided $1.5 billion in credits during this period.

6. A brief description by a member of the British Cabinet of the problem during this period of convertibility is contained in Hugh Dalton, *High Tide and After: Memoirs, 1945–1960* (London: Frederick Muller, Ltd., 1962), pp. 254–71.

7. H. M. Treasury, *United Kingdom Balance of Payments, 1946–1957*, p. 58.

8. Dalton, *High Tide and After*, p. 193.

9. Cmd. 8195, "Economic Survey for 1951," par. 130.

10. *Ibid.*, par. 22.

11. *Ibid.*, par. 73.

12. Cmd. 8509, "Economic Survey for 1952," par. 7.

13. *Ibid.*, par. 1.

14. *Ibid.*, Table 1, p. 9.

15. *Ibid.*, par. 36.

16. Cmd. 8800, "Economic Survey 1953," par. 7 and Table 3, p. 9.

17. *Ibid.*, Table 1, p. 7.

18. *Ibid.*, par. 123.

19. Cmd. 8768, "Statement on Defence, 1953," p. 4.

20. Cmd. 9108, "Economic Survey 1954," par. 73.

21. Computed from data in Cmd. 8800, "Economic Survey 1953," p. 9; Cmd. 9728, "Economic Survey 1956," p. 30; Cmd. 113, "Economic Survey 1957," p. 31.

22. H. M. Treasury, *United Kingdom Balance of Payments, 1946–1957*, pp. 54–55, and Cmd. 1188, "United Kingdom Balance of Payments 1957 to 1960," p. 19.

23. *Ibid.*

24. Computed from Central Statistical Office, *Annual Abstract of Statistics*, No. 96 (London: H. M. Stationery Office, 1956), p. 226; and Central Statistical Office, *Monthly Abstract of Statistics*, No. 185 (London: H. M. Stationery Office, 1961), p. 112.

25. Cmd. 9728, "Economic Survey 1956," par. 73.

26. "Research out of Balance," *Economist*, September 8, 1956, p. 813.

27. Cmd. 9691, "Statement on Defence, 1956," p. 5.

28. *Ibid.*

29. Dalton, *High Tide and After*, p. 196.

30. Anthony Eden, *Full Circle: The Memoirs of Anthony Eden* (Boston: Houghton Mifflin, 1960), p. 349.

31. Dalton, *High Tide and After*, p. 206.

32. The sterling area includes all the Commonwealth countries (except Canada), South Africa, Iceland, Burma, Southwest Africa, Ireland, Jordan, Libya, Kuwait, and the British-protected states in the Persian Gulf.

33. See "1955–56, Supplementary Estimate, Army," July 4, 1955, p. 7 in *House of Commons Sessional Papers, XXXI, 1955–56* (London: H. M. Stationery Office, 1956).

34. See Cmd. 669, "Memorandum of the Secretary of State for War relating to the Army Estimates 1959–60," p. 3.

35. Interview.

36. Interview.

37. Interview.

38. Interview.

39. Interview.

40. Cyril Falls, "A Window on the World," *Illustrated London News,* August 25, 1962.

11/ Defense and Politics

A NUMBER of conditions helped to account for the United Kingdom's long-secure position as a great power. Britain's geographic location partially isolated it from the military and political upheavals which periodically swept Europe after the wars of the French Revolution. Control over much of the periphery of the Eurasian land mass was possible because Britain's naval and military forces could be deployed rapidly from numerous strategic bases and overseas territories under British jurisdiction. World-wide political influence rested on the stability and decision-making effectiveness of the United Kingdom's system of parliamentary democracy. The United Kingdom also enjoyed, because of its highly developed economy, rank among the leading industrial countries of the world; Britain's economy provided the technical and logistical strength needed to sustain its military and, particularly, its naval power. The industrial prowess which allowed it to export manufactured goods went hand-in-hand with London's activities as banker and financier for much of the world's trade. The commercial and financial ties linking London with the rest of the world supplemented the political, administrative, and symbolic institutions of the Empire and, later, the Commonwealth, and provided additional mechanisms through which British power and influence could be exerted.

As the only major western European nation to survive World War II without a change in its political system, Britain was well suited for an active role in international affairs after 1945. It made a major contribution to the economic and political reconstruction of western Europe, and Britain's part in building the North Atlantic Treaty Organization was second only to that of the United States. The process of decolonialization, which began in 1947 with the grant of independence to India and Pakistan and now nears completion, insured Britain a prominent, if temporary, voice in the affairs of the nations in the Middle East, Africa, and southern Asia.

The important international role played by Britain in the early years after World War II obscured the numerous weaknesses in the British economy and resource base. Although its economy was less severely damaged than those of most European countries, the costs of World War II were nevertheless very great. Between 1939 and 1945 wealth accumulated over many decades was consumed rapidly: overseas investments were sold or traded; shipping losses cut the merchant fleet to a fraction of its prewar size; as a result of the diversion of investment to defense, plants and equipment became obsolescent or worn out in many sectors of the economy. The costs of World War II were demonstrated by both the scarcity of goods and the physical controls that were maintained after 1945. Rationing of food, furniture, and clothing was necessary until 1948. Many common necessities—household pans, for example—were not available for several years. A severe coal crisis in the winter of 1947 caused shortages in fuel and power; even as late as 1950 the supply of these two basic commodities was insufficient to meet consumer demand.[1]

In 1945 British industry enjoyed a competitive advantage

over its European competitors. This quickly disappeared, however. With the stimulus provided by Marshall Plan assistance, European countries, West Germany in particular, rapidly repaired the damages of World War II. As European recovery progressed, these countries provided increasingly stiff competition and captured a larger share of total world exports. Britain's competitive position was weakened further by the extensive defense effort of the United Kingdom, a disproportionate effort as compared to that of the other European countries. At the same time the divestment of empire, increasingly expensive to maintain, weakened Britain's commercial advantages in exporting to the overseas colonial areas.

With the economic and political recovery of western Europe and the establishment of independent states in the colonial areas, opportunities for British leadership declined. To continue to play a major role in international affairs nevertheless remained an important national goal. International politics in the 1950's presented unusual dangers, and the growing awareness of the extraordinary cost of failure was intensified by the widespread concern in Britain over the wisdom and certainty of America's cold-war leadership. But it was more and more difficult to ignore the gulf between national resources and the multitude of political problems whose outcome the United Kingdom desired to influence. The gap was most stunningly demonstrated by the Suez intervention in 1956. While some observers wondered if the attributes of judgment, experience, and moderation had not also been lost, the experience provided British officials and political leaders a particularly dramatic appreciation of the growing limitations on unilateral national action.

An important goal of British political leaders in the years since World War II has been to maintain, even enhance, their country's international position. Thus, as the resource limitations have become more severe and apparent, the prestige implications of policy choices have increased in importance. Britain has tried to maintain its international influence both by strengthening its special relationship with the United States and by consolidating its position as head of the Commonwealth.

BRITAIN AND THE UNITED STATES

Britain and the United States have always enjoyed rather special ties, if only because of the common language and culture of the two countries. Historically, there was little question of Britain's status. World War II demonstrated the enormous resource differences, however, and as the United States has accepted greater international responsibilities, Britain has been relegated to a secondary role. What could be done to maintain at least a degree of influence over American policy? Military policy has provided a lever—one, incidentally, which also supports a prestigious role in other aspects of international politics.

The connection between Anglo-American relations and international prestige and military policy is suggested by the various supplementary motives which have been attached to the decisions to manufacture nuclear weapons and to form a strategic bomber force. It should be emphasized that the desire to influence American policy or to enhance Britain's international prestige do not in themselves explain either of these choices. The wartime strategic bombing effort and the United States Strategic Air Command were progenitors of the British strategic nuclear force. But in each of the several decisions that led to this force, considerations of Britain's world leadership role and its desire to influence American policy played an important part.

The decision to produce atomic weapons was made in 1946. During World War II Britain had co-operated with the United States in the Manhattan Project; it expected at the end of the war either to receive atomic weapons or to share in their control. These calculations were upset by the U.S. Congress with the passage in 1946 of the MacMahon Act, which made it impossible for the United States to furnish its allies either weapons or data. The Attlee government thereupon initiated an independent development program. The task did not appear to be an impossible one because British scientists were familiar with the engineering techniques developed in the Manhattan Project. Production of atomic weapons was also expected to result in some valuable non-military benefits. Because of the shortage of coal, nuclear-powered electrical generating plants were economically competitive; in addition, the fissionable nuclear materials needed for atomic weapons would be a by-product. Most important, a weapons-development program would enable Britain to meet the American definition of great power status implicit in the MacMahon Act, which promised American assistance to those nations that made substantial "independent" progress in the development of atomic weapons. As Prime Minister Attlee explained:

. . . It was right. We couldn't get co-operation with the Americans. That stupid MacMahon Act prevented our acting fully with them. And they were inclined to think they were the big boys and we were the small boys; we just had to show them they didn't know everything.[2]

For the Churchill government after 1952, production of the hydrogen bomb and formation of a strategic nuclear force were motivated by similar considerations: "Personally, I cannot feel that we should have much influence over . . . [American] policy or actions, wise, or unwise, while we are largely dependent, as we are today, upon their protection," argued Sir Winston Churchill in the 1955 defense debates. "We, too, must possess substantial deterrent power of our own."[3] Nor was the objective limited to influencing American policy. Sir Winston's successor as prime minister, Sir Anthony Eden, was convinced that nuclear weapons offered his government exceptional opportunities for "influenc[ing] the ambitions of others."[4] Prime Minister Eden's views had been greatly strengthened by his experience at the Geneva conference in

1954, where, he recalls, he became "sharply conscious of the deterrent power of the hydrogen bomb." [5]

The subsequent generation of political leaders, which emerged in the mid-1950's, accepted without apparent qualification the judgment of their elders: "The independent contribution [to the Western deterrent] gives us a better position in the world," Mr. Macmillan reported to a TV audience in early 1958. "The fact that we have it makes the United States pay a greater regard to our point of view, and that is of great importance." [6] The late Hugh Gaitskell, the leader of the Labor party between 1955 and 1962, believed that an independent strategic nuclear force was necessary if Britain wished to influence the United States. He argued as follows in the 1960 defense debates:

> The real case for our having our own independent nuclear weapons is fear of excessive dependence upon the United States. It springs from doubts about the readiness of the United States Government and the American citizens to risk the destruction of their cities on behalf of Europe. It depends also, I think, on fear that an excessive dependence on the United States might force upon us policies with which we did not agree, because we would be in such a weak position to argue with the United States.
> My hon. Friend . . . [Mr. R. H. S. Crossman] suggested . . . that we no longer took the view that the possession of nuclear weapons was of any value in discussing matters with the Americans. I am afraid that I still do think it of some value. [7]

Whatever advantages the possession of nuclear weapons and the means to deliver them give British statesmen in their dealings with the United States or other foreign countries, the strategic nuclear force has implications for domestic politics as well. An independent force is a symbol, as was the fleet, of Britain's independence and world-leadership role. It provides evidence that Britain is a great power, with the right to be consulted on major international issues. This seems particularly important in a period when the traditional emblems of Britain's position, the Empire, for example, have become meaningless. Indeed, nuclear weapons and an independent strategic nuclear force have frequently been equated with great power status: " . . . If we want to remain a first-class power," Sir John Slessor, a retired Chief of Air Staff, advised in February, 1954, "we cannot possibly leave to an ally, however staunch and loyal, the monopoly of this instrument of such decisive importance in these massive issues of war and peace." [8] A prominent member of the Church of Scotland agreed: "Britain without the bomb," suggested the Archbishop of York, "might become a satellite of a nation which possessed it." [9] A more recent expression, before the American Chamber of Commerce in London in late 1958, came from Randolph Churchill: "Britain can knock down twelve cities in the region of Stalingrad and Moscow from bases in Britain and another dozen in the Crimea from bases in Cyprus. We did not have that power at the time of Suez. We are a major power again." [10]

The importance for domestic politics of Britain's status in international affairs cannot be better illustrated than by noting one relatively isolated event of recent years. This was the attempt in 1957 to employ nuclear *strategy,* as distinct from the strategic nuclear force itself, for symbolic purposes. The defense white paper, normally published in February, was delayed until early April, ostensibly to provide the new minister of defense, Duncan Sandys, with an opportunity to review and to reformulate British strategy. Throughout this period, the months immediately after the Suez intervention, the Macmillan government's strategic reappraisal was given considerable publicity. The combination of publicity and delay helped stimulate public interest; Mr. George Brown, the Labor spokesman, even charged that "this White Paper is being sold a wee bit highly." [11] Next, presentation showed that what until 1956 had been a *"contribution"* to "the Allied deterrent" [12] had become in the Defense White Paper of 1957 "nuclear deterrent power of . . . [Britain's] own." [13] Finally, in their discussion of the strategy announced in the white paper, government spokesmen implied that the strategic nuclear force would be employed as a first-strike force, rather than limited to retaliation in the event of an attack on Britain itself.

The white paper's emphasis on nuclear strategy, the overtones of unilateral action, and the stress on Britain's independent force—all had obvious symbolic and prestige implications. The basic objective of the policy was obscured, as was recognition that at that time the strategic force was in all probability too small for independent use. The policy was designed to achieve a measure of control over American use of Strategic Air Command by casting the British force in a "trigger" role.[14] Although similar to the "massive retaliation" doctrine enunciated by Secretary of State Dulles and therefore vulnerable to the same charges of inadequacy, such a policy maximized British influence on American military decisions. British political leaders needed to be ambiguous about the circumstances in which the strategy was applicable: precision would have revealed the policy's weaknesses as strategic doctrine and thereby undermined its prestige and symbolic implications.

THE COMMONWEALTH

The second element in Britain's position as a great power is its position as the leader of the Commonwealth. Through the economic, political, and symbolic institutions which constitute this relationship, Britain has been able to exercise extensive political influence in the emerging areas of the world, especially in Africa and South Asia. Commonwealth leadership is highly valued because it is a peculiarly British responsibility, not shared with other nations. It is important, too. In the British view political stability and military security in Africa and the areas adjacent to the Indian Ocean cannot reasonably be ignored by the West in the cold war. The Commonwealth thus symbolizes an independent and prestigious non-European leadership position.

The system of strategic bases was historically at the heart of the Commonwealth's security arrangement. Facilitating control of the major sea routes, bases provided for the rapid deployment and supply of British military and naval forces; bases were also symbolic of the international role associated with Commonwealth leadership. This was particularly true of Suez: "It is the Clapham Junction of Commonwealth communications, and the keystone of the architecture of Imperial defence," Julian Amery once claimed. "If we pull out of Suez we cut ourselves off from the greater half of the Commonwealth and we abandon our friends in it to face the Soviets alone or to become dependents of the United States." [15] With the loss of Suez and numerous other bases, those remaining—Hong Kong, Singapore, Aden, Cyprus, Malta, Gibraltar—are considered the irreducible minimum which will permit British forces to operate in the overseas areas. For many in the decision-making elite, to withdraw from the remaining bases or to reduce British forces in the overseas areas is to abdicate responsibility and to forfeit an opportunity to exercise influence in these critically important areas. These sentiments have been, of course, most evident in the Conservative party, especially among its older and more influential elements. The depth of that attachment was demonstrated by the acerbity and tensions within the party both after the 1954 withdrawal of the military garrison from the base in Suez and following the Suez intervention in 1956. Similar feelings, strengthened by years of service abroad and the close co-operation among Commonwealth countries in military affairs, are also evident among military groups, particularly senior officers. As one retired senior officer put it, "No bases, no strategy." [16]

As its contribution to the joint Commonwealth security arrangements, Britain provides conventional forces, including ground units trained in police and internal-security operations, and naval and air contingents adept in showing the flag. The alternative use for forces of this type is in NATO. These two commitments thus compete for resources, especially the

limited supply of army manpower: an allocation to one inevitably influences the forces which can be made available in
the other. The NATO commitment, however, has none of the
domestic prestige implications of the Commonwealth obligation. In fact, a larger contribution to NATO tends to signify
an increased European role, the antithesis of the independent
leadership position assumed by Britain's Commonwealth relationship and overseas strategy.

The significance of Commonwealth leadership in domestic
politics has decreased in recent years, mainly because the
ranks of the political and military hierarchies are increasingly
filled with younger men whose attachment to the Commonwealth is less than that of their elders.[17] Yet, despite the reduced prestige and symbolic implications of the Commonwealth, the military commitment in the overseas areas has
probably grown in importance. One reason is that a fairly
large number of political and military leaders question the
desirability of maintaining a strategic nuclear force. The force
which the United Kingdom can afford, it is argued, is too small
to be militarily significant; to the extent that the British force
serves a deterrent function, it duplicates an already adequate
American capability. Thus, the independent British strategic
nuclear force does not, in this view, have the positive value
claimed for it in Anglo-American or Commonwealth relations.
Instead, the argument continues, the resources now being devoted to Bomber Command and the Polaris submarine force
should be diverted to conventional forces.[18] An increase in conventional capability would insure that Britain could continue
to play its present part in the overseas areas. It might also
enable the United Kingdom to strengthen its contribution to
NATO—a move which would be valued highly by the United
States. In other words more adequate conventional forces,
which some observers believe would be possible if there were
no strategic nuclear force, would increase Britain's prestige
all around—in the Commonwealth, on the Continent, and with
the United States.

MANPOWER AND DOMESTIC POLITICS

The influence of domestic economic and political considerations on defense policies may also be illustrated by a discussion of military manpower problems. In this instance defense objectives were modified because they conflicted with domestic economic and political goals. The issue in question—the decision in 1957 to end National Service in 1960—was one of crucial importance for British security policies.

The Attlee government decided in 1947 to continue the system of conscription initiated in 1938 and used throughout World War II. Peacetime National Service was initially justified by the need to maintain large, trained, manpower reserves. By 1949, however, conscripts constituted a large part of total service manpower, including a sizeable share of the personnel in operational units. Throughout the early years of the 1950's National Service continued to be a major source of service manpower—about half in the army, one-third in the air force, and one-tenth in the navy. The importance of National Service was actually greater because the very high probability of required service acted as an incentive and spurred voluntary enlistment in the forces.

Peacetime National Service was widely recognized as necessary; it was nevertheless unpopular. When the program was initially proposed in 1947, it drew strong opposition, including a back-bench revolt which the Labor government quelled only by reducing the period of service to one year. Although open opposition decreased when the cold war intensified in 1948, the basic dislike of National Service among political leaders remained. Evidence of this position is provided by the extensive political support given government proposals for military pay increases. Service pay was increased five times between 1950 and 1960. In each instance it was expected that the greater financial attractiveness of military service would improve the flow of volunteers into the forces. Perhaps the most that can be claimed for these increases, however, is that after

1957 pay was not a disincentive to voluntary enlistment.[19]

There were numerous reasons for the unpopularity of conscription, but both opponents and proponents shared the belief that National Service was an uneconomical method of securing manpower for the military services. In the first place, conscription was wasteful. The constant influx of new, untrained conscripts necessitated the maintenance of a large training establishment. If conscription could be ended, it would be possible to shift personnel in training centers to other duties, thereby reducing the over-all size of the forces. Second, an end to National Service would cut the number of men in the "pipeline"—the troops in transit between assignments—because the movement of personnel to and from overseas stations, no longer dictated by the two-year period of service, would be less frequent. Finally, it was generally accepted that National Service was the major deterrent to long-term voluntary enlistment. If the number of conscripts in operational units could be reduced, it was expected that service morale, particularly in the army, would undergo a corresponding improvement. Higher morale, in turn, would lead to an increased flow of enlistees into the forces.[20]

The service departments were also dissatisfied with National Service. The two years that conscripts served were too short for successful training in many of the specialized skills required of modern military organizations. All the uniformed services had a strong tradition of all-regular forces, and most senior officers desired to return to volunteer forces as quickly as possible. By the mid-1950's the number of volunteers entering the navy was nearly sufficient for its requirements. Recruiting for the Royal Air Force had also improved; only in the army did the problem remain acute. The War Office, nevertheless, was not strongly opposed to ending National Service. A reduction in army manpower was then under consideration; if it was assumed that the pay increases due in 1956 would lead to improved regular recruiting, it was reasonable to believe that reduced army manpower needs could be met.[21]

With the easing of East-West tensions after the Korean War, the dissatisfaction of political leaders with National Service again became apparent. Even before the 1955 general election, in which the Labor party proposed a reduction in the period of service, the need for conscription was questioned by politicians from both parties.[22] But it was difficult to obtain reasoned discussion of the issue. The government did not wish to initiate a debate on a policy which it believed was unpopular. The Opposition's dilemma was that if it proposed an end to conscription, it was vulnerable to charges of irresponsibility; if it did not, it would lose to the government the electoral advantage which most politicians believed would fall to the party responsible for ending National Service.

The growing dissatisfaction with National Service in 1955 coincided with one of Britain's recurrent economic crises. According to Prime Minister Eden, the problems that year stemmed from "prosperity." [23] Prices were rising and manpower was in short supply—the unemployment rate was at its postwar low of less than 1 per cent. Total demand was also very heavy: the level of domestic investment was one-sixth above that of 1954; annual defense-production expenditures amounted to £550-600 million, the highest rate since World War II; and consumption expenditures were larger than ever before. As consumption and investment drew goods from the export markets and as imports increased in response to the record level of output and the need to replace stock depleted in 1954, the balance of payments position deteriorated.[24] To meet the crisis, the government in midsummer instituted a series of corrective measures. These included a "credit squeeze," an increase in certain construction-loan rates, and, in October, a special budget.[25]

As an additional palliative, to ease the pressure on the labor force, a reduction in military manpower was decided upon.[26] Sir Anthony Eden announced the cuts in service force levels at the Conservative Party Conference in early October. Forces were to be reduced during the following two and one-half years by one hundred thousand, a not unreasonable reduction in view of the 1954 agreement with Egypt to evacuate the Suez Canal Zone, which allowed the redeployment of about eighty thousand troops.

One year later, in July, 1956, the Eden government ordered a further review of defense policy:

> The Minister of Defence, Mr. Selwyn Lloyd, reported to me in July [1955] that unless existing programmes were revised the cost of defence would rise during the next four years from £1527 million to £1929 million in 1959. The economy of the country could not be expected to stand this mounting strain. We had to call a halt in defence expenditure and hold it over a period of years.[27]

This review also "created an opportunity to reduce the strength of the armed forces," [28] and it was decided to lower force levels to 445,000 by 1960, a total cut of 225,000. The largest reductions were to take place in the army and air force. Civilian labor was to substitute as far as possible for uniformed personnel in supply and service units so that these economies could be realized "without sacrificing the power to strike back at any aggressor." [29]

One of the consequences of the 1955 and 1956 reductions in service force levels was to increase dissatisfaction with conscription. In the administration of National Service few exemptions were granted, and virtually every qualified male entered the forces. As long as manpower levies remained about the same as the number of men becoming eligible for service each year, the system created few problems. But after the 1955–56 force reductions the number of conscripts available exceeded the needs of the military departments. Conscription rolls thus increased in length; conscripts, called into the forces by their date of registration, entered service at an older age. The period between school-leaving and commencement of service was therefore lengthened—with an increasingly disruptive effect on individual plans for schooling and jobs. In short, with smaller forces the system of National Service was more and more ill suited for Britain's military manpower needs. For most political leaders, however, there was no alternative to conscription except voluntary enlistment. Compulsory military service was considered an onerous, burdensome duty, an obligation which had to be shared equally by all citizens. Although a selective-service system similar to the one in the United States was occasionally proposed, the deeply ingrained attitude of "fair shares" made it impossible to adopt procedures which would select a few for service from among the many eligible and qualified for this duty.

The force reduction of 1956 was interrupted by the Suez intervention in October, 1956, when about thirty thousand reserves were mobilized. In the aftermath of Suez, during the uncertain early days of the Macmillan government, the decision was made to end National Service and to rely exclusively on all-volunteer forces. The policy was conditional, and the government promised to continue conscription if the army did not recruit at least 165,000 regulars by 1960.[30] Politically, the government stood to benefit, because National Service was unpopular both with politicians and the general public. The military consequences were to reduce Britain's conventional forces by about eighty thousand men. Since a large part of the reduction occurred in the army, the loss of ground-combat strength was particularly severe. The commitments most seriously affected were NATO and the overseas areas, because military capabilities in these areas are directly related to force levels.

The loss of conventional war capability was not viewed as a serious problem by the Macmillan government, however: it believed that strategic nuclear weapons would more than compensate for the reduction. Indeed, the end of National Service provided an additional justification for an independent strategic nuclear force. The alternatives the government posed to Parliament in the 1957 defense debates were as follows: " . . . If we refuse to rely on the deterrent, we cannot at the same time urge the abolition of National Service." Mr. Iain

Macleod, the minister of labor and national service continued by noting: "We cannot urge the abolition of National Service unless we are prepared either to rely for our protection for all time and in all circumstances upon a foreign but friendly country or are prepared to take the grim decision to make the bomb. . . . "[31] For Mr. Macmillan it was a choice between the same alternatives: " . . . The end of conscription must depend upon the acceptance of nuclear weapons."[32]

The decision to end conscription constitutes one of the most crucial policy choices since 1945. The shift to all-regular forces culminated a series of sharp reductions in service manpower. More importantly, force levels now depend on voluntary recruitment, a somewhat uncertain source of manpower, or a return to conscription, an alternative which would be difficult for any government to order. With conventional forces valued more highly than in 1957, voluntary recruitment imposes a severe limitation on the size of the British Army. The *advantages* of this decision should not be ignored, however. Manpower reductions brought in turn a reassessment and reconsideration of both Britain's objectives and the ways in which military forces could contribute to these goals. That less should be attempted in the 1960's than in the 1950's and that the 430,000 men currently in the services provided more balanced forces than the 800,000 did in mid-1955 seems clear beyond dispute. Even those critics who argue that Britain's conventional capability must now be increased have implicitly accepted the decision: they would settle for an increase of 10,000 to 15,000 men in the army's strength.

1. See A. J. Youngson, *The British Economy, 1920–1957* (Cambridge: Harvard University Press, 1960), pp. 158–74.

2. *Listener*, January 22, 1959, p. 156.

3. 537 H. C. Deb. 1905.

4. Anthony Eden, *Full Circle: The Memoirs of Anthony Eden* (Boston: Houghton Mifflin, 1960), p. 412.

5. *Ibid.*, p. 139.

6. Cited in 583 H. C. Deb. 635.

7. 618 H. C. Deb. 1136–37. There has been wide acceptance of the idea that it is desirable, even imperative, that Britain influence American decisions. This was based initially on the assumption that it was necessary to avoid a rash or precipitous American act, especially the use of nuclear weapons. (The late President Kennedy, for example, was highly regarded because of the firmness and restraint he demonstrated in the Cuban crisis of 1962.) This reason has more recently been joined by another—the fear that the United States will not use nuclear weapons in Europe's defense. An interesting comment on the ability of British leaders to influence American choices is contained in R. H. S. Crossman, "The Truman Doctrine," *The Charm of Politics* (London: Hamish Hamilton, 1958), pp. 20–25.

8. *Listener*, February 11, 1954, p. 244.

9. *Ibid.*, June 24, 1954, p. 1081.

10. *The Times*, November 14, 1958. The Campaign for Nuclear Disarmament accepts the assumption that Britain needs to enhance its status as a great power. One of the CND's main reasons for renouncing nuclear weapons is that it would permit Britain to "give a moral lead," and thereby assume a more important and prestigious international role.

11. 568 H. C. Deb. 1777, and Denis Healey, "Britain and NATO," in Klaus Knorr (ed.), *NATO and American Security* (Princeton: Princeton University Press, 1959), pp. 221–22.

12. Cmd. 9691, "Statement on Defence 1956," p. 4. (Italics mine.)

13. Cmd. 124, "Defense: Outline of Future Policy," p. 3.

14. Healey, "Britain and NATO," pp. 224–25.

15. 512 H. C. Deb. 648.

16. Interview.

17. S. E. Finer *et al.*, *Backbench Opinion in the House of Commons, 1955–1959* (New York: Pergamon, 1961), pp. 76–121, 191.

18. The major difficulty with this argument is that few of the resources now being devoted to the strategic nuclear force could be transferred to conventional forces. The main limitation on conventional forces is manpower—not money. An increase in the strength of the British Army would seem to require a return to conscription. Few observers believe this is likely.

19. See, for example, the comments by Nigel Birch, 524 H. C. Deb. 1023–24, and by Lord Monckton, 549 H. C. Deb. 1020–21.

20. The best general survey of the manpower problem is contained in Cmd. 545, "Report of the Advisory Committee on Recruiting." On conscription see Cmd. 9608, "National Service." Manpower policies are also discussed in M. R. D. Foot, *Men in Uniform: Military Manpower in Modern Industrial Societies* (New York: Praeger, 1961), pp. 129–49.

21. Manpower levels were then under review by the Hull Committee, noted in Chapter VIII (p. 157). This committee recommended that the army be reduced to about two hundred twenty thousand men. Army manpower in 1956 amounted to about four hundred thousand.

22. For example, the motion introduced by the Opposition in the 1954 defense debates read, in part: " . . . The Government . . . has made no proposals for a reduction in the length of National Service" (524 H. C. Deb. 1048).

23. Eden, *Full Circle*, pp. 347–65.

24. Central Statistical Office, *Annual Abstract of Statistics*, No. 93 (London: H. M. Stationery Office, 1956), p. 103.

25. Eden, *Full Circle*, pp. 351–52, and National Institute of Economic and Social Research, "Chronological Tables," *Economic Review*, No. 10 (1960), pp. 40–45.

26. Eden, *Full Circle*, p. 350.

27. *Ibid.*, p. 414.

28. *Ibid.*, p. 417.

29. *Ibid.*, p. 414.

30. See Chapter II, p. 41 n.

31. 568 H. C. Deb. 1958.

32. *Ibid.*, 2040.

12/ Conclusions

HISTORICALLY, British defense policy was designed to protect the home islands against an attack from the European mainland and to maintain security, stability, and British domination in the overseas colonial areas. Naval forces were the principal instrument utilized in achieving these objectives—from the time of the Spanish Armada until the beginning of the twentieth century, Britain's superiority on the high seas was nearly absolute. Naval control of the ocean moat separating the United Kingdom from Europe was conceived as the main barrier against an invasion from the Continent. In conjunction with Britain's numerous overseas bases, naval squadrons were employed both to control the sea routes linking the United Kingdom and its overseas possessions and to protect merchant shipping moving supplies into British ports. The missions falling to the army were less precisely defined. Its responsibility in the event of a war in Europe, at least after 1911, was to be prepared to intervene on the Continent to preserve the European balance of power; in the overseas areas the army garrisoned the strategic bases and provided cadres for native troops which maintained security within the colonial areas.

The maritime-intervention strategy which dominated British security policies until World War II has been replaced since 1945 by what may best be described as an alliance-deterrence strategy. Security in the overseas areas now depends on army garrisons in the few remaining strategic bases, on the Royal Navy's carrier task forces and Commando units, and on a small air-lifted strategic reserve. Defense of Britain itself is an integral part of the security of western Europe and rests on the military and political strength of the North Atlantic Treaty Organization. To NATO the United Kingdom allocates much of its operational air and naval forces; British Army of the Rhine, its principal military contribution to the Alliance, is the first army unit stationed on the Continent during peacetime since the Napoleonic Wars. Finally, the United Kingdom has built and continues to maintain a force of manned bombers equipped with hydrogen weapons. With the exception of the Commando, these adaptations in defense policy were initiated prior to 1954.

The current alliance-deterrence strategy has proven substantially more expensive than the traditional maritime posture. Except for the period of the World War I, annual defense costs between 1890 and 1938 averaged about 3 per cent of the Gross National Product. The current defense budget amounts to slightly over 7 per cent of the GNP; during the Korean War, when the postwar rearmament program was initiated, expenditures exceeded 12 per cent of GNP—four times the average prewar outlay for defense. Despite a steady reduction in military manpower levels since 1953, the current strength of the forces is about 430,000, some 100,000 more than the average between 1920 and 1938. With the end of peacetime conscription in 1960, the services returned to the traditional pattern of all-volunteer forces.

The increase in the magnitude of the defense effort notwithstanding, Britain's military forces have been seriously overcommitted in recent years: obligations have exceeded the readily available military capabilities. The government's improvisations, as during the Berlin crisis of late 1961, attest the validity of the charge. Fortunately, the consequences have not been serious, since situations requiring the operational use of military forces have not often occurred simultaneously.[1]

The problem of overcommitment is exacerbated by the development of forces which provide some sort of military response at every possible level of conflict. The strategic nuclear force, whose annual cost is generally estimated to be between 10 and 15 per cent of the defense budget, has made no direct contribution to the resolution of those conflicts in which the United Kingdom has been involved. Similarly, the value of this force as a deterrent is questionable, overshadowed as it is by the larger and more technologically advanced American strategic force. Maintaining a strategic nuclear capability necessarily reduces the resources which can be devoted to forces capable of lower levels of response. The wide variety of equipment employed by forces capable of responding to every level of conflict also demands a correspondingly broad research and development effort. This spreading of limited resources makes it difficult to obtain the economies associated with large scale production. With declining force levels the services now require an even smaller number of any given item of equipment, which further intensifies the problem of scale in research, development, and production.

Two possible solutions to the problems of overcommitment and dispersion of effort are: to increase the size of the defense effort, or to reduce Britain's over-all security obligations. There are understandable difficulties in each. The cost of an increase in the size of the defense effort can be expressed in terms of sacrificed domestic goals—less education, fewer roads, higher taxes, or lower levels of social-welfare expenditures. To cut commitments is equally difficult. If forces are withdrawn from the overseas areas Britain's Commonwealth ties will be weakened. A smaller contribution to NATO would constitute an additional strain in the Atlantic Alliance, undermine Britain's special relationship with the United States, and further diminish London's influence on the Continent. Either action could be interpreted as an admission that Britain can no longer maintain its present role in the affairs of the world.

The question of overcommitment is closely involved with another crucial issue—the security of Britain and western Europe. The principal questions are: (1) Should Britain continue to maintain an independent strategic nuclear force? (2) If so, what plans should be made for the use of this force? (3) How large a conventional contribution should the United Kingdom make to NATO?

There is general agreement on the basic military situation in western Europe. The Soviet Union's nuclear strength is estimated at 800 to 900 missiles (mainly medium-range ballistic missiles) and approximately 1000 medium and 200 heavy bomber aircraft. The nuclear war capability of the Western Alliance is substantially greater, consisting of over 1,000 intercontinental ballistic missiles and some 1,500 to 2,000 aircraft, about equally divided between medium and heavy bombers.[2] With the exception of the United Kingdom's force of some 180 V-bombers, however, Western retaliatory strength is composed solely of American forces. The probability that the Soviets would employ their strategic nuclear forces in Europe is regarded as minute—U.S. Strategic Air Command is viewed as an adequate deterrent against such an attack, although some Britons and Europeans hold that the American promise of retaliatory action is unreliable.

The Warsaw Pact's conventional capabilities pose a more complex problem. It possesses larger and better deployed ground forces than those of the Western Alliance, even though recent increases in troop strength have greatly improved NATO's defensive position.[3] One possibility that arises from this imbalance in conventional forces is a massive assault spearheaded by Soviet forces. While the likelihood of such an action is undoubtedly low, its potential for damage is enormous and the contingency demands careful attention. A more probable danger lies in unpremeditated conflict developing from a crisis in Berlin, an incident along the East-West border, or an uprising in eastern Europe. If such an encounter spread rapidly in scope, NATO would face the same dilemma posed by a massive conventional attack—its shortcomings in conventional forces would necessitate the difficult choice between losing much of central Europe or employing nuclear weapons.

Very broadly, there are two approaches to the question of Britain's role in the defense of western Europe. The main point in the critics' position is that the United Kingdom's strategic nuclear force is not necessary. Because of its size and growing obsolescense, the V-bomber force is not a credible deterrent. Bomber Command is also, unlike U.S. Strategic Air Command, highly vulnerable to Soviet attack. It therefore constitutes a provocation. For these reasons the resources devoted to Britain's independent deterrent should be reallocated to conventional forces—an action which would enhance the U.K.'s ability to conduct conventional operations both in the overseas areas and in NATO. The same argument applies to the decision to replace the aging bomber force with a fleet of five Polaris missile submarines. The large capital outlay for this force, still to come, would be better spent on conventional forces. In addition, the secondary consequences of a third national nuclear force are undesirable: it destroys the strategic balance between American and Soviet forces; it encourages other nations to build their own national nuclear forces; and it increases the difficulties in establishing arms-control agreements in western Europe. Finally, critics point out that by the end of the decade the United Kingdom's independent nuclear force will not be independent at all but subject to control by an ally, since Britain will depend on the United States for the supply of one of the principal components (Polaris missiles) of the weapons system. When coupled with the assumption that the United States will employ its nuclear forces in response to an attack on western Europe, critics conclude that an independent nuclear force has little value. Even if an American response to a Soviet attack is not assured, a NATO or European nuclear force would provide a more suitable deterrent than an independent British force.[4]

The second aspect of current defense policy which the critics would change concerns NATO's conventional capabilities. It is argued that NATO's conventional forces must be strengthened if the alliance is to be able to contain a large-scale Soviet conventional attack without resorting to nuclear weapons. An increase in conventional capabilities would reduce the need to use nuclear weapons and thereby improve the chances of avoiding a thermonuclear war. The United Kingdom can do its share by increasing the size and operational readiness of British Army of the Rhine—and it is believed that an initiative in this direction would be a powerful incentive to similar action by other NATO members.

Finally, the government's plans for the use of the strategic nuclear force are criticized, since it is believed that they tend to increase, rather than limit, the chances of an all-out war. If, as the government proposes, the strategic nuclear force were used against virtually any conventional attack, the Soviets would most likely reply in kind, probably with large-scale nuclear attack. If NATO possessed adequate conventional forces, the alliance would be able to respond in kind over a range of contingencies. Forestalling the use of nuclear weapons, even for a matter of hours, might provide the margin of time needed to resolve the issue by other means.

The government accepts the same basic definition of the military situation in Europe; its solution, however, contrasts sharply with that of the critics.[5] This difference approaches that between defense and deterrence: the critics wish to be able to defend Europe against a range of possible attacks; the government seeks to avoid an attack. A Soviet attack, official strategists contend, is very apt to bring on a full-scale conflict in western Europe: even a small non-nuclear attack would

expand rapidly into a large-scale war. There would be little
over-all difference, at least to Europeans, between a full-scale
conventional war and a nuclear exchange; therefore, any
Soviet attack must be met by a nuclear response. Making this
explicit, the government asserts, further reduces the possibility of a deliberate attack. Additional justification for this
policy—and the independent nuclear force—is provided by the
belief that the American guarantee to defend Europe is uncertain—will the United States risk destruction of its cities to
reply to a Soviet attack on European capitals? As a corollary,
some prominent official strategists believe that large conventional forces weaken the credibility of the threat of a nuclear
response. Finally, the government maintains that existing
NATO forces are sufficient to insure against the more probable
contingencies—border incursions or other provocative actions
by the Warsaw Pact nations.

The merits of these conflicting positions on Britain's role in
western European defense have been argued for several years.
Both positions are complicated by the question of political
relations between Europe and the United States. If western
Europe evolves in the direction desired by General de Gaulle,
the U.K.'s diplomatic position will become very difficult: it will
be separated from the United States by vast distance and
from Europe by sharply different ideas on the nature of the
Atlantic Community. In this event a national nuclear force
(and the related scientific and technical capabilities) might
have considerable value as a bargaining device to facilitate
Britain's diplomatic relations with a unified Europe. But if
Europe and the United States evolve into a relatively cohesive
Atlantic Community, the "grand design" envisaged by the
late President Kennedy, the case for Britain's independent
strategic nuclear force is not especially strong. The critical
issue in this situation is not whether to give up nuclear
weapons, but the equally difficult question of how to accomplish
this task in a way which appears credible to other nations.[6]

Those who advocate forces capable of responding to a range

of communist provocations in western Europe buttress their case by the concept of "interdependence." They point out that security problems transcend national boundaries and that defense now hinges on the joint efforts of several countries. This is clearly the case, and in virtually every respect—at home or overseas—the attainment of Britain's security objectives depends to some extent on the forces of other countries. Since interdependence may thus be said to exist in fact, national policies should recognize it. Specifically, a greater degree of co-operation and sharing is in order. There are two possible approaches: each partner can concentrate on the production and supply of selected items of equipment utilized by all; or each partner can assume a specialized and limited part of the over-all security mission. The objective in either case is to achieve the economies which accompany specialization.

Although a condition of interdependence may exist, the willingness of a nation to shape policies which recognize this fact varies greatly. Differences in the size of national-resource bases generate varying degrees of acceptance for sharing and specialization. The economies of scale are already available to the larger partner, and the advantages it obtains from sharing are often negligible. It is therefore less willing to accept policies which recognize interdependence than are its smaller partners, to whom the benefits are correspondingly greater.

Several special difficulties lie in the path to interdependence by means of equipment standardization. Standardization requires broad international agreement on the specific design characteristics of military equipment. The almost complete failure of NATO standardization groups to agree, even on items as simple as infantry rifles, suggests the difficulties involved. Nor do the problems end with an accord on specifications. Standardization involves foreign exchange flows and the balance of payments position, and it is difficult, if not impossible, to distribute contracts in such a way as to balance the benefits and costs to any single country. Finally, defense production contracts are of special concern in the domestic politics of most countries. The assumptions that each nation should be self-sufficient in the production of defense equipment and that national products are of superior quality provide powerful arguments to those economic interests which benefit from defense spending. These reasons, plus the relatively few direct benefits that the American services receive from equipment standardization, are normally cited by British officials to explain what they consider the great reluctance of the U.S. Department of Defense to co-operate in joint equipment ventures.[7]

There are numerous examples of the second approach, a division of the over-all security mission among allies, by which defense policies may reflect a condition of interdependence. Security tasks are divided by geographic areas; for example, Britain has responsibility for the area East Africa–Malaya, while the United States accepts responsibility for Southeast Asia and the western Pacific. Division on a functional basis also exists, with the United States providing tactical and strategic nuclear weapons for Europe's defense. But critics would extend this functional division—those who believe that Britain should not maintain an independent strategic nuclear force are a case in point. The barriers to relying on an ally to perform some part of the security mission are numerous, however. Military policies are dualistically interdependent—with the policies of one's allies, but also with domestic political and economic policies. While the United Kingdom's strategic nuclear force is but a minor part of the alliance's strategic forces, it has major implications for Britain's domestic politics: Bomber Command is a symbol of the country's great power status, and the possession of a national nuclear capability is widely regarded as a relevant instrument for the conduct of foreign relations. Finally, in the absence of political integration in the Atlantic Community, a functional division of the security mission raises the question of political control. In the case of nuclear-equipped forces, the obstacles are particularly serious. Indeed, the government's lack of enthusiasm for the Mixed-Manned Nuclear Force proposed by the U.S. is based partially on the inadequacy of the methods of political and military control.

The differences on substantive issues between the government and its critics have been widened by a number of recent policy debacles. These include military failures during the Suez intervention and the cancellation of the Blue Streak and Blue Water missile systems. Sharp differences on policy, in turn, have served to stimulate criticism of the ways in which security policies are formulated. Much of this criticism concentrates on interservice rivalry and bargaining. These phenomena are viewed as symptoms of inadequate control by political leaders and the cause of duplication and waste in the defense establishment. Interservice politics are also held responsible by some observers for what is considered a slow and inadequate adjustment to a rapidly changing strategic situation. The implication of much of this criticism is that proper arrangement of the machinery of government would result in appropriate policies.

Despite a preoccupation with institutional arrangements, some observers have tended to ignore the important organizational changes which have taken place in recent years. It is useful in this regard to compare British and American practices, particularly since several of the procedures recently initiated in the U.S. Department of Defense have captured the imagination of commentators in Britain. One major innovation, the five-year force plan, was adopted in the United States in 1962. Under this system defense spending is projected over a five-year period. A similar procedure, the five-year forecast budget, was instituted in Britain in 1958. In the United States the five-year force plan was largely the product of the RAND Corporation; the procedures adopted in Britain were devised "in-house," the product of civil servants. Improved financial management methods, the system of program control, were initiated shortly after the forecast budget was adopted. Similar arrangements were not established in the Department of Defense until 1962.[8]

British observers have also encouraged the government to adopt other procedures utilized by the U.S. Department of Defense. One concerns the use of civilian consultants, a valuable suggestion which the Ministry of Defense has accepted in principal but done little to implement. The ministry's reluctance is understandable. The use of consultants is not extensive elsewhere in British government. Also, British political practices make it difficult to obtain one of the major benefits associated with consultants and research institutions in the United States—creating a body of skilled, informed analysts who can be appointed to political office. Finally, the absence of extensive commentary by observers outside the government suggests that qualified consultants might be hard to obtain, and officials question whether meaningful assistance could be obtained in this way. Most officials contend that policy decisions would be improved more, and more quickly, if the relatively small civil and military staffs in the defense departments were increased in size.

A second procedure urged on the government is the use of "cost-effectiveness" analyses. Although studies of this type have been part of the weapons-selection process for a number of years, the cancellation of major weapons systems—Blue Streak is an example—is normally cited as evidence of the need for this form of analysis. While the decision to develop Blue Streak may well have benefitted from additional analysis, some of the difficulties the project encountered may reasonably be ascribed to the characteristic uncertainty of weapons development.[9] Uncertainty of three kinds plagued Blue Streak: actual costs outran original estimates; engineering problems were slower in resolution than expected; and a similar but cheaper weapons system (Skybolt) became available from the United States. The Blue Streak cancellation, in short, illustrates the limitations of analysis: cost-effectiveness studies at best display, rather than resolve, the uncertainties which are inherent in all defense policy decisions.

It is perhaps unfortunate, but it is nevertheless true, that the problems facing defense policy-makers cannot be solved by proposals as easily arranged as organizational changes: the issues are more complex. Some of the difficulties, including those characteristics of the policy process most criticized by observers, could be eliminated if the example of the Kennedy administration were followed. An increase in the defense budget of about 20 per cent would quickly dissolve most of the tensions among the services; in addition, many of the present inadequacies of Britain's military forces could be corrected. Even then, however, one source of muddle would remain. All defense planning is troubled by uncertainty: uncertainty over the actions of the enemy and of one's allies, uncertainty stemming from the defense-equipment requirement for the most advanced techniques and methods of science and technology, uncertainty in estimating the costs and development time of new weapons,[10] and uncertainty resulting from the need to plan a decade or more into the future. In the case of British military policies, there is an additional source: What future international role should Britain attempt to play?

Security policies pose unusual difficulties because they are interdependent with both domestic and foreign policies and because they present an extraordinary array of uncertainties. For this reason controversy over policy choices is normal— in fact, highly desirable. A coherent debate between policy-makers and critics outside the government is a valuable part of this process. In Britain, unfortunately, that dialogue is weak and sporadic. Much of the commentary on defense problems concerns process rather than substantive issues of policy: it is much easier to question the quality of the civil service or to deplore interservice rivalries than to analyze the complex substantive issues of defense policy. Criticism of the policy process, moreover, inhibits responsible officials in their attempts to resolve the issues. By penalizing disagreement and providing a disincentive to the development of alternative solutions to very complex problems, criticism contributes to a deterioration in the quality of policy.

In the absence of extensive commentary on the substantive issues of policy by intellectuals and leaders of the political opposition, it is all the more important that disagreement take place within the government. Organizational arrangements must be designed to this end. Separatism and divisions within the defense establishment promote disagreement and the development of alternatives; centralization and the avoidance of disagreement, qualities held desirable by most observers, paper over issues and inhibit the presentation of different solutions to problems. The other consequences of separatism within the defense establishment are also valuable. Separatism improves policy flexibility. It ties loyalties away from the organizations responsible for operational functions—and thereby facilitates internal change and adjustment.

Britain's relatively decentralized defense policy-making structure may also claim some modest successes in terms of effective and successful security policies. This judgment is supported by Britain's numerous contributions to free world security. The United Kingdom's over-all effort, defense spending as a percentage of the national product, has been exceeded only by the United States and matched only by France. British forces have made a substantial contribution to peace and security in parts of the Mediterranean and Middle East, much of Africa, and the area between Aden and Singapore. Military power has been an effective instrument of British and Western statecraft within these areas. The successes include the defeat of communist guerrillas in Malaya and similar, though smaller scale, operations against insurgents in Kenya and Cyprus.

The United Kingdom is, and has been, one of the mainstays of the North Atlantic Treaty Organization. Although the size of Britain's conventional contribution to NATO is widely regarded as inadequate, British Army of the Rhine is nevertheless one of the larger and better equipped national forces in Allied Forces Central Europe. That BAOR is larger than the government feels is necessary points to another attribute of British policy: its responsiveness to the needs of the various alliances to which the country belongs, as opposed to the more narrowly nationalistic policies that might be pursued.

The rapidity of change in security policies provides further justification for decentralized organization. From a maritime-intervention strategy at the end of World War II the United Kingdom has moved to an alliance-deterrence strategy. The shift has been accomplished quickly; with the important exception of the Suez intervention, the process of adjustment has been marked by a reasonably close parallel between prevailing notions regarding the role Britain should play in international politics and military policies which support this role. This achievement is significant, since the factors leading to policy adjustment have been different. Defense, because of its extensive demands for domestic resources, has tended to adjust to scarcity of men and money. Conceptions of the nation's international role have been under less severe or immediate pressure. The possibility has therefore existed, and of course still remains, that a gap might develop between aspirations and resources. But in contrast to France, where a similar problem contributed to the fall of the Fourth Republic, defense policies have not been a source of domestic difficulties. The armed forces have been a highly reliable instrument of national policy; such radicalism as has appeared has been concentrated in the Campaign for Nuclear Disarmament, a mass movement whose strength has not increased since 1958.

The gap between commitments and forces in being and the limited flexibility which the government's strategy allows in Europe are serious shortcomings. These deficiencies exist, however, because military policies conflict with other national goals. Quite aside from its military implications, there are persuasive reasons for keeping an independent strategic nuclear force. It has prestige implications, domestically and internationally; to maintain such a force is to recognize that, in the absence of political integration, control of a supranational force presents serious difficulties; and a national nuclear capability may have considerable utility in Britain's future relations with the Continent. At the same time, the economic and political pressures for smaller conventional forces also have been very great. The numerous direct and secondary advantages of large military deployments in the overseas areas, even at the expense of Britain's NATO commitment, are of benefit to the West and have broad appeal in the United Kingdom. The size and disposition of British forces, in short, admit the real world, with its conflicting objectives and limited resources.

Security policies, in brief, exhibit the qualities associated with all public policies in the United Kingdom: they rest on a broad consensus, evolve slowly but constantly, and involve a compromise among many conflicting objectives. The strengths of these defense policies can be attributed to the manner of policy-making in Britain's parliamentary democracy—the process of "muddling through." Friction and competition among relatively independent organizational components stimulate change. The desire for service autonomy leads to the development of alternative solutions and thus enhances the quality of policy. Extreme variation is moderated to produce viable policies which rest on the support of the many individuals responsible for policy-planning and execution. If policy planners could accurately forecast the future, a highly centralized policy organization might then be in order. But defense policies are plagued by uncertainties; the difficulties are compounded by the doubts surrounding Britain's future. A broad spectrum of military capabilities, several organizational structures, and a tradition of evolutionary change seem peculiarly well adapted to these circumstances. All increase Britain's ability to respond to a rapidly changing security environment. All insure against premature choices which, because of Britain's changing international role, might prove impossible to rectify.

1. Civil unrest in Cyprus and East Africa and the threat of action by Indonesia against Malaysia strained British forces severely in late 1963 and early 1964.

2. See Institute for Strategic Studies, "The Military Balance 1963–1964," (London, 1963), pp. 3–4, 11–12.

3. *Ibid.*, pp. 4–5, 7–9, 14–24.

4. A related problem is Britain's policy on the MLF—the mixed-manned nuclear force proposed by the U.S. The United Kingdom has agreed to participate in a mixed-manned experiment involving one vessel, largely at the insistence of the present prime minister, Sir Alec Douglas-Home. The Labor party thus far has opposed the proposal.

5. There are, of course, deviates in both camps, particularly over the size of BAOR and Britain's strategic nuclear force.

6. See "Britain's Bomb: Keep or Renounce?", *Economist*, February 15, 1964, pp. 587–89, and the letters to the editor from Alastair Buchan and Sir John Slessor which appeared in the *Economist*, February 22, 1964, p. 669.

7. Interviews.

8. A senior official in the Treasury suggested in mid-1963 that the quality of staff work in the defense departments was superior to that prepared by the civil departments in British government.

9. See Merton J. Peck and Frederic M. Scherer, *The Weapons Acquisition Process: An Economic Analysis* (Boston: Division of Research, Graduate School of Business Administration, Harvard University, 1962), especially pp. 17–54.

10. Officials in the Ministry of Defense have perhaps enjoyed the recent plight of their colleagues in the Ministry of Works. The costs of the renovation of the government houses on Downing Street (nos. 10, 11, and 12) and the adjacent Treasury chambers was underestimated by 100 per cent. Construction required about twice as much time as originally planned. It is hardly necessary to suggest that modern weapons systems involve more complex computations than structural repair.

Bibliographic Note

STUDIES on British military policies are not numerous, although in recent years there has been an increase in the number of works published. Britain's security position at the end of World War II is examined in Chatham House Study Group, *British Security* (London: Royal Institute of International Affairs, 1946); the strategic situation on the eve of the Korean War is one of the subjects treated by SIR CHARLES WEBSTER, MAJOR GENERAL SIR IAN JACOB, and E. A. G. ROBINSON in *United Kingdom Policy. Foreign, Strategic, Economic: Appreciations* (London: Royal Institute of International Affairs, 1950). Because of the author's role in the formulation of British defense policies during the period 1950–52, particular attention should be given to SIR JOHN SLESSOR'S *Strategy for the West* (New York: Morrow, 1954). The security problems of the late 1950's, along with some comments on the process of defense policy-making, is considered in E. J. KINGSTON-MCCLOUGHRY'S *Global Strategy*

(New York: Praeger, 1957) and *Defense: Policy and Strategy* (New York: Praeger, 1960). In his essays in *Deterrent or Defense: A Fresh Look at the West's Military Position* (New York: Praeger, 1960), B. H. LIDDELL HART, the dean of Britain's military analysts, gives a number of insights into various aspects of the United Kingdom's strategic position. A careful reading of *On the Prevention of War* (New York: St. Martin's Press, 1963), by the late JOHN STRACHEY, will suggest the important influence which the work of various American authors, particularly BERNARD BRODIE, HENRY KISSINGER, and HERMAN KAHN, has had on British students of security policies.

Security policies in the NATO area are the subject of ALASTAIR BUCHAN's excellent and important book, *NATO in the 1960's: The Implications of Interdependence* (New York: Praeger, 1960). *Arms and Stability in Europe: A British-French-German Enquiry*, a report by ALASTAIR BUCHAN and PHILIP WINDSOR (London: Chatto and Windus, 1963) is the most recent effort of the Institute of Strategic Studies and of Mr. Buchan, its director, to sort out the complex strategic issues now faced by the Atlantic Alliance. DENIS HEALEY, the member of Parliament currently serving as the Labor party's "shadow" minister of defense, has provided an excellent review of the evolution of British military policies in NATO in his essay, "Britain and NATO," in KLAUS KNORR (ed.), *NATO and American Security* (Princeton: Princeton University Press, 1959), pp. 209–35. Another Labor MP, F. W. MULLEY, who has served as one of the United Kingdom's representatives to the Western European Parliament and also as "shadow" air minister under Mr. Gaitskell, has provided a useful analysis of the security problems in NATO in *The Politics of Western Defense* (New York: Praeger, 1962). The Army League's, *The British Army in the Nuclear Age* (Barnet, Herts.: Stellar Press, 1959) and the League's earlier pamphlet, *The Army in the Nuclear Age* (Barnet,

Herts.: Stellar Press, 1955), stress the importance of conventional forces, both in NATO and the overseas areas.

The commentary on British military policies in the overseas areas in quite limited. Special attention should be given to Colonel DEWITT C. ARMSTRONG's "The Changing Strategy of British Bases" (Ph.D. dissertation, Princeton University, 1960), an examination of the evolution of British strategic thinking as it pertains to overseas bases. Strategic mobility, an extremely critical factor in military deployments in the overseas areas (particularly in Africa and Southeast Asia), is considered in NEVILLE BROWN, *Strategic Mobility* (London: Chatto and Windus, 1963).

There is an extensive body of literature which poses disarmament, in greater or lesser degree, as an alternative to current defense policies; these writings deserve mention, if only because they have attracted considerable public sympathy in Britain. Most widely known of the several advocates of nuclear disarmanent is BERTRAND RUSSELL, whose recent works on the subject include *Common Sense and Nuclear Warfare* (New York: Simon and Schuster, 1959), *Has Man a Future?* (New York: Simon and Schuster, 1962), and *Unarmed Victory* (New York: Simon and Schuster, 1963). COMMANDER SIR STEPHEN KING-HALL advocates a combination of unilateral nuclear disarmament and passive resistance in *Defense in the Nuclear Age* (Nyack, N.Y.: Fellowship Publications, 1959). Other proposals are outlined in WAYLAND YOUNG, *Strategy for Survival: First Steps in Nuclear Disarmament* (London: Penguin, 1959). In *Disengagement in Europe* (London: Penguin, 1958), MICHAEL HOWARD reviews the several proposals for disengagement which were widely discussed in the mid-1950's, including an alternative similar to the one advanced by the late HUGH GAITSKELL in *The Challenge of Coexistence* (Cambridge: Harvard University Press, 1957). *The Control of the Arms Race; Disarmament and Arms Control in the Missile Age* (New York:

Praeger, 1961), by HEDLEY BULL, is an extremely provocative study—the only serious analytic examination of arms control and disarmament problems which has been written in Britain thus far.

There are a number of useful articles on the social and political implications of the Campaign for Nuclear Disarmament. Two of the best are H. A. DEWEERD's "British Unilateralism: A Critical View," *Yale Review*, LI, No. 4 (1962), 574–88, and HEDLEY BULL's "The Many Sides of British Unilateralism," *The Reporter*, March 16, 1961, pp. 35–37. Additional commentary is provided by NORMAN BIRNBAUM, "The Campaign for Nuclear Disarmament" and DREW MIDDLETON, "The Deeper Meaning of British Neutralism," both in ROBERT THEOBOLD (ed.), *Britain in the Sixties* (New York: H. W. Wilson, 1961), and by CONSTANTINE FITZGIBBON, "Politics and the Novel: A Letter to Patrick O'Donovan," *Encounter*, June, 1961, pp. 71-73.

The literature on post–World War II British foreign policies is quite limited. The foreign policy of the 1945–51 Labor government is analyzed in M. A. FITZSIMONS, *The Foreign Policy of the British Labour Government*, 1945–1951 (Notre Dame: University of Notre Dame Press, 1953). LEON EPSTEIN also reviews this period in *Britain—Uneasy Ally* (Chicago: University of Chicago Press, 1954); his careful examination of the attitudes on major foreign-policy issues held by different political groups makes this work a useful complement to Fitzsimons' study. C. M. WOODHOUSE, *British Foreign Policy since the Second World War* (London: Hutchinson, 1961) and F. S. NORTHEDGE, *British Foreign Policy: The Process of Readjustment, 1945–1961* (New York: Praeger, 1961) are general surveys of British foreign policies since the end of World War II. LORD STRANG's interpretative essay, *Britain in World Affairs: The Fluctuation in Power and Influence from Henry VIII to Elizabeth II* (New York: Praeger, 1962), views recent British foreign policy in the perspective of Britain's nineteenth and early twentieth-century international role. *America in Britain's Place: The Leadership of the West and Anglo-American Unity* (New York: Praeger, 1961), by LIONEL GELBER, examines the strains in Anglo-American relations which have occurred as a result of America's assumption of free-world leadership. ANTHONY NUTTING argues in *Europe Will Not Wait* (New York: Praeger, 1960) that Britain must take a more active part in the evolution of a unified North Atlantic Community. A number of insights into the United Kingdom's foreign-policy problems between 1951 and late 1956 are contained in *Full Circle: The Memoirs of Anthony Eden* (Boston: Houghton Mifflin. 1961). SIR ANTHONY, the foreign secretary under Sir Winston Churchill, also provides a lengthy rationale for the policies of his own government during the Suez intervention of 1956. *Backbench Opinion in the House of Commons, 1955–1959* (New York: Pergamon, 1961), by S. E. FINER, H. B. BERRINGTON, and D. J. BARTHOLOMEW, demonstrates in a highly original and systematic way the attitudes of Parliamentary backbenchers on a number of important substantive issues of defense and foreign policy, including Commonwealth relations, nuclear weapons, and German rearmament.

A general survey of economic problems and policies since 1945 is contained in A. J. YOUNGSON, *The British Economy, 1920–1957* (Cambridge: Harvard University Press, 1960) and SIR ROY HARROD, *The British Economy* (New York: McGraw-Hill, 1963). *The British Economy, 1945–1950* (London: Oxford University Press, 1952) and its companion work, *The British Economy in the Nineteen-Fifties* (London: Oxford University Press, 1962), both edited by G. D. N. WORSWICK and P. H. ADY, provide intensive treatment of many problem areas, especially the postwar balance of payments position and the difficulties in adapting fiscal and monetary policies to Britain's always vulnerable economic position. HUGH DALTON, Labor's chancellor of the Exchequer between 1945 and 1947, gives an insider's view of the economic position immediately after World War II, particularly the financial strains created by Britain's foreign and military policies, in *High Tide and After: Memoirs, 1945–1960* (London: Frederick Muller, 1962). ALAN T. PEACOCK and JACK WISEMAN, *The Growth of Public Expenditure in the United Kingdom* (Princeton: Princeton University Press, 1961) is an especially valuable record of governmental expenditures. Other useful works include: C. A. R. CROSLAND, *Britain's Economic Problem* (London: Cape, 1953); A. C. L. DAY, *The Future of Sterling* (London: Oxford University Press, 1954); G. D. H. COLE, *The Post-War Condition of Britain* (New York: Praeger, 1957), and Political and Economic Planning, *Growth in the British Economy: A Study of Economic Problems and Policies in Contemporary Britain* (London: Allen and Unwin, 1960). ANDREW SHONFIELD, *British Economic Policy Since the War* (London: Penguin, 1958) and MICHAEL SHANKS, *The Stagnant Society* (London: Penguin, 1961) argue that Britain's economic malaise—inflation, the loss of overseas markets, and a relatively slow growth rate—are the result of inefficient management, antiquated union practices, and the rigidities created by class and a status-ridden educational system. These works, the latter especially, also illustrate the tenor of much of the recent commentary on Britain's problems, whether economic, political, or military. The *Economist* is a valuable source of information and comment on current economic problems and policies; the annual *Economic Survey,* prepared by the Treasury, provides an excellent year-by-year review of the government's economic policies.

Some of the economic aspects of Britain's defense effort are treated in "Britain's Defence Budget: The Real Cost," *New Statesman and Nation,* February 27, 1954, pp. 255–58; A. C. L. DAY, "The Cost of Defence," *Survival,* II, No. 2 (1960), 81-85, is a pioneering effort on the subject. A useful compilation of defense financial statistics is contained in D. C. PAIGE's carefully researched article, "Defence Expenditures," *Economic Review,* No. 10 (1960), pp. 26 ff, and in F. T.

BLACKABY and D. C. PAIGE, "Defence Expenditure—Burden or Stimulus," *Survival*, II, No. 6 (1960), 242–60. The defense sector is described in detail in Economist Intelligence Unit, *The Economic Effects of Disarmament* (London): Economist Intelligence Unit for the United World Trust, 1963). For further details on the implications of defense policy for various industrial groupings, see ELY DEVONS, "The Aircraft Industry"; THOMAS WILSON, "The Electronics Industry"; and A. K. CAIRNCROSS and J. R. PARKINSON, "The Shipbuilding Industry," in DUNCAN BURN (ed.), *The Structure of British Industry* (2 vols.; Cambridge: Cambridge University Press, 1958).

The military manpower problem is treated in Command 545, "Report of the Advisory Committee on Recruiting" (The Grigg Report), 1958; conscription policies are explained in Command 9608, "National Service." M. R. D. FOOT devotes a chapter to this issue in *Men in Uniform: Military Manpower in Modern Industrial Societies* (New York: Praeger, 1961). An examination of the officer-recruitment problem as it pertains to the army is contained in the Army League's *A Challenge to Leadership: An Examination of the Problem of Officer Recruitment for the British Army* (Barnet, Herts.: Stellar Press, 1962).

D. N. CHESTER and F. M. G. WILLSON, *The Organisation of British Central Government*, 1914–1956 (London: Allen and Unwin, 1957), is a general description of organization and administration in British government. *New Dimensions in Foreign Policy: A Study in British Administrative Experience, 1947–59* (New York: Macmillan, 1961), by MAX BELOFF, is especially valuable for an understanding of the administrative and policy-making process in those departments concerned with defense and foreign policies. The budgetary process is considered in great detail in SIR HERBERT BRITTAIN, *The British Budgetary System* (New York: Macmillan, 1959). The important role of the Treasury in controlling and co-ordinating governmental expenditure is clearly demonstrated in S. H. BEER's *Treasury Control: The Co-ordination of Financial and Economic Policy in Great Britain* (London: Oxford University Press, 1957). Parliamentary control of public expenditures is examined in BASIC CHUBB, *The Control of Public Expenditures: Financial Committees of the House of Commons* (London: Oxford University Press, 1952). The research and development program and how the process can be optimally organized are discussed in Office of the Minister of Science, *Report of the Committee on the Management and Control of Research and Development* (London: H. M. Stationery Office, 1961).

The history of the Committee of Imperial Defense, including its establishment and evolution into the Ministry of Defense, is the subject of FRANKLYN A. JOHNSON's *Defence by Committee: The British Committee of Imperial Defence, 1885–1959* (New York: Oxford University Press, 1960). Three white papers, Command 6923 (1946), Command 476 (1958), and Command 2097 (1963), all entitled "Central Organisation for Defence," document the establishment and subsequent changes in the organization of the Ministry of Defense. The informal reorganization of the Ministry of Defense in the period 1955–57 is treated by VICE-ADMIRAL J. HUGHES HALLETT in "The Central Organisation for Defense," *Journal: Royal United Services Institution,* November, 1958, pp. 488–93. MICHAEL HOWARD compares British and American experiences in defense organization in "Organisation for Defence in the United Kingdom and the United States, 1945–1958," in H. G. THURSFIELD (ed.), *Brassey's Annual, 1959* (New York: Macmillan, 1959), pp. 74 ff. LAURENCE W. MARTIN has furnished an excellent summary of the policy process as it evolved in the critical period after the Suez intervention in "The Market for Strategic Ideas in Britain: The 'Sandys Era,'" *American Political Science Review,* LVI, No. 1 (1962), 23–41. C. G. GREY, *A History of the Air Ministry* (New York: Norton, 1941), SIR CHARLES WALKER, *Thirty-six Years at the Admiralty* (London: Lincoln Williams, 1933), and HAMPDEN

GORDEN, *The War Office* (London: Putnam, 1935), are the only existing studies of the service departments. It is hoped that these badly outdated works will soon be replaced by a volume on the organization of the defense establishment in Allen and Unwin's "New Whitehall Series."

The social, political, and professional characteristics of the regular officer corps have attracted relatively little serious study. The most extensive effort, a too brief parallel of MORRIS JANOWITZ's study of the American military professional, is PHILIP ABRAMS' excellent essay "Democracy, Technology, and the Retired British Officer," in SAMUEL P. HUNTINGTON (ed.), *Changing Patterns of Military Politics* (New York; Free Press of Glencoe, 1962). For a historical perspective of civil-military relations in Britain, there is no equal to CECIL WOODHAM SMITH's classic on the Crimean War, *The Reason Why* (New York: Dutton, 1960). In "Great Britain: The Crimean War to the First World War," in MICHEAL HOWARD (ed.), *Soldiers and Governments* (London: Eyre and Spottiswoode, 1957), pp. 25–50, ROBERT BLAKE summarizes the developments during a later period. A highly critical view of the army officer is offered by SIMON RAVEN, "Perish by the Sword," in HUGH THOMAS (ed.), *The Establishment* (New York: Potter, 1959), pp. 49–79. ANTHONY SAMPSON paints a blander but more accurate portrait in *Anatomy of Britain* (New York: Harper and Row, 1962), pp. 251–69. A number of autobiographies of individuals who held positions of high responsibility in the postwar defense establishment command special attention from students of civil-military relations or defense policies. These include *The Central Blue: The Autobiography of Sir John Slessor, Marshal of the RAF* (New York: Praeger, 1957), by the chief of the Air Staff during the Korean War, SIR JOHN SLESSOR; Field Marshal the Viscount Montgomery's *The Memoirs of Field-Marshal Montgomery* (New York: Signet, 1958); *Conflict without Malice* (London: Odhams, 1955), by EMANUEL SHINWELL, secretary of state for war and later minister of defense during the Attlee government; and LORD ISMAY, *The Memoirs of General Lord Ismay* (New York: Viking, 1960).

In addition to the works noted above, special attention should be paid to several documentary sources. These include the annual Statement on Defense (the defense white paper), which normally appears each February, and, until they became a part of the defense white paper in 1962, the "Memorandum" prepared by the minister of each service department, which provides additional information pertaining to the part of each of the separate services in the over-all security program. *Hansard* (Parliamentary reports), particularly the daily reports of defense debates, is also a basic source of information and political opinion. Other documentary sources include the reports of select committees of Parliament and the proceedings of committees convened by the government to study particular problems.

The daily and weekly press provides excellent coverage of defense affairs. The most thorough is contained in *The Times*, the *Guardian*, and the *Daily Telegraph*. The *Economist*, the *New Statesman*, and the *Spectator*, the most widely read of Britain's weekly journals of opinion, and the major Sunday papers, the *Observer*, the *Sunday Times*, and the *Sunday Telegraph*, supplement the major London daily papers as sources of editorial reaction to government policies. *Brassey's Annual* and the *Journal: Royal United Service Institution* are favorite publications for service authors. Many of the most important articles on British defense policies which appear in the publications listed above are reprinted in *Survival*, the bi-monthly publication of the Institute of Strategic Studies.

Some of the data used in this study were obtained in personal interviews. Interviews were conducted during two periods—December, 1961–February, 1962, and July–August, 1963. A majority of the sixty interviews were with officials, both civil and military, in the service departments, the Ministry of Defense, the Ministry of Aviation, the Treasury, the Foreign Office, and the Cabinet Office. The remainder of those interviewed included parliamentarians of both major political parties, officials in the party headquarters, and commentators, writers, and scholars specializing in defense affairs. To facilitate the discussions and to avoid the possibility of any embarrassing situations which might arise because of my position as a member of the United States armed forces, I have refrained from attributing statements by name. With few exceptions, however, the text indicates the general category of the respondent, e.g., "a civil servant," or "an officer on the Joint Staff."

British defense policies in the months and years ahead appear inextricably tied to the impending general election, which must be held sometime before November, 1964. If the Conservative party under Sir Alec Douglas-Home returns a majority to Parliament, there is little reason to expect any substantial change in defense policies, at least in the immediate future. The Labor party, however, has implied that it intends a number of major policy shifts; at the time of writing there is an excellent possibility—since it has maintained a sizeable lead (from 4 to 10 per cent in public opinion polls) over the Tories since the summer of 1963—that Labor will win the election. The defense policies which might be expected from a Labor government are thus a subject of considerable interest. HAROLD WILSON, the Labor leader, offers his preview in "Britain's Policy If Labor Wins," *Atlantic*, October, 1963, pp. 61–65. In "Labor's Defense and Foreign Policy," *Foreign Affairs*, April, 1964 pp. 391–98, PATRICK C. GORDON WALKER, the probable choice as foreign secretary in a Labor government, asserts that Britain would keep the present V-bomber force. It would not replace this force when it becomes obsolescent, however, nor would it support the proposed MLF (the "mixed-manned nuclear force"). The defense correspondent for the *New Statesman*, ANTHONY VERRIER, examines in "British Defense Policy under Labor," *Foreign Affairs*, January, 1964, pp. 282–92, the military, economic, and political implications of the alternative policies currently being

pressed upon Mr. Wilson by his advisers in the party. PAUL
JOHNSON's analysis, "Will Wilson Keep the Bomb?", *New
Statesman,* December 13, 1963, pp. 866 ff., suggests some of
the reasons why a Labor government might deem it advisable
to maintain Britain's strategic nuclear capability. The *Economist's* thoughts on the strategic nuclear force, "Britain's Bomb:
Keep or Renounce?", February 15, 1964, pp. 587–89, should be
read in conjunction with the comments which this article attracted from ALASTAIR BUCHAN and SIR JOHN SLESSOR in the
February 22, 1964, issue (p. 669).

Index

Abrams, Philip, 269

Acheson, Dean, 3

Aden: air movements to, 14; military forces in, 219, 235, 257; unified command in, 17

Administrative Class of Civil Service, 110–12; in Admiralty, 126

Admiralty, 90, 92, 93, 123, 124–29; criticism of 1957 White Paper, 167; Fairlead conference, 125, 167; and naval tradition in Britain, 126–27; personnel in, 125–26; procurement responsibilities, 143, 145; research functions of, 127–28; strength of, 147, 169; see also Navy

Ady, P. H., 265

Africa: British political influence in, 234; military forces in, 10; see also Kenya

Agreement on policy choices, 159–62

Air barrier, problem of, 12, 14

Air Force, Royal, 18, 84, 87; and Air Ministry, 135–41; Bomber Command, 26–27, 138–39, 140–41, 236, 249, 253; budget allocations for, 170; commitment to NATO, 139; defense of air bombardment, 25–26; division of interests of, 174; manpower in, 37, 182; in overseas areas, 139; procurement activities, 143; Prospect conference, 125, 166; research programs, 138, 143, 145; rivalry with other services, 136–37; and strategic nuclear force, 138–40; support of army operations, 140; Transport Command, 140, 141

Air League of the British Empire, 84

Air-lift strategy, 11–15; air barrier as problem, 12–14; development of transport capacity, 12; and storage of supplies, 14

Air Ministry, 90, 93, 123, 135–41, 143, 144; alliance with Ministry of Supply, 144–45; organization procedures, 137; procurements for, 145

Air support, tactical, 17–18

Aircraft carriers: conversion of, 17; importance of, 128–29; use of, 18, 23

Aircraft production, 89, 90; expenditures for, 27; Ministry of, 138, 142

Alliance-deterrence strategy, 246, 258

Amery, Julian, 235

Ammunition, production of, 89

Antisubmarine warfare, concern for, 22–23

Armstrong, DeWitt, 263

Army: air force support of operations, 140; budget allocations for, 170; commitment to NATO, 134–35; conscription of men, 35–36 (*see also* Conscription); corps in, 132; division of interests of, 174; equipment needs, 131; in Europe, 134–35; internal fragmentation of, 131–32; manpower in, 37, 182 (*see also* Manpower); in overseas areas, 10–11, 134–35 (*see also* Overseas security); personnel needs, 131; postwar missions of, 132; recruiting of men, 134, 157, 158, 238, 242; regimental system in, 131; research program of, 132–33; reserve forces, 87; responsibilities of, 245–46; technical experience in, 116; and War Office, 129–35; *see also* British Army of the Rhine; Military; War Office

Army Antiaircraft Command, deactivation of, 23

Army Emergency Reserve, 87

Army League, 69, 84, 86, 262, 267

Army Reserve Bill of 1961, 40

Asia: British political influence in, 234; military forces in, 10

Association of British Chambers of Commerce, 99

Atomic weapons; *see* Nuclear weapons

Attlee, Clement, 45, 47, 51, 57, 65, 106, 117, 160, 196, 213, 218, 231, 237

Aviation, civil, 143

Aviation, Ministry of, 90, 92, 94, 96, 105, 123, 138, 141–47; *see also* Service departments

Backbenchers, 46, 47, 50, 51, 66; committees of, 67–68; importance of, 70–72; information sources of, 69–70

Balance of payments and defense, 205–24; and defense demands, 208–16; and defense deployments, 216–24; and dollar reserves, 214–15; and domestic investments, 215; and raw material purchases, 211–12

Baldwin, Stanley, 23

Ballistic Missile Early Warning System, 27

Bargaining and decision-making, 154–56, 162–69

Bartholomew, D. J., 265

Bases, overseas, importance of, 128, 235

Bastable, C. F., 181–82

Beamish, Tufton, 69

Beaverbrook, Lord, 138, 142

Beer, S. H., 268

Beloff, Max, 267

Berlin crisis of 1961, 39, 184, 247

Berrington, H. B., 265

Bevan, Aneurin, 51, 56, 61, 67

Birch, Nigel, 50

Birnbaum, Norman, 264

Blackaby, F. T., 267

Blackett, P. M. S., 73

Blue Steel project, 27, 32, 140

Blue Streak project, 27–28, 139, 254, 255

Blue Water missile system, 140, 223

Bomber Command, 26–27, 138–39, 140–41, 236, 249, 253

Bow Group, 70
Brassey's Annual, 270
British Aircraft Corporation, 90
British Army in the Nuclear Age, The, 69, 262
British Army of the Rhine, 132, 134, 135, 220, 221, 246, 250, 258; cost of, 20; reduction of, 20, 49; tactical nuclear weapons in, 21
British European Airways, 93, 98
British Institute of Public Opinion, 56, 57, 59, 61
British Legion, 87
British Limbless Ex-Servicemen's Association, 87
British Overseas Airways Corporation, 93, 98
British Peace Committee, 84
Brittain, Herbert, 267
Broadhurst, Harry, 27
Brodie, Bernard, 262
Brown, George, 49, 58, 158, 196, 233
Brown, Neville, 263
Buchan, Alastair, 75, 169, 262, 272
Budget: allocations in 1949-50, 170; balanced budget doctrine, 188-89; ceiling for defense costs, 201; decisions on, 155-56, 157, 161, 163; defense budget process, 196-202; five-year forecast, 197, 200, 254; program control, 200; projections in, 197; relation to defense spending, 195; *see also* Expenditures
Bull, Hedley, 264
Burn, Duncan, 267
Butler, R. A. B., 187, 188, 219

Cairncross, A. K., 267
Cambridge, 108, 109
Campaign for Nuclear Disarmament, 59, 61, 82-84, 258
Canberra bombers, 139
Cardwell, Mr., 130

Carriers; *see* Aircraft carriers
Censure Motion: in 1955, 51; in 1960, 51
Chandos, Lord, 167
Chatham House Study Group, 261
Chester, D. N., 267
Chiefs of Staff Committee, 152, 153, 162, 164, 165
Chubb, Basic, 268
Churchill, Randolph, 233
Churchill, Winston, 45, 46, 106, 117, 136, 142, 160, 186, 187, 195, 231, 265; opinions on conscription, 55; rearmament program of, 56; and White Paper of 1954, 67
Civil aviation, 143
Civil control of armed forces, 106
Civil defense, 24
Civil servants, 110-12; in Admiralty, 125-26; in Air Ministry, 137; club membership of, 111; educational background of, 111; family background of, 111; importance in policy process, 116-19; relations with military, 116-19; in reorganized defense establishment, 153; in service departments, 160-61; in War Office, 130-31; *see also* Service departments
Civilian consultants, use of, 255
Civilianization programs, and military strength, 38-39
Clerical Class of civil servants, 110, 111
Club membership: of civil servants, 111; of Conservatives, 109; of military officers, 113
Coast Artillery, 23, 175
Coastal Command, 163
Cole, G. D. H., 266
Collins, John, 83
Commando ships, 15-17, 23, 246
Committee of 100, 61, 82, 84
Committees, back-bench, 67-72
Common Market, 4

Commons, House of: defense debates in, 46; function of, 44
Commonwealth, 234–36; and domestic politics, 236; security arrangements, 235
Communist infiltration of organizations, 84; *see also* Russia
Compromise and decision-making, 154–56
Conscription of men, 36; ending of, 172, 240–42; public opinion poll data on, 54–55; unpopularity of, 237–38; *see also* National Service
Conservative Research Center, 69
Conservatives: attitudes toward government expenditures, 186–87; club membership of, 109; educational backgrounds of, 108–9; Labor support of, 47, 48; ministers in service departments, 107–8; policies of, 271; public opinion on, 62; social origins of members, 109
Consultants, civilian, use of, 255
Consumer price index, 189
Consumption expenditures, 239
Contracts, industrial, awarding of, 88–102
Convertibility of sterling, 206–8, 209
Costs of defense; *see* Expenditures for defense
Cousins, Frank, 60
Cranwell, RAF college at, 112
Crosland, C. A. R., 266
Crossman, R. H. S., 50, 157–58, 171
Crowley, John, 166
Cyprus, military forces in, 11, 132, 184, 235, 257
Czechoslovakia, 184

Daily Herald, 53
Daily Telegraph, 73, 74, 270
Dalton, Hugh, 56, 209, 218, 265

Day, A. C. L., 266
Debt-servicing charges, 193, 208
Decentralized defense policy-making structure, 257–58
Decision-making: agreement on policy choices, 159–62; arbitrary decisions, 172–73; bargained policies, 154–56, 162–69; competition and diversity in, 175–76; criticisms of policy process, 171–77; outcome of, 169–71; and vested interests, 173–75
Defense: allied-deterrence strategy, 246, 258; cost of, 33–35 (*see also* Expenditures for defense); graduated deterrence doctrine, 49; massive retaliation policies, 48, 51; nuclear and conventional forces, balance of, 48–52; public opinion on policies, 54–62; resources for, 33–40; Trades Union Congress opinions on policies, 60–61; white papers on (*see* White Papers)
Defense Committee, 152, 197, 198
Defense Council, 152
Defense Department of U.S., 253, 254
Defense Ministry, 88, 105, 123, 143; authority of Minister of Defense, 156–57; and budget process, 197–98; civilian consultants for, 255; reorganization of, 151–54; *see also* Service departments
Defense Research Committee, 154, 164
Defense Scientific Staff, 153–54
Defense Secretariat, 153
Defense Staff, 152–53; chief of, 157
Deficit financing, 190
Deployment of defense forces, 235; and balance of payments, 216–24; commitments to NATO, 18–24, 184, 220, 221, 235–36, 241, 246, 257, secondary effects of, 222; occupation troops, 184; in overseas areas, 220, 221, 235, 241, secondary effects of, 221–22

Deterrence strategy, 49, 51, 160, 233–34; alliance-deterrence strategy, 246, 258; graduated deterrence doctrine, 49

Devons, Ely, 267

DeWeerd, H. A., 264

Douglas-Home, Alec, 271

Duff, Peggy, 83

Dulles, John Foster, 49, 234

Durant, Henry, 61

Eccles, David, 168

Economic factors: in civil defense program, 24; and defense costs, 239; interdependence with defense program, 208–16; in reduction of forces in Europe, 20–21; *see also* Budget; Expenditures

Economic services, expenditures for, 191, 192

Economics of Defense in the Nuclear Age, The, 78

Economist, 73, 168, 215, 266, 270, 272

Eden, Anthony, 19, 35, 58, 156, 163, 184, 186, 219, 231, 239, 240, 265

Educational background: of civil servants, 111; of military officers, 112–13; of political leaders, 108–9

Eisenhower, Dwight D., 28, 34

Electronics, production of, 89, 90

Engineering industries, output of, 211–13, 215

Engineers, shortage of, 215

Enthoven, Alain, 153

Epstein, Leon, 264

Eton, 108, 109, 113

European defense, 18–24; *see also* North Atlantic Treaty Organization

European Defense Community, 19

Ever-Readies, 87

Executive Class of civil servants, 110, 111

Expenditures: consumption, 239; debt-servicing charges, 193, 208; for defense, 89, 181–202 (aircraft expenditures, 28; annual production costs, 239; availability of resources, 185–96; ceiling on, 156; central governmental expenditures, 185–91; competitors for revenues, 191–96; conflict with production for export, 210–11; cost-effectiveness studies, 255–56; costs of NATO commitments, 220; cost of strategic nuclear force, 247; costs of World War II, 228; crises affecting, 185–86; defense budget process, 196–202; defense demands for resources, 182–84; inflationary pressures, 189–91; in non-sterling area, 220; for nuclear submarines, 32; overseas expenditures, 216–24; percentage of Gross National Product, 33, 35, 182, 183, 185, 187–88, 191, 194, 246; public opinion poll data on, 55–59; reduction of, 11–17, 209; relation to total budget, 195; revenue sources, 187–88; in sterling area, 219; types of defense purchases, 211); for economic services, 191, 192; and investment incentives, 194, 215, 239; for social services, 191, 192

Exports: decline of, 229; and defense production during Korean crisis, 210–13; importance of, 205–16; of military equipment, 223

Fairlead conference of Admiralty, 125, 167

Family background: of civil servants, 111; of Conservatives, 109; of Labor party members, 109; of military officers, 113

Federation of British Industries, 99

Financing, deficit, 190

Finer, S. E., 84, 265
Fisher, Warren, 161
FitzGibbon, Constantine, 264
Fitzsimons, M. A., 264
Flyingdales Ballistic Missile Warning Station, 139
Forster, E. M., 83
Foot, M. R. D., 267
Foot, Michael, 83
Ford Foundation, 75
France: attitudes of De Gaulle, 31, 251; rejection of European Defense Community, 19; relations with Britain, 184; relations with Germany, 21
Front-bench spokesmen, 48, 50, 53, 69

Gaitskell, Hugh, 4, 60, 232, 262, 263
Gaulle, Charles de, 31, 251
Gelber, Lionel, 265
Geneva conference in 1954, 231–32
Germany: anti-Germanism, 83; Berlin crisis of 1961, 39, 184, 247; military contributions of, 19, 20–21, 184, 220; rearmament of, 51, 52; relations with France, 21; troop deployments in, 135, 222
Gibraltar, military forces in, 10, 219, 235
Godber, Lord, 167
Gorden, Hampden, 269
Gordon Walker, Patrick C., 271
Graduated deterrence doctrine, 49, 51
Greece, military forces in, 11, 219
Grey, C. G., 268
Gross National Product, and expenditures for defense, 33, 35, 182, 183, 185, 187–88, 191, 193, 194, 246
Guardian, 73, 270
Guns and ammunition, 89

Haldane, Mr., 130
Hall, Stephen King-; *see* King-Hall, Stephen
Hallet, Hughes, 155, 268
Hansard, 270
Hard-money philosophy, 190
Harrod, Roy, 265
Hart, B. H. Liddell, 262
Harvey, A. V., 71
Hawker Siddeley Group, 90
Head, Antony, 50, 164
Healey, Denis, 49, 262
Hitch, Charles J., 78, 199
Hoare, Samuel, 136
Home Guard, demobilization of, 23
Hong Kong: dockyards closed in, 38; military forces in, 219, 235
Howard, Michael, 263, 268, 269
Hull, Richard, 131, 157
Hull committee, 172
Huntington, Samuel P., 269

Illustrated London News, 223
Imperial Defense College, 113
Imports and exports, importance of, 205–16
Industrial lobby, 88–91
Industry: in advertising role, 96–98; as adviser or technical consultant, 94–96; cancellation of projects of, 96; contacts with government research establishments, 92; criticisms of, 100–101; modernization of, 194; negotiations with government, 91–102; production decisions, 91 (*see also* Production); as salesman and innovator, 92–93
Inflationary pressures, 189–91
Information sources: from Institute of Strategic Studies, 75–76; from opposition, 69; from press reporting, 73–75; from research staff, 69–70

Institute of Strategic Studies, 75–76, 262, 270

Intellectual community, influence of, 72–79, 255, 257

Interdependence, concept of, 252–53

International position of Britain, 227–30; Anglo-American relations, 230–34; Commonwealth, 234–36

Interservice rivalry, 75, 155, 159, 162; bargaining with, 163–65; and policy defects, 171, 173; publicity of, 166; and separatism, 174, 175–76, 257

Interviews, data from, 270–71

Investments: domestic, increase of, 215, 239; incentives for, 194

Ismay, Lord, 270

Jacob, Ian, 261

Janowitz, Morris, 269

Johnson, Franklyn, 268

Johnson, Paul, 272

Jordan, 17

Journal: Royal United Service Institution, 270

Kahn, Herman, 262

Kennedy, John F., 32, 139, 251, 256

Kenya, military forces in, 5, 11, 132, 184, 219, 257

King-Hall, Stephen, 263

Kingston-McCloughry, E. J., 126, 159, 261

Kissinger, Henry, 262

Knorr, Klaus, 262

Korea, reduction of British forces in, 20

Korean War: classified information in, 45, 46; and expenditures for defense, 34, 183, 246; interservice relations during, 164; manpower levels during, 183, 184; rearmament during, 18–19,
23, 51, 56, 61, 67, 209, 210–15; tax rates during, 188

Kuwait, operations in, 17

Labor, shortage of, 218, 239

Labor and National Service, Ministry of, 88

Labor party: attitude toward National Service, 237, 239; backbench committees in, 67; divisions in, 52–53, 62; educational backgrounds of politicians, 109; family backgrounds of members, 109; ministers in service departments, 107; Miscellaneous Occupations in, 52; occupational backgrounds of members, 52; policies of, 271; Professions in, 52; weaknesses in opposition, 47–53; Workers in, 52

Libya, reduction of British forces in, 20

Lloyd, Selwyn, 240

Lobby, industrial, 88–91

London University, 109

Lords, House of, 46

McCloughry, E. J. Kingston-; *see* Kingston-McCloughry, E. J.

Macgregor, D. H., 189

McKean, Roland N., 78

Maclean, Fitzroy, 50

Macleod, Ian, 241–42

MacMahon Act, 230–31

Macmillan, Harold, 32, 35, 38, 45, 58, 74, 129, 151, 155, 157, 158, 168, 181, 190, 232, 233, 241, 242

Maitland, John, 71

Malaya, military forces in, 5, 11, 132, 184, 257

Malta: dockyards in, 38; military forces in, 222, 235

Manhattan Project, 25, 230, 231

Manpower: civilianization programs, 38–40; conscription of, 36 (*see also* Conscription); de-

Manpower—*Continued*
termination of size of, 157; and domestic politics, 237–42; for labor, shortage of, 218, 239; levels of, in defense forces, 182; postwar service levels, 35–40; recruiting of, 38, 134, 157, 158, 238, 242; reduction of forces, 20–21, 38–39, 58, 88, 114, 209, 239–42; scientific, shortage of, 215–16

Marines, Royal, 17

Maritime strategy, 9–10; *see also* Navy

Marshall Plan, 229

Martin, Laurence, 268

Mason, Roy, 166

Massive retaliation doctrine, 48, 51

Mediterranean area, military forces in, 10

Mediterranean Command, 17

Metal industry output, 211–13, 215

Middleton, Drew, 264

Military: civil control of, 106; civil-military relations, 116–19; and civilianization programs, 38–40; club membership of officers, 113; commitments to NATO, 18–24, 184, 220, 221, 235–36, 241, 246, 257; conscription of men, 35–36 (*see also* Conscription); criticism of policy formations, 75; educational background of officers, 112–13; expenditures overseas, 216–24 (*see also* Expenditures for defense); family background of officers, 113; influence over American policy, 230, 234; interservice conflicts, 75, 136–37 (*see also* Interservice rivalry); manpower problems, 237–42 (*see also* Manpower); occupation troops, 184; overcommitment of forces, 247–48; overseas (*see* Overseas security); pay and pension increases, 87; purchases from industry, 92–93; recruiting of men, 38, 134, 157, 158, 238, 242; reductions of forces, 19–21, 38–40, 58, 88, 114, 209, 239–42; reserve forces,

organization of, 87; service associations, 84–86; standardization of equipment, 252; technology changes in, 184; *see also* Air Force; Army; National Service; Navy

Minesweepers, need for, 22

Ministers, contact with back-bench committees, 68

Ministries; *see specific ministries*

Mixed-Manned Nuclear Force, 33, 254

Modernization of industries, 194

Monckton, Lord, 196

Montgomery, Field Marshal, 46, 155, 269

Motor transport production for military, 89

Mulley, F. W., 262

Munitions: Controller of, 142, 143; Ministry of, 141–42; production of, 89

Nassau Agreements, 32, 71, 129

National Association for Employment of Regular Sailors, Soldiers, and Airmen, 88

National Insurance and Health Contributions, 188

National Service, 35–36, 133; attacks on, 61; ending of, 50, 237–42; public opinion poll data on, 55; *see also* Conscription of men

National Union of Manufacturers, 99

Navy, Royal: afloat support, 16; aircraft in, 136; aircraft carriers in, 15, 16, 17, 18, 23, 128–29; amphibious task group, 17; budget allocations for, 170; capabilities of, 129; choice between submarines and carriers, 128–29; Commando ships, 15–17, 23, 246; commitments to NATO, 22–23; criticism of 1957 Defense White Paper, 167; division of interests of, 174; maintenance of, 9–10; manpower in, 37, 182; overseas

Navy, Royal—*Continued*
bases for, 128, 235; for overseas security, 15–18; peacetime activities of, 127; Polaris missiles, 32, 35, 71, 72, 129, 139–40, 236, 249; responsibilities of, 245, 246; and strategic nuclear force, 139–40; submarines in (*see* Submarines); technical experience in, 115; *see also* Admiralty

Navy League, 81, 84, 85

New Scientist, 73

New Statesman, 73, 270, 272

Newspapers, role of, 73–75, 270

North Atlantic Treaty Organization (NATO): air force commitment to, 139; bomber force in, 31; Britain's role in, 228; conventional capabilities of, 250–51; costs of commitments to, 220; military commitments to, 18–24, 184, 220, 221, 235–36, 241, 246, 257, secondary effects of, 222; naval commitments to, 22–23; nuclear force of, 249–50; policy in 1954, 49; size of forces of, 134–35

Northedge, F. S., 264

Nuclear disarmament; *see* Campaign for Nuclear Disarmament

Nuclear force, strategic, 19–20, 24–33; air force role in, 138–40; atomic development program, 26; attractions of, 50; balance with conventional forces, 48–52; cost of, 247; criticism of, 30–31, 49, 75, 236, 249, 250; defenders of, 31–32; early warning system with, 27; effectiveness of, 28–32; first-strike force, 234; formation of, 230–34; joint-European strike force, 31; justification for, 241–42, 259; massive retaliation doctrine, 234; navy role in, 139–40; and resource demands, 184; second-strike role of, 29, 30, 32; vulnerability to attack, 29–30

Nuclear weapons: in British Army of the Rhine, 21; production of, 230–33; public opinion poll data on, 59–62

Nutting, Anthony, 265

Observer, 52, 73, 168, 270

Officers' Pensions Society, 87

Opposition members, as information source to backbenchers, 69

Overseas security, 10–18; air-lifted central strategic reserve, 11–15; deployment of forces, 220, 235, 241, secondary effects of, 221–22; military commitments to, 241; and military expenditures, 216–24; naval bases, 128, 235; naval task force, 15–17; tactical air support, 17–18; unified commands for, 17

Oxford, 108, 109

Paget, Mr., 69

Paige, D. C., 266, 267

Palestine, British military forces in, 11

Parkinson, J. R., 267

Parliament: back-bench members, 46, 47, 50, 51, 66, 67–72; consequences of debate, 53–62; as critic of defense policy, 43–62; front-bench spokesmen, 48, 50, 53, 69; House of Commons, 44, 46; House of Lords, 46; influence of, 65–72; lack of information in, 44–46; lack of interest in defense, 46–47; limitations on, as critics of defense policies, 44–53; and pressure groups, 84–86; weakness of Labor party in opposition, 47–53; *see also* Conservatives; Labor party

Peacock, Alan, 266

Peck, Merton J., 78

Pensions, service, increase in, 87

Polaris missiles, 32, 35, 71, 72, 129, 139–40, 236, 249

Political leaders of service departments, 105–10

Politics and defense, 227–42; Commonwealth, 234–36; and defense spending, 181–202; manpower and domestic politics, 237–42; United States and Britain, 230–34

Politics of decision-making, 151–77; agreement versus bargaining, 159–69; criticisms of policy process, 171–77; *see also* Decision-making

Poll data on public opinion, 54–62

Press commentaries, 73–75, 270

Pressure groups: consultation with government departments, 86–102; and defense policies, 81–102; industrial lobby, 88–91; and Parliament, 84–86; and public opinion, 82–84

Price index, consumer, 189

Priestley, J. B., 83

Procurements for service departments, 142–44

Production: of atomic weapons, 230–33; for defense, annual rate of, 239; feasibility studies, 91; and manpower shortage, 218, 239; Ministry of, 142; operational requirements, 91; project studies, 91

Prospect conference of RAF, 125, 166

Public opinion: influence of intellectual community, 72–79, 255, 257; lack of interest in defense issues, 53; poll data on, 54–62 (on conscription, 54–55; on expenditures for defense, 55–59; on nuclear weapons, 59–62); and pressure groups, 82–84

Publicity of interservice battles, 166

Radio Industry Council, 99

RAND Corporation, 72, 254

Raven, Simon, 269

Rearmament during Korea, 18–19, 22–23, 51, 56, 61, 67, 209; exports and defense production during, 210–13; and reserve position, 214–15

Recruiting in military services, 38, 134, 157, 158, 238, 242

Reorganization: of defense establishment, 151–54; of Ministry of Supply, 143–44

Research: in Admiralty, 127–28; in air force, 138, 143, 145; army program of, 132–33; government facilities for, contacts with industry, 92; in service departments, 142–44; staff in, as source of information for backbenchers, 69–70; in War Office, 145

Reserve forces, organization and size of, 87

Reserves, dollar, rearmament affecting, 214–15

Resources: availability of, 185–96; consumed by defense, 33–40 (cost of defense, 33–35; manpower, 35–40; *see also* Expenditures for defense; Manpower); defense demands for, 182–84 (and military commitments, 183–84; and strategy choices, 184; and technology changes, 184); division of, 174, 181

Retired Officers' Association, 87

Revenues: competitors for, 191–96; sources of, 187–88

Robinson, E. A. G., 261

Royal Air Force; *see* Air Force

Royal Marines, 17

Royal Military College of Science, 116

Royal Navy; *see* Navy, Royal

Royal Ordnance Factories, 89

Russell, Bertrand, 83, 263

Russia: advances in military technology, 23; conventional strength of, in Europe, 50; fear of aggression from, 31, 33, 48, 49, 134, 184, 250; nuclear strength of, 248; submarines of, 22, 168

Sampson, Anthony, 269

Sandys, Duncan, 34–35, 144, 157, 164, 168, 172, 196, 233

Scherer, Frederic M., 78

Schrivenhan, Royal Military College of Science at, 116
Scientific Staff, Defense, 153–54
Scientists, shortage of, 215–16
Separatism in service departments, 174, 175–76, 257
Service associations, significance of, 84–86
Service departments, 123–47; Admiralty, 123, 124–29 (*see also* Admiralty); Air Ministry, 135–41 (*see also* Air Ministry); Aviation Ministry, 90, 92, 94, 96, 105, 123, 138, 141–47; civil servants in, 110–12 (*see also* Civil servants); different departmental strengths, 169–71; homogeneity of members, 160, 177; interdepartmental agreement, 160–61; interservice rivalry (*see* Interservice rivalry); merged with Ministry of Defense, 151–54; military officers in, 112–16; political leaders of, 105–10; procurements for, 142–44, 145, relative abilities of, 147, 169; research in, 142–44; separatism in, 174, 175–76, 257; vested interests of, 173–75; War Office, 129–35 (*see also* War Office)
Shanks, Michael, 266
Sharples, Richard, 69
Shinwell, Emanuel, 45, 109, 155, 169, 269
Shipbuilder's Conference, 99
Shipbuilding industry, 89
Shonfield, Andrew, 266
Singapore: military forces in, 235, 257; storage of supplies in, 14
Skybolt missiles, 28, 32, 139, 255
Slessor, John, 114, 137, 160, 164, 233, 261, 269, 272
Smith, Cecil Woodham, 269
Social service, expenditures for, 191, 192
Society of British Aerospace Companies, 99–100
Soldiers, Sailors, and Airmen's Family Association, 87

Soviet Union; *see* Russia
Spectator, 73, 270
Stability and Survival, 70
Standardization of equipment, 252
Sterling, convertibility of, 206–8, 209
Sterling-area countries, 206–8, 219–20; Rest of the Sterling Area, 208, 220
Stockpiling of supplies, 14, 24
Strachey, John, 49, 69, 155, 173, 262
Strang, Lord, 264
Strategic Air Command, 26, 50, 230, 234, 248, 249
Strategic nuclear force; *see* Nuclear force, strategic
Strategic reserve, air-lifted, 11–15
Submarines: antisubmarine vessels, 22–23; Polaris-firing, 32, 35, 71, 72, 129, 139–40, 236, 249; Russian, 22, 168
Suez: intervention in 1956, 229, 235, 240, 241, 254, 258 (defense costs in, 34–35; naval operations in, 15–16; size of defense program during, 58; strategic reappraisal after, 233); loss of, 11; naval base in, 10
Sunday Telegraph, 73, 270
Sunday Times, 73, 270
Supply, Ministry of, 90, 100, 132–33, 141, 142; alliance with Air Ministry, 144–45; orientation of, 145–46; reorganization of, 143–44
Survival, 76, 270

Taxation rates, 185–86, 187, 188
Taylor, A. J. P., 83
Taylor, Maxwell, 165
Technology: in army, 116; military, changes in, 184; in navy, 115; shortage of manpower for, 215–16
Territorial and Auxiliary Forces Association, 87

Territorial Army, 87
Theobold, Robert, 264
This Is the Road, 186
Thomas, Hugh, 269
Thorneycroft, Peter, 71, 190
Thursfield, H. G., 268
Times, The (London), 70, 73, 167, 270
Tories; *see* Conservatives
Trade, international, importance of, 205–16; *see also* Exports
Trades Union Congress, 86, 99; opinion on defense policies, 60–61
Transport Aircraft Requirement Committee, 100
Transport and Civil Aviation, Ministry of, 143
Transport Command of air force, 140, 141
Trenchard, Hugh, 25, 135, 136, 138
Trincomalee, dockyards closed in, 38
TSR2 aircraft, 140

Underway Replenishment Group, 15
Unemployment rate, 218, 239
Unilateralism, 48, 59–62, 229, 234; attitudes on, 83–84
United States: Anglo-American relations, 230–34; anti-Americanism, 83; Atomic Energy Act of 1946, 25; bargaining among service departments, 165; Defense Department, 253, 254; Loan Agreement of 1945, 207; military commitments of, 19; naval commitments to NATO, 22; political relations with Europe, 251; security tasks of, 253; Strategic Air Command, 26, 50, 230, 234, 248, 249; strategic capability of, 21

Valiant aircraft, 26, 27, 139

Verrier, Anthony, 271
Vested interests and policy-making, 173–75
Victor bombers, 26, 29
Vulcan aircraft, 26, 27, 29

Walker, Charles, 268
War Office, 88, 92, 123, 129–35; civil servants in, 130–31; fragmentation of army, 131–32; procurement responsibilities, 143; research in, 145; strength of, 147, 169; weakness of, 130–32; *see also* Army; Military
Warsaw Pact, 248, 251
Way, Richard, 131
Weapons Acquisition Process, The, 78
Weapons Development Committee, 154
Webster, Charles, 261
Weeks, Lord, 167
Westlands, 90
White Papers, 43, 270; of 1953, 213; of 1954, 11, 19, 24–25, 67; of 1956, 216; of 1957, 16, 23, 58, 67, 124, 134, 167, 181, 233; of 1958, 48, 168; of 1962, 18; of 1963, 72, 151
Wigg, George, 21, 44, 50
Willson, F. M. G., 267
Wilson, Harold, 51, 271
Wilson, Henry, 136
Wilson, Thomas, 267
Windsor, Philip, 262
Wiseman, Jack, 266
Woodhouse, C. M., 264
World War II, costs of, 228
Worswick, G. D. N., 265

Young, Wayland, 263
Youngson, A. J., 265

Zilliacus, Konnie, 48